W9-AGL-619

Saladin in his Time

SALADIN
IN HIS TIME

P. H. Newby

BARNES
&NOBLE
B O O K S
N E W   Y O R K

This edition published by Barnes & Noble, Inc.
by arrangement with Harold Ober Associates.

1993 Barnes & Noble Books

ISBN 0-88029-775-1

Printed and bound in the United States of America
M 11 10 9 8 7 6 5 4 3

Contents

Near East
(about 1170 AD)

Frankish territory

0   500   1000 km

Note

Medieval Arabic names are long and complicated because they were intended to carry a lot of information. They include not only the domestic name (Yusuf, or Joseph, in the case of Saladin) but the father's name and sometimes, in the interests of genealogy, a line of ancestors. In addition there were tribal names, honorific names, nicknames and names to show where the owner came from.

Saladin was known to his contemporaries as al-Malik al-Nasir Salah al-Din Abu 'l-Muzaffer Yusuf ibn Ayyub ibn Shadi. This is a title consisting of an honorific name followed by two domestic names, the more important being Yusuf. He was also the son of Ayyub (Job) who was the son of Shadi. His title, al-Malik al-Nasir, has been translated as 'the king strong to save (the Faith)'. Many honorific names ended in Din, meaning 'religion' or 'faith', and Salah al-Din means the 'well-being' or 'honouring' of religion. The Crusaders turned this name into Saladin as they turned the name of his brother, Seif al-Din al-Adil, into Saffadin.

Other popular names were Nur al-Din, the Light of Religion, Imad al-Din, the Pillar of Religion, and Beha al-Din, the Lustre of Religion. Many people were known by nicknames, the Cadi al-Fadel, for example, 'the talented Cadi', although his proper name was Abu Ali al-Rahim al-Lakhmi al-Ascalani (of the tribe of Lakhm, from Ascalon).

The transliteration of Arabic names is difficult and usually attempted with the help of accents, lines over stressed syllables and the Arabic *hamza* (written ') for a kind of guttural glottal stop. These refinements are a distraction to the general reader and I have followed Stanley Lane-Poole, whose *Saladin and the Fall of the Kingdom of Jerusalem* (1898) is still the basic study, in leaving them out.

The Moslem era is reckoned from the 'Flight', the Hejirah, of the

[11]

Note

Prophet from Mecca to Medina in AD 622 and ideally all dates in a work relating to Moslem history should be given as AH as well as AD. For example, Saladin was born in AH 552 which corresponds to the period 19 September AD 1137 to 8 September AD 1138. The two systems do not coincide because the Moslem year is made up of 12 lunar months and is therefore some 11 days shorter than the solar Christian year. The Moslem months retrogress through the seasons every 32½ years; so the month of fasting, Ramadan, can be midwinter when a Moslem child is born and midsummer when he is 16 years old. There is, therefore, some complexity in relating AH to AD. Because they are more familiar to Western readers and for simplicity the years have been given according to the Christian calendar alone.

Why no Saracens? The word has gone out of favour. It was originally applied to the Beduin who harassed the Imperial frontiers in late Classical times, was widely used by the Crusaders as a general term for all the soldiers of Islam, but never by the Moslems themselves. Contrary to popular belief in the West, Islam was an urban religion, not from the desert, and any word implying that Moslem civilization was an expression of nomad culture could be seriously misleading.

P. H. N.

❧ 1 ❧
The Moslem and Christian Background

When Kaiser Wilhelm II visited Damascus in 1898 he had the neglected tomb of Saladin repaired and covered with a new and rather ugly structure over which a silver lamp was suspended. This bore his own monogram and that of the reigning Sultan of Turkey, a mark of respect for the old Moslem hero who had recaptured Jerusalem from the Franks in 1187 that was in keeping with a European tradition going right back to the time of Saladin himself, for he was as good an example of the Noble Enemy as could be found. He was considered so noble and chivalrous that it was popularly supposed by the French that he had a French mother or grandmother. The English thought she must have been English. He became Christendom's favourite Moslem. He had been knighted according to the European ritual, or so it was believed, and he left money to Christian foundations. This was not in fact so, but Dante gave him favourable mention in *The Divine Comedy*. Saladin was more of a man of blood than some modern biographers have pretended but much of his high reputation in the West was deserved. It would be natural to suppose that the strength of his position in Moslem territories made it easy for him to be magnanimous. But for much of the time his position was not strong.

An almost unceasing struggle for power and territory went on, not only between Moslems and Franks but between Moslems themselves. Following the successful First Crusade of 1099 a Frankish empire was set up in the Holy Land and Moslem strength to resist it drew mainly on Egypt, Syria and lands further east. But from time to time a Moslem city or even the vizier of a country as important as Egypt would make an alliance with the Franks to advance their own interests. Spies and informers were everywhere, checking for disloyalty, treachery and treason. A Moslem leader in this jungle who released prisoners, pardoned enemies and gave away the wealth that fell into his hands sounds very confident of himself and of general Moslem support. But this confidence Saladin never had.

He came from no princely family and was not one of the predominantly Turkish ruling class. They despised him as an upstart and were jealous of his success. His background was not even respectably Arab or Persian. He was a Kurd whose family came originally from a highland village in Greater Armenia; and Kurds were difficult people, touchy about their honour, and with their own tribal ways and their own language. Turks looked down on them in this way rather as a Norman might look down on a Scottish Highlander. Even after he had established himself as a great fighter for Islam Saladin was often at odds with the ruler (in name at least) of all Moslems, the Caliph in Baghdad, who thought him too ambitious, an adventurer who was also an outsider. Supposedly Saladin was rallying Moslems against the infidels but this was a cloak; his real aim, his enemies said, was to establish a dynasty and even, some extremists suggested, topple the Caliph himself. What else could be expected of a man who had come to power not by inheritance or the will of the Caliph but by seizing the territories and possessions of the very family who had shown him favour?

Saladin's position was repeatedly under challenge, so his good qualities must have flowed from some profounder source than an assured status. He himself, being very pious (after a not very devout youth) would have ascribed whatever virtues he possessed to the will of God, whose creature he was. From one contemporary Moslem chronicler he attracted malice; but he also attracted panegyrics, and behind both kinds of exaggeration it is possible to glimpse a man who, although very much a product of his harsh and brutal times, had uncommon gifts and steadfastness. Unusually for a man with his background he had no fear of the sea. For a lot of the time he was like the master of a ship in a storm, with a mutiny brewing below decks that could destroy everyone.

Whatever bad relations there might be from time to time between Saladin and Baghdad he always regarded himself as answerable to the Caliph for his actions. The Caliphate was the one political institution in Islam that gave any promise of permanence and therefore stability. But almost from the beginning, soon after the death of the Prophet Mohammed in AD 632, there was conflict over the succession. Mohammed, the founder and head of the new theocratic state, left no clear guidance on his 'successor' (the word Caliph means just that), and there was violence. What began as dynastic squabbling became a religious divide in Islam when the fourth Caliph, Ali the Prophet's cousin and son-in-law, was murdered and his son Husein was killed in battle. For many, Ali and Husein were glorious martyrs and a whole sect of Islam, the Shia (the word means sect) was animated by revenge. The Shia tapped ancient, pre-Islamic beliefs that salvation came through sacrifice and this led to the forming of esoteric interpretations of the Koran and an expectation of further divine guidance through a succession of holy leaders, or imams.

Another way of understanding the tension between orthodox Islam (Sunni) and the Sect (Shia) is as cultural evolution. Islam was originally an Arab culture, strongly influenced by those parts of the Hellenic world the Moslem Arabs overran, particularly in Syria. The first orthodox dynasty of Caliphs, the Umayyads, ruled from Damascus. In the eighth century they had an empire that stretched from India to Spain and from the steppes of central Asia to the upper Nile. They were bitterly resented by the Shia whose views could increasingly be seen as an expression of Persian ways and traditions. To them the Umayyads seemed to have been taken over by the world they had conquered. The Caliphs were not Islamic enough. This hostility played a part in the overthrow of the Umayyads by their cousins the Abbasids (descendants of al-Abbas, uncle of the Prophet) who were nevertheless as orthodox as the house they displaced, but more devout. Damascus ceased to be the imperial capital. In the year 766 the Abbasids founded Baghdad as their seat of power and the Moslem world was now run not by Arabs and Syrians but by a cosmopolitan establishment in which Persians were prominent. Within fifty years, in the time of the Caliph Harun al-Rashid the new city of Baghdad had become the greatest between Constantinople and China. This was high noon for the Caliphate. The Abbasids ruled for 500 years with varying degrees of power, quite nominal when the Seljuk Turks came in from Central Asia and took control. The Abbasids were the Caliphs Saladin had to reckon with, and at a time when they were regaining some of their old power as a result of the disintegration of the Seljuk regime.

[15]

The continuity provided by the Caliphate was all the more important because there was no religious establishment to keep a light burning in times of darkness. There was nothing in Islam comparable to the Latin or Orthodox Christian Churches in the West, no priestly hierarchy, no ecclesiastical or monastic institutions with any real worldly power. The supreme religious authority was the Koran, God's final message to mankind communicated by the Angel Gabriel to the man, Mohammed, whose spiritual authority sprang from that fact. He had nothing of the Divine about him. But he was God's Messenger and unique. None of his successors had that status. They were not Popes or Patriarchs, their office was not religious and no one looked to them for spiritual guidance. They were political leaders whose office was entirely of this world; yet no orthodox Moslem, not even Turks, forgot that in a mysterious way they inherited something of the temporal authority of the Prophet himself.

The Turks were not the only newcomers to usurp the authority of the Caliphs, but their power was the most firmly established and it outlived the Abbasid Caliphate itself. Hard things have been said about the Turks. To Hilaire Belloc they were 'dwarfish, slant-eyed Tartars, crouched on the saddle of their small swift horses bringing nothing constructive but Death' (*The Crusades*, 1937). Sir Charles Eliot, author of *Turkey in Europe* (1900) said of the Turks that 'their history has been a large but strange one. Their contributions to the art, literature, science and religion of the world are practically nil. Their destiny has not been to charm or to improve, hardly even to govern but simply to conquer.' But the intervention of the Seljuk Turks (named after a tribal leader) in Western Asia came at a moment in the eleventh century when because of civil war, sectarian strife and maladministration the Caliphate was near extinction, and they gave the institution a new lease of life.

The bold simplicity of Islam appealed to the Turks. They were willing converts and became sternly orthodox. As befitted no-nonsense soldiers they accepted that the Koran meant exactly what it said and could not be examined for secret meanings. They rescued the current Caliph from a short-lived Persian dynasty who were anything but orthodox, treated him with honour, gave him limited powers and used his authority for their own political ends. Later Caliphs were murdered if they showed independence and more compliant substitutes found. The Seljuks established a Sultanate with an empire that stretched from the Mediterranean to the Caspian Sea and to India. Within this empire the arts and sciences flourished, universities and astronomical observatories were established and men of real distinction, usually Persians, held high office. When the Seljuk Sultanate itself began to fall apart, largely because of that endemic affliction of Moslem societies, dynastic rivalries, the Abbasid Caliphate was still there, drawing on its residual authority to re-establish the old order. But now there were Turks everywhere; Turkish generals, Turkish governors, Turkish regiments—some of them mercenary, some just Turkish tribesmen on the make— because what they were best at was fighting; so much so that the Crusaders referred to all Moslem troops as Turks, no matter whether they were really Egyptian, Arab, Syrian or Kurdish. Saladin himself was thought of as a Turk. Arabs were no longer the dominant Moslems but this is not self-evident because many non-Arabs, Saladin included, bore Arab names.

A prime victim of the Turks was the Eastern Roman or Byzantine Empire ruled from Constantinople. After a remarkable revival of its power and influence in the tenth century the Empire was already in decline and its weakness made the loss of its territories in Asia Minor to the Turks almost inevitable. At Manzikert in Greater Armenia the Byzantine army was destroyed and the Emperor Romanus Diogenes taken prisoner. The year was 1071. The Seljuk Kingdom in Asia Minor, or Rum as they called it, then established became in the course of time independent of the Seljuks of Iraq and Persia and such a threat to Constantinople that the Emperor Alexius Comnenus appealed for military assistance from the West and so brought on the First Crusade. Yet at the time of the Battle of Manzikert the Turkish leadership was less interested in disposing of the Byzantine Empire than in attacking fellow-Moslems in Egypt where a rival Caliphate to the Abbasids was in power, and had been for just over 100 years.

The Fatimid Caliphs of Cairo denied the authority of the orthodox Abbasid Caliph in Baghdad and asserted instead their own claim to be in the line of succession from the Prophet through his daughter Fatima and her husband, the martyred Caliph Ali. In other words it was a Shia dynasty, first established in Tunisia in AD 909 before moving to Egypt in AD 972. Because the line came down

[17]

through an eighth-century imam, Ismail, the family was known as Ismaili. At their greatest the Ismaili Fatimids controlled North Africa, the Yemen and the Hedjaz in addition to Egypt and Greater Syria. Their new city of Cairo, newer even than Baghdad, was with the neighbouring older Fustat the greatest in Africa, and their fleet was second only to the Byzantine. From the Turkish point of view a war against the Fatimids offered not only the usual attractions of plunder and power but the extra relish of knowing that the enemy was not just infidel like the Byzantine Greeks but heretical. The Turks did not get as far as the Nile valley but they did put an end to Fatimid power in Syria and Palestine.

Western Europe at this time had a rough equivalent to the Turks. Just as the Turks had come out of Asia, so the Northmen came out of Scandinavia. They both took over richer, more populous territories than those they left behind; they both adopted a new religion (often in a more bigoted form than that held by those who had converted them); both were assimilated to new societies, the Normans much more than the Turks because, being comparatively few in number (coming in warrior bands rather than as migrating tribes) they gave up their own language in favour of French before moving on to the conquest of England, seizing Sicily from its Moslem rulers and attacking southern Italy, then part of the Byzantine Empire. For the Turks Arabic was the language of religion and law, just as Latin was for the Normans, but for all other purposes they kept their own language. Both peoples were energetic and rapacious and saw themselves as natural conquerors; the Turkish tribesmen settled as herdsmen and agriculturalists in the lands they occupied in Anatolia; the Normans, like the Seljuk Turks of Iraq and Persia, emerged as a ruling class. Both were intent on the dismemberment of the Byzantine Empire and the occupation of Constantinople. It is ironical that many of the princes and knights who, at the urging of Pope Urban II, answered the appeal by the Emperor Alexius Comnenus for help against the Turks were Normans or of Norman descent and saw the Emperor as their eventual and natural victim.

Between Western Christendom and Byzantine Orthodoxy there were differences in theology and in the status of organized religion. During the Dark Ages in the West the Roman Church became indispensable for the maintenance of any sort of government and this led later to claims of temporal authority that no Patriarch of the

Eastern Orthodox Church would have dreamed of; there the continuity of Imperial rule was unbroken. The Emperor did not need priests and monks to administer the law, teach in schools and be generally responsible for running state affairs. He had his own civil servants. As Head of the Roman Church the Pope had spiritual and temporal powers for which there was no equivalent in Byzantium; and, as successor to Peter, claim to authority over all the Christian Churches, East and West. This claim was not accepted by the Orthodox and other Eastern Churches. When the Crusaders marched, with Papal blessing, through Byzantine territory on their way to Palestine they saw Christianity in a different form and despised it, just as the Orthodox priests despised the Latin rite and resanctified any of their altars on which it had been practised. The differences were not just religious. Fear, resentment, envy of the other's qualities (the superior civilization and wealth of Byzantium, the drive and military prowess of the Franks) made real cooperation against the Moslems impossible, and so helped the eventual success of Saladin. It is surprising to learn that Saladin and the Byzantine Emperor were in alliance against the Franks and Germans at the time of the Third Crusade, just as Fatimid Egypt had been in alliance with the Emperor to stave off the Seljuk Turks. Power politics ignored ideology then just as, more cynically, in our own time.

The success of the First Crusade in 1097 did not cause as much despondency among Moslems as a whole as might be expected, although the butchering of the inhabitants of Jerusalem was not forgotten. Little was known in Baghdad about Western Europe. At first the Crusade was thought of as just another of the Byzantine Emperor's forays. Even the Fatimids, who had once counted Sicily as their province, still traded extensively with the Italian states and should therefore have known better, misunderstood the invaders' intentions and tried to negotiate a division of territory in Syria and Palestine with them. Moslems thought they were threatened more by divisions within their own world than by this attack from the West. What is evident from the Western point of view is that the Crusaders were lucky in their timing.

Had they arrived a few years earlier the formidable Seljuk Sultan Malik Shah would have been alive and events might have turned out differently. But Malik Shah died in 1092 and his sons fought for the succession in a way that showed they were indifferent to anything but securing the real centres of power which they located in Iraq and Persia. By the time the various Turkish successors to the Seljuks had established themselves as independent rulers in such centres as Mosul and Aleppo, the Crusaders were in firm possession of conquered territories: the Principality of Edessa (dangerously far to the east), Antioch, Tripoli and the Kingdom of Jerusalem itself. Even so they never succeeded in taking that key military city in North Syria, Aleppo, nor the rich city of Damascus, and so controlling the trading and military routes across the desert between Mesopotamia and the Nile valley.

The first Crusaders had many motives, political and economic as well as religious, but the one with broadest appeal was the securing of freedom for Christian pilgrims to visit the Holy Places. In earlier times this had not been a great issue. Except for the period of the mad Fatimid Caliph al-Hakim (996–1021) who demolished the Holy Sepulchre in 1009, pilgrims were welcomed and money made out of them; but when the Turks took over from the Fatimids a new spirit of intolerance was shown and pilgrims had a rough time, particularly those from the West. The Church of the Holy Sepulchre (rebuilt by the Byzantine Emperor) and the Holy Places at Bethlehem and Nazareth had, after a period when the Latin Church controlled them, now reverted to the guardianship of the Byzantine Emperor and the Orthodox Church, and they had their own reasons for treating pilgrims who observed the Roman rite as not being fully Christian. Under Turkish overlords the Relic of the True Cross, part of that discovered in the time of the Emperor Constantine, was carried through the streets of Jerusalem during festivals while pilgrims of whatever Christian persuasion, Latin, Orthodox, Armenian, Coptic, Jacobite, Maronite, prostrated themselves in the dust, much to the scorn of the Turkish and other Moslem soldiers who regarded them as idolators and spat accordingly.

There is not much evidence in the early years of the twelfth century, when a Christian king reigned in Jerusalem, that Moslems regarded the recovery of that city as a great religious duty. To Western Christendom it had been intolerable that the land of Christ's ministry, and particularly the city of his death and resurrection, should be in the hands of Moslems. It was intolerable, too, for Jews that the site of Solomon's temple should be profaned by the rituals of an alien creed. But although Moslems venerated the city because of the references to it in the Koran and in certain Traditions they did not, to begin with, yearn to possess it as a religious necessity, as they would have yearned to repossess Mecca and Medina if those holy cities had been in infidel hands.

Nevertheless Jerusalem and the Sahil (which was the rest of Palestine extending up and into modern Lebanon) was holy to Moslems for the same reason it was holy to the Jews and the Christians; it was the land of the patriarchs and the prophets. The three religions are rooted in the history of the Semitic peoples, and Mohammed, who at first hoped to persuade the Jews of Medina to accept the Koran as God's ultimate revelation of the truths imparted to Abraham and Moses, originally turned to face in the direction of Jerusalem, not Mecca, to pray. Abraham was the first Moslem, the first, that is to say, who testified to the One God who then tested his submission (the word Moslem means 'submitted') by asking him to sacrifice his son Isaac, traditionally on the sacred rock of Moriah. To this rock Mohammed was miraculously transported one night on the steed Al-Burak in the company of the Angel Gabriel. By means of a ladder of light Mohammed ascended into heaven and eventually found himself in the presence of God who gave instructions on the devotions his followers should perform. The magnificent Dome of the Rock had been built over Moriah nearly 500 years before Saladin's time by the Caliph Abd al-Malik. The scarcely less ancient al-Aqsa Mosque (the 'farther' mosque) ranks only after the mosques at Mecca and Medina. Another place of special sanctity was the Cave of Machpelah at Hebron where Abraham, Sarah, Isaac, Rebecca, Jacob and Leah were buried. All that land between the Euphrates and the so-called River of Egypt (a wadi running down to the sea near El Arish) was regarded as having been specially blessed by God; Mohammed, according to tradition, had said it was of particular holiness, 'that is to say, purity'. It was that part of the world where for Moslems it was best to live and die.

The man who is usually given the credit for starting the Holy War, the counter-Crusade, to recover this territory for the Moslems was Zengi, the ruler of Mosul. In 1130 he gained a bloody victory over the Crusaders just south of Aleppo. In 1144 he recovered the rich and ancient city of Edessa from the Franks mainly because they had dropped their guard and the city was there for the taking. It was not primarily an act of religious fervour on his part; he had spent a lot of energy not on attacking the Franks but on an abortive attempt to seize Damascus, now an independent Moslem city.

Zengi was a brutal and intemperate Turk who had shown himself an effective military leader. He had been an administrator in the service of the Caliph but his campaigning had been as a vassal of one or other of the successors to the Seljuk Sultanate, mostly against fellow-Moslems. The taking of Damascus seems to have been the height of his ambition. Then he would have been master of the three key cities of Damascus, Aleppo and Mosul, controlling movement between Mesopotamia on the one hand and the lands of Egypt, the Seljuk Sultanate of Rum and the Crusader states on the other. Thereafter he might, who knows, have attacked the Latin Kingdom but not, one feels, out of religious enthusiasm. The son who succeeded him in 1146 was, however, a very different man from his ferocious father. Nur al-Din turned out to be the ideal Moslem prince; devout, a great believer in the equality of all men before God and the law, of simple even austere tastes, and a good soldier. It was in his time that the idea of recovering Jerusalem so that it could be purified of the unbelievers gained momentum. Christian reverence for the Holy Places to some extent fed Moslem reverence for their sacred precinct there, the *haram*. Nur al-Din ordered a pulpit to be made against the day he entered Jerusalem in triumph and could install it in the Al-Aqsa Mosque. But the time was not ripe, partly because the Franks had good leadership and partly because Nur al-Din could not keep a sufficiently large fighting force together for any length of time.

Zengi's other sons acknowledged Nur al-Din's suzerainty and ruled in their various cities in North Syria and in the 'island' (Jezireh) between the great bend of the Euphrates and the Tigris. The Turkish emirs who served them and their overlord had been well rewarded for their loyalty. They were proud of being Turkish and proud of serving such a successful family as the Zengids. This did not prevent them from siding with one brother against another when quarrels broke out, or even changing sides to secure some advantage. But it was a more settled world than the one Zengi himself had been born into. There was more money about, trade began to prosper again and the Turkish emirs saw these benefits as the natural consequence of Zengid power. To usurp the Zengid succession would cause resentment and it was Saladin's destiny to do just that.

Nur al-Din and the other Zengids had no support from Egypt where the once powerful Fatimid Caliphate had degenerated to the point where an individual caliph might rule little more than his own Twin Palaces and viziers fought civil wars. The political divide between Egypt and Syria was a source of strength to the Frankish states. They could agree to a truce with one of them and attack the other, usually Egypt because it was such a rich and vulnerable country. In later years Egypt was seen by the Crusaders as the key to power in the Middle East. But not yet. Their eyes were too firmly fixed on the Holy Places. The Moslems also, even in Nur al-Din's time when a Holy War to drive the Franks out of Palestine began to grip their imagination, had no grand strategy. Nur al-Din had no thought of invading Egypt as a preliminary to an attack on Jerusalem. If he marched on the Nile the Franks, as he saw it, would march into Syria behind his back. He could not fight both the Fatimids and the Franks at the same time. When it did come, the Syrian take-over of Egypt was reluctant.

In the middle of the century the Crusader states were reasonably well united under good leadership while the Moslems were divided. As time went by these positions were reversed. The Franks ran into trouble over the succession in the Latin Kingdom, there was tension between the old families established there since the First Crusade and newcomers from Europe; power was increasingly assumed by the military orders, the Templars and Hospitallers, who acknowledged no authority but the Pope and quarrelled with each other. The Moslems, however, moved from disunity to unity and this was largely due to Zengi and his son Nur al-Din. The case of Damascus is instructive. The city was so independent it regularly collaborated with the Franks and presented no great threat to them. But after the Second Crusade of 1147 which, ironically, had the city as its principal objective, it was taken over by Nur al-Din. After that, first of all under Nur al-Din and even more so under Saladin it was a main base in the fight to drive the Franks out.

The most dramatic step towards mobilizing Moslem resources against the Franks was the hesitant annexation of Egypt by Syria and the end of the Fatimid Caliphate in 1171. For the first time it was possible to think of the Latin Kingdom of Jerusalem being caught in Moslem pincers. Saladin's part in this, as Nur al-Din's lieutenant, set him on the road to empire. He had no thought of it before going

[23]

down to Egypt where it was almost as though he stumbled on the realities of power. The security of his own position among the Moslems actually required a war against the Latin Kingdom; and the wealth of Egypt, in men and materials and gold, was necessary to wage it successfully. The unexpected death of Nur al-Din meant that Saladin's main hope of holding Egypt and Syria together was as Nur al-Din's spiritual successor; it was politically necessary for him to establish the same kind of moral ascendancy. His advantage over Nur al-Din was his ability to command the wealth of Egypt as well as the regiments of Syria and the Jezireh.

It detracts in no way from Saladin's achievement that the wind veered in favour of the Moslems and against the Franks during his lifetime. A lesser man could not have held together the sometimes conflicting ambitions of his supporters or won enemies over to his side. His triumph was personal and darkened at the end only by the sober expectation that it was too personal to be lasting.

The romantic Western legend of Saladin was given a new impetus by Sir Walter Scott's *The Talisman*, and even Lane-Poole's scholarly biography of 1898 is under its influence. It has provoked modern historians into a certain amount of debunking. So far from being the noble champion of Islam he was, they say, an ambitious and ruthless man whose main purpose was to establish an empire for himself and members of his family, even if it meant fighting fellow-Moslems as vigorously as he fought the Franks. Up to a point this is feasible but it leaves the near anarchy of the time out of the reckoning. Saladin was only reluctantly ambitious to begin with. Once having established himself he could survive only by anticipating the inevitable threats to his position. A leader could not be virtuously passive and remain a leader, or even alive. Saladin is a more credible personality if he is seen as a man with the wit and ability to maintain the initiative, admittedly in a way that served his own interests, while serving quite genuinely the interests of Islam as a whole. As Sir John Hackett has said in a review of the most recent work of scholarship, *Saladin: The Politics of the Holy War*, by M. C. Lyons and D. E. P. Jackson: 'In the bloodstained jungle of twelfth-century Syria the Saladin of *The Talisman* would hardly have stood a chance.'

Just what the real Saladin was trying to do is still a matter for argument and neither the romanticists nor the debunkers can hope to have it all their own way. The truth is more interesting. But his story cannot be told just as a sequence of events open to different interpretations with Saladin receiving good or bad marks accordingly. If we are to know how he perceived the world we must first know something of the tastes, assumptions and outlook he shared with other educated Moslems of his time. It is against that background that his true stature can be measured.

❧ 2 ❧

Damascus and the Syrian Inheritance

Damascus was the place where Saladin felt most at home. It was already a city when Abraham passed that way. The Pharaohs of Egypt knew it as Dimashka, a fortified trading centre that paid tribute to them, as well it could afford to. The place was prosperous when it was not being plundered. Caravan routes from the Nile valley, from Mediterranean ports, from Anatolia and, above all, from Babylonia met there at a time so remote the camel was not used as a beast of burden; the oil, wine, flax, linen, salt, alum, dried fish, papyrus, hides, honey, lapis-lazuli, turquoise, copper, silver, gold, were transported in paniers on the backs of mules or donkeys. Nothing of that Dimashka now remains and little enough from later and more familiar periods.

The Great Mosque occupies the shell of the Christian church of St John the Baptist and a Greek inscription can still be seen there saying 'Thy Kingdom, O Christ, is an everlasting Kingdom and thy Dominion is from Generation to Generation'. This church, to take the story back earlier, had usurped the Temple of Jupiter built when the city was a Roman metropolis and business was transacted in Greek or Aramaic. The real sense of antiquity comes, however, not from any building but from a more elusive quality. The spirit of the place, the continuity with the past, is in cold, running water.

The rapid and shallow Barada rises in the Anti-Lebanon mountains some 100 kilometres away, picks up tributaries and is fed by up-bubbling springs in its own stony bed. The water is chill to the touch because it was originally melted snow or winter rain trapped and stored in the limestone to be released with remarkable steadiness throughout the year, even during the hot, dry summer. After running through a narrow valley it bursts into the high plain—the Ghuta, which would otherwise be barren—divides into seven, the Rivers of Damascus, and creates an oasis of about 200 square kilometres before spending itself finally in the desert. Damascus is a city of running water. It flows through ancient stone conduits into streets, market squares, houses and mosques where it appears in fountains and basins that are as much the centre of living as fire is in the north.

From the old suburb of Salahiye on the slope of Mount Qassiun to the north of the city the oasis looks like a green prayer mat set before the immensity of the Arabian desert. Away to the west Mount Hermon is snow-capped even in July. From those heights Cyprus can be seen on a clear day, a smudge in the blue remoteness. Damascus stands at the frontier between the Mediterranean world and Asia. Approached from Mesopotamia or the Hedjaz it is a port all the more alluring because of the sun-struck plains of sand and stone through which the traveller must pass before reaching it. There is a tradition that the Prophet Mohammed himself declined to enter the city because he wished to enter Paradise but once. Its gardens of apricot, fig and pomegranate trees, with streams running through them, might well stand for the reward awaiting the faithful of which the Koran speaks.

In Islam the merchant and trader had great status. The Prophet himself was one and his successor after abu-Bakr, the Caliph Umar, said, 'There is no place where I would be more gladly overtaken by death than in the market place, buying and selling for my family.' Under the Umayyad Caliphs, who were of the family of the pious businessman Umar, from about AD 650 to 750, Damascus was the greatest of trading cities. To the list of goods traded through Dimashka could be added silk, precious stones from the East and white slaves from the North. A lot of money was made out of the slave trade. But when the Abbasids took over they reduced Damascus to the status of a provincial city and their new round city of Baghdad with its three great concentric walls became the imperial capital in its place. Even so Damascus remained rich and populous enough to attract Zengi; but when he tried to take the city from its current Moslem ruler he had no success. He did, however, take Baalbek, its dependent city some 100 kilometres away and install there as governor a very capable Kurdish officer called Ayyub. This Ayyub was the father of Saladin. The events that brought the family to Baalbek, later to Damascus, illustrate very well the complicated power politics of the time and help to explain why Saladin was later to struggle not only with the Franks but with the family of his father's one-time lord, the *atabeg* Zengi of Mosul himself.

The Seljuk empire depended for its functioning on the granting of land, or the revenue that could be raised from that land, in return for annual tribute or military service to the Sultan. The fief, or *iqta* as it was called, was seen by the ruler as payment for services rendered and the grant was nothing like so absolute as in Western feudalism. The fiefs could be swapped around and all that mattered was that the changes should not be brought about in a way to cause anyone to lose face or, what amounted to much the same thing, money. In the case of cities, like Mosul for example, the local ruler could be expected to provide quite big contingents for the Sultan's forces and he was, to begin with, usually a member of the Sultan's family; this feudal obligation was met, or not met sometimes, with the rancour and suspicion that often spring up between relations. If one of these local rulers died leaving a young son (a frequent occurrence for life was short) it was Seljuk practice—and it was unique to them—to put in a trusted military guardian called an *atabeg*. The word means 'tutor' and in theory the *atabeg* was educating the young prince for the succession. But such, it was generally recognized, was the uncertainty of life and the difficulty of knowing what God might decide that it became practice for the *atabeg* to marry the late ruler's widow. Just as the Seljuk Sultan was the real ruler of the Empire and the Caliph's rule was nominal, so the real ruler of Mosul would not be the Seljuk princeling himself but the Turkish *atabeg* who, as time went by, took as much independence as he could grasp and tried to establish his own dynasty. This is what Zengi, son of a one-time slave or *mamluk* of the great Seljuk Sultan Malik Shah, had done. (The word *mamluk* means 'possessed' yet implies no inferiority. Perhaps 'retainer' is a better translation.)

Ayyub, in a more modest way, had also got on since he came down with his brother Shirkuh from their native Kurdish village near Dawin in Armenia, not far from present-day Tiflis. The Kurds have lived so long in these parts that they have claim to be the original inhabitants; but from time to time, independent and proud though they might be, they looked for profit and advancement. So with Ayyub and his brother. By favour of a Greek-born administrator of Baghdad Ayyub had been made governor of the fortified town of Tikrit on the Tigris. The Caliph Mustarshid and the Sultan Masud started to fight each other and Zengi, in support of Masud, had rather surprisingly been defeated. In flight he came to the Tigris opposite Tikrit and asked for Ayyub's help in getting him across the river to safety.

Ayyub and his younger brother Shirkuh were a contrast. Shirkuh, an impetuous, shortish man, with a cast in one eye, a greedy eater and fat for a Kurd, was a good soldier with qualities of leadership that made him a brilliant commander in the field. Ayyub was more of an administrator; he was worldly-wise and circumspect. Whatever the loyalty of the moment might be or who his patron was he was mainly concerned with the advancement of himself and the other members of his family. The arrival of Zengi with an appeal for assistance meant, he would have realized, an opportunity of some sort. But what? As a Baghdad appointee he had a plain duty to deny Zengi any assistance. But that would bring down on him the wrath of the Caliph's adversary, Masud. What Ayyub was really being called on to assess that spring day in Mesopotamia was the probable outcome of the struggle for power. He decided in favour of Masud and provided boats so that Zengi and the remnants of his army could be ferried to the safety of the west bank. Surprisingly he was not immediately removed from his job; no doubt he wrote a plausible letter to Baghdad justifying himself and not until six years later were he and Shirkuh given their marching orders because Shirkuh had killed a Christian clerk for no good reason. This normally would not have caused the raising of an eyebrow in Baghdad. The real reason was that Ayyub's loyalty had become so suspect that even his powerful friends in Baghdad could no longer protect him.

The tradition is that his son Saladin was born the very night the family were forced to leave Tikrit. They went to Mosul where Zengi recognized that he had a debt to pay. The next year Ayyub was Zengi's governor of Baalbek in Syria with the expectation that in due course he would move on to Damascus when, as was confidently expected, that city too would surrender to his master.

But Zengi's conduct at the taking of Baalbek made the citizens of Damascus all the more determined not to surrender. Baalbek held out for two months against Zengi in the autumn of 1139 and the garrison opened the gates only when given a guarantee of freedom, safe conduct out of the citadel and assurances of security for the

[29]

inhabitants. Zengi gave this pledge on the Koran and then broke it by ordering the massacre of the soldiers and taking the women and children into slavery. This shocked not only the population of Damascus but everyone else too, and for Ayyub, who was present, it was a warning he would have passed on. Such conduct was not only barbarous, it was against the teachings of the Koran, and from a worldly point of view it was unwise. It only stiffened resistance next time. Saladin, when it was his turn to accept the surrender of cities on agreed terms, never went back on his word. Zengi may well have provided, in family talk, the decisive cautionary precedent.

Baalbek was not the obvious place for the nurturing of a Moslem hero. Architecturally it is part of Europe; the great temples of Jupiter and Bacchus—still largely complete before the devastating earthquake of 1170—are Roman and must have seemed ostentatiously pagan to Ayyub and his family. They date from the second and third centuries AD and stand on the largest stones ever hewn. Some of the columns are the tallest from antiquity. It was this massive stonework that attracted the Moslems. With comparatively little trouble the temples could be transformed into a kind of castle. On the grandiose steps of the Temple of Bacchus a fortress tower was built and linked by a curtain wall with the ramparts that ran round the whole temple area. At strategic points towers were built on to the Roman masonry and—though this came some time later—the complex was surrounded by a moat.

The site is high, some 1,150 metres above sea level, so, in contrast with Tikrit or even Damascus, the climate was invigorating; even the hot summers could be crisply cool at night and during the winter charcoal braziers burned continuously in the living quarters. Fur coats were worn. All around was the fertile Beka'a valley. Fields of wheat and beans were broken up by groves of apricot and mulberry trees. There were vineyards and fig orchards surrounded by poplar trees for shade and for the supply of that increasingly scarce commodity, timber. The Lebanon range ran some miles away to the west, already stripped of most of its cedars and looking reddish with purple shadows or no shadows at all, depending on the angle of the sun. To the east ran the Anti-Lebanon range, where there were Christian villages in which nothing but Aramaic, the language of Jesus, was spoken. Here, in the Baalbek Great Mosque, largely built from material plundered from the temples, Saladin underwent his early education which at this stage largely consisted of learning as much of the Koran by heart as possible, studying grammar and how to write the beautiful Arabic script. Saladin spoke Kurdish at home, Arabic in the mosque and, in all likelihood, Turkish when he started his military training.

Zengi was murdered by some of his servants in September 1146 and almost immediately the ruler of Damascus marched on Baalbek to claim his own, which was more than he would have dared in Zengi's lifetime. Zengi's successor was his son Nur al-Din but he was too busy establishing himself in the succession to be of any assistance. Ayyub, then, had the alternative—either to defend Baalbek to the bitter end or come to an arrangement. Being Ayyub he came to an arrangement. The strength of his position was such that he was able to strike quite a bargain—the citadel of Baalbek would be surrendered if he was suitably rewarded. He received a house in Damascus, ten villages near Damascus by way of *iqta* and was confirmed in his governorship of Baalbek too. Such were the rewards of diplomacy. Everyone seems to have behaved sensibly. Certainly a lot of lives were saved.

Ayyub had qualities that were clearly much in demand— intelligence and efficiency probably—because not only did he remain castellan of Baalbek but in a few years became the head of the Damascus militia, a defence force that could play an aggressive role when necessary. It reads like a classic case of the outsider exploiting local differences to lever himself, as an apparent neutral, into a position of power. And there were many local differences. It is a mistake to think of the inhabitants of a medieval Syrian city like Damascus as being under the arbitrary rule of its prince. The citizens were well organized in guilds and societies; they were a spirited lot and firmly Sunni with all that implied for an insistence on their rights under the law. For many years the ostensible rulers had been the sons and grandsons of a certain *atabeg* Toghtekin, but it was a weak dynasty. The merchant class under a kind of mayor (known as the *rais*) who was often a distinguished legal figure, were engaged in a curiously unacknowledged struggle with the Caliph's appointee (for such the members of the Toghtekin clan were) and it would be very understandable if a respected Kurdish bureaucrat from another province turned out to be the compromise candidate everyone agreed on. Ayyub became commander of the very force, the militia,

[31]

which until then had been the prerogative of the *rais*. Everyone seemed pleased.

Damascus was the main objective of the Second Crusade of 1148 led by the German Emperor Conrad and the French King Louis VII. As Damascus was readier than any other Moslem state to collaborate with the Latin Kingdom this is surprising, but the Europeans were not ready to listen to the advice of the resident Franks and thought mainly of what the acquisition of this rich city would do for their individual fortunes. The Crusade was a fiasco. The Europeans penetrated as far as the gardens outside the city walls only to be confused by the network of walls and streams. From wooden towers concealed among the trees they were harassed by militia bowmen and, according to one account, there was a tactical miscalculation that led the Franks to the north-east side of the city where the defences were strongest and there was no supply of water. The position of Damascus is not naturally strong; its citadel was unique in Syria in being built not on a hill but on flat ground, backing on to the river. But even so, since the fall of Antioch in 1098 no besieged city (with the exception of Acre and there were special reasons for that) was taken during the Crusading period when a relieving army was in the field; the relieving army in this case was that of Nur al-Din, son of Zengi, marching down from Aleppo. It did not engage the Crusaders, but rumour of Nur al-Din's approach was enough to clinch their withdrawal. No Crusader was ever to set foot in Damascus except as an emissary, a tourist or, most commonly, as a prisoner of war.

Whether Ayyub and his family were in Damascus at this time is not known. Most likely he was seeing to the defences of Baalbek in case the Crusaders struck there. Of more significance for the future was Ayyub's rise to a position of political and military power in Damascus at the very time that his brother Shirkuh was being promoted to senior command in Nur al-Din's military establishment. Although in opposite camps the two brothers were in regular communication, one result of which was that in 1152, when Saladin was 14, he was sent to join his uncle in Aleppo, given an *iqta*, and set on a career that would lead to his becoming one of Nur al-Din's emirs. Like Zengi before him, Nur al-Din (and therefore Shirkuh) always intended the conquest of Damascus, so it may seem strange that the young Saladin was allowed to take up a position of potential

Damascus and the Syrian Inheritance

hostility to the city where his own father occupied a prominent position. But this is to underestimate Ayyub. When, as was inevitable, the Aleppo army, strengthened by contingents from Nur al-Din's Mesopotamian vassals, presented itself before the walls of Damascus in 1154, Ayyub was able to persuade his fellow citizens that resistance was not in the interests of the city. While the last member of Toghtekin's family to rule Damascus argued from the battlements with Nur al-Din's emissaries, the real negotiations were going on between Ayyub and Shirkuh. The upshot was that the city surrendered, the ruler was compensated with an important fief elsewhere and Ayyub, the great survivor, was made governor and granted the unusual honour of being allowed to sit in Nur al-Din's presence when everyone else had to stand.

Devoted servant of the House of Zengi as he was, the old fox Ayyub would have conveyed to his new lord that over the years he had worked for nothing but the addition of Damascus to its empire. Everyone acted as though this claim was true without necessarily believing it. A man's real motives were known to God alone. All mortal men could do was judge by results which God decided anyway.

The expectation of life was short and youths were given the responsibilities of men. At 16 Saladin had his own establishment (a wife as well if the usage of the time is evidence), would have mastered a great deal of religious instruction and law, was well versed in the Traditions concerning the Prophet, and he would, under the guidance of his uncle Shirkuh, have learned how to fight and to hunt. Some historians, Hilaire Belloc for one, have suggested that Saladin was more of a scholar than a soldier, but there is no evidence for this other than the favour of Nur al-Din who, a different man from his ruthless father, would naturally respond to a youth with his own serious interests. If Saladin had wanted to spend his time among books rather than in the saddle there was nothing to stop him. He could, like his friend and fellow Kurd Aisa al-Hakkari, have been a Cadi, or judge. But he did not see himself that way. He had a great deal of his father Ayyub in him and his father's gifts were for administration and diplomacy. Since administrators had to be soldiers too—perhaps first and foremost—he had to be proficient in combat: swordsmanship, the management of the horse, archery and above all how to thrust with a lance when mounted.

Shirkuh's advice would be: 'Hold it tight under your arm. Don't wave it about! Hold it to you tight, so that it carries the whole weight of your own body *and* the weight of the horse!' As Shirkuh was a recognized champion who had killed Raymond of Antioch in single combat in 1149 he would be listened to with particular attention. Hunting and hawking were the usual pastimes. Gazelles were hunted in the desert on horseback which was one way of perfecting the techniques of using a bow at full gallop, a Turkish speciality. Lions still roamed in northern Syria and were hunted on foot with a spear. The Prophet himself was a lover of horse racing so there was plenty of that to watch and take part in. More hazardous was a primitive form of polo, involving a great crowd of players, or riding at full gallop with a spear to hit a swinging target. A favourite indoor game was chess.

It was a time when real power was centred on the cities, under Turkish control usually, but something of the old aristocratic Arab way of life lingered on in the country districts and smaller towns. Shayzar, a town and castle overlooking the Orontes, is the one we know most about because of the memoirs of a member of the family that ruled there, Usamah ibn Munqidh. They provide a vivid picture of country life in Syria, particularly during the early part of the century. It was less regulated than in the cities. Agriculture was despised by the original Arab champions of Islam rather as trade was by later European aristocracy, and the attitude persisted. The local prince was less concerned with his crops than he was with the traditional occupations of a gentleman—hunting, fighting and writing poetry.

Shayzar was well to the north of Baalbek, within Aleppo's sphere of influence. There were many Armenians and Kurds in the area; from time to time migrant Turkoman tribesmen appeared, living by horse-breeding and plunder. There was plenty of open space for wanderers, like the semi-nomadic Arab tribe of the Uqailid on the middle Euphrates. Men came and went across what look like firm frontiers on the map of history, from Shayzar into the Christian Principality of Antioch, from Damascus to Latin Jerusalem and on to Fatimid Cairo, and from Baalbek through the passes of Mount Lebanon to the nearest Mediterranean port, Beyrout in the territories of the Christian Count of Tripoli. Outside the cities the control of territory was always in question; there was no knowing just whom a traveller would run into. All the more important, then, for a Moslem ruler to hold key cities, to see that their defences were sound and that communication between them was quick and secure. For the first time in Syria the mounted and well-guarded envoys saw their work supplemented by carrier pigeons.

At the age of 18 Saladin was sent down from Nur al-Din's court at Aleppo and made deputy to his uncle in the military governorship of Damascus. He was responsible among other things for the maintenance of order, the punishment of criminals and the enforcement of regulations concerning dress. According to the Spanish Moslem Ibn Jubayr, who had already visited Cairo and Baghdad, Damascus was, in spite of its secondary status in the Caliphate, the most populous city in the world. Behind the city walls the streets were narrow and dark, lined with three-storey houses of mud and reeds (fire was a constant danger), the bazaars noisy with metal workers and fragrant with spices, thronged with a great mixture of racial types. The many hot baths were an inheritance from Roman times. There was a large free hospital, twenty colleges for students of law and religion, convents where Sufis (the mystics of Islam) used music and dance to arouse ecstasy. The Orthodox Christian church, St Mary's, was brilliant with mosaics, and worshippers there were freely allowed to follow their religion. The rich Jewish community of some 3,000, many of them refugees from the Latin Kingdom of Jerusalem, ran their own university. Two race tracks lined with poplar trees were 'like rolls of green brocade'.

The most splendid building there was the Great Mosque for which the Umayyad Caliph Walid was largely responsible. Within the three-aisled basilica of the original church the walls were covered with mosaics representing the great cities of the Moslem world, and overhead was an onion-shaped dome, the Dome of the Eagle, within which was a gilded and painted cupola. From the height of the dome men could be seen in the great courtyard reduced to the size of small children, a dizzying experience. The mosque possessed a couple of brazen falcons. Every two hours they dropped brass balls from their beaks into brass cups, from where the balls returned to the interior of the device. At night a water clock operated a system of lights behind coloured glass. But more important than these marvels was the teaching that regularly went on in the mosque, the learned doctor

[35]

with his back to a pillar and his students around him, sometimes moved to tears of appreciation by the elegance of his exposition.

There were, and are, three minarets, one of them the very first ever built. The Minaret of the Bride was not just a watch-tower or place from where the muezzin could make his call to prayer but a building with sizeable apartments for occupation by scholars who, as was then customary, passed from one centre of learning to another. The topmost one was occupied for two years by al-Ghazali (AD 1058–1110), so eminent a theologian that he has been described as the chief of Moslems after Mohammed himself; his contribution to the intellectual debate that had been going on in Islam for centuries was such that, to his successors, no further illumination seemed possible.

He powerfully influenced the intellectual world in which Saladin lived. Had it not been for al-Ghazali Saladin would have been more of a fundamentalist than in practice he was because al-Ghazali was largely responsible for making mysticism respectable in orthodox eyes. Sufis (from *suf*, the wool of the garment they wore) had been imprisoned and even decapitated in the past for their presumption in striving for a direct and immediate experience of the Godhead. For al-Ghazali the Sufi path was one that led out of the despair into which at a crucial period of his life he had fallen. His 'dark night of the soul' came when he was a professor at the Nizamiya university in Baghdad and found that for all his mastery of scholastic theology he was without the spiritual experience necessary, in his view, for that truly religious life which would ensure bliss in the world to come. His illumination came after years of ascetic contemplation. Out of the experience he wrote *The Revival of the Religious Sciences* which showed that true religion was not achieved merely by rituals or by mastering a lot of information (important though both of these were) but through a living awareness of divine values. There was no substitute for the seed-bed of despair. Al-Ghazali remained Moslem but such was the rigour of his procedures, using Aristotelian logic on the theistic philosophies of his time and so fortifying the claims of Islamic dogma that he was able to extend the Sunni spectrum of what was considered orthodox. When Ayyub was at Baalbek he established a convent for Sufis there, by the standards of his father's time quite a daring concession to the modern movement.

Islam was, however, not so much a theological as a legal system.

Damascus and the Syrian Inheritance

The Koran was the very utterance of God himself communicated to Mohammed by the Angel Gabriel. It was not just a revered document any more than the inscribed tablets brought down from Sinai by Moses were. It was God speaking. Moslems regard the Koran as the final revelation of God's will to mankind. It provides, therefore, the fundamental teaching for the Faithful but it does not treat of all possible circumstances. As Islam expanded out of the mercantile communities of Mecca and Medina to take in so much of the civilized world the sacred text needed interpreting for the new circumstances—not theologically, but socially and legally. The statements and acts of the Prophet, preserved in Traditions carefully tested for authenticity, provided another source of authority. Al-Ghazali himself wrote that in the absence of authority there was no alternative to the exercise of independent reason. To be within orthodoxy, and authoritative, this judgement had come to be formed in different ways, by analogy with existing texts, by a consensus of the learned, by a guarded use of speculation or, in the narrowest sense, an insistence on the exclusive authority of the Traditions.

There are no priests in orthodox Islam because there are no sacraments for them to administer. Preachers and prayer-leaders exist but the real intellectual leadership was provided by religious lawyers who belonged to one or other of the main schools—the Maliki school of Medina, for example, which was, as might be expected from its location, conservative, emphasizing the exclusive validity of the Traditions and not unduly concerned with the peculiar problems of Persians, Indians and Maghrebis. The Hanafi school of Baghdad accepted the need for speculation. The Shafiy school of Cairo stood some way between the conservative Medina and the liberal Baghdad schools, and this golden mean of its founder Mohammed ibn-Idris al-Shafiy became the dominant rite in Palestine and Syria. Saladin and his master Nur al-Din were members and did a great deal, by building colleges and teaching mosques (mudrassas) to advance the middle-of-the-road views it advocated. These schools (and there was a fourth, the Hanbali, which was more traditional) were all happily accommodated under the one orthodox roof; literally so, because there were teaching mosques, like Al-Azhar in Cairo later on, where each school was assigned its teaching area.

[37]

Damascus and the Syrian Inheritance

The rule of law (Sharia, the 'high way') was the best check on tyranny, and Nur al-Din was one of the rulers who took pride in the way an ordinary citizen could bring a suit against him which would be judged in open court. He sought no immunity. Property, inheritance, marriage, the duties and privileges of merchants, the whole fabric of ordered life was regulated by laws interpreted by the adjudicating Cadi. Sharia law did not apply to the Christian and Jewish minorities (the *dhimmis*, or people of the covenant) who ran their own courts. Friction between the various ethnic and religious groups in the city was minimized by gates between their respective quarters that were locked at night.

Unlike Christianity but very like Judaism the teachings of Islam require practical expression in the daily life of its believers, not only prayers at set times but personal hygiene and even the right posture to adopt in going to sleep. Al-Ghazali, who in his search for truth tested the limits of human knowledge as well as giving detailed guidance on acts of worship, wrote on the correct way to perform ablutions. As a student of all these matters Saladin was conscientious but he did not as a young man carry his piety to the lengths of austerity the Koran demanded; for example he drank wine, like so many of his contemporaries. Other pleasures were authorized by the Prophet himself who confessed: 'I have loved two things in the world, women and pleasant scents. But I have found refreshment of my heart only in prayer.' God determines everything and man can only submit in humility, passively unless summoned by some undeniable imperative, like the fighting of a Holy War, when this passivity becomes a sometimes fanatical aggressiveness. What then happens is received with either joy or grief, but in any case fatalistically.

Saladin had vexatious dealings with the learned but endlessly argumentative Cadi of the city of whom it was said the angels complained because he wanted God to give him a special Day of Judgement to himself. But it was not the Cadi who caused Saladin to leave. His first spell of administration in Damascus was brief. He discovered that the chief accountant was dishonest and either because he could not press the charge or because he felt himself to be compromised he handed in his resignation to his uncle Shirkuh and returned to Aleppo where he entered Nur al-Din's inner circle, 'never leaving him whether on the march or at court'.

The Battles for Egypt

The Latin Kingdom had been in existence for over half a century and by now Syrian Moslems had grown to know the Franks pretty well. They despised the knights for their boorish behaviour, their belief in the Trinity, which they regarded as mere polytheism, and the Franks' acceptance of trial by combat and by ordeal as judicial procedure. Usamah, the Arab gentleman from Shayzar, described in his memoirs what he had seen in the town of Nablus: an elderly farmer accused of helping brigands being set to fight a blacksmith with cudgels to prove his innocence and a suspected robber being dropped into a great butt of water to see whether he could touch the bottom. The farmer was killed, the water 'rejected' the robber and, his guilt being thus proved, he was blinded. For a man like Usamah brought up in Sharia law these proceedings were further evidence of the barbarity of the Franks.

The Frankish knights were, in the main, French speakers from France, Normandy and Flanders, Normans from Sicily and Italy, and knights from Spain. There were a small number of Germans and even fewer English. The Moslems were rather hazy about where all these men came from and were generally incurious about the West. In Baghdad there was more interest in the east and north; a study was made of the Mongols long before they threatened to attack but no comparable study was made even of Byzantium and few Moslems learned a European language. Many of the native-born Franks knew Arabic and some, like Reynaud of Sidon, were informed about Arab history and literature.

The typical Frankish knight was more heavily armed, physically bigger and stronger than his enemies but he was also, Moslems believed, immeasurably more stupid. Franks disdained tricks, artifices and stratagems such as the feigned retreat. They marched in the heat of the day in full armour. They were, perhaps, so cold by nature as to be not quite human. The relative freedom which women enjoyed in the Latin Kingdom was regarded as evidence of low vitality in the Frankish male. Ever since the Prophet's favourite wife had been wrongly suspected of a flirtatious affair the Koranic revelation concerning women had been to keep them in a proper state of seclusion. This did not prevent women from exerting power behind the scenes and having carefully preserved rights, as in the matter of property. But male chauvinism had become such a characteristic of Moslems that when they heard of what appeared to be a complete lack of sexual jealousy in the Latin Kingdom they could ascribe it only to ignorance and lack of feeling.

Many amusing stories went the rounds. The mildest of them concerned the Frank who, out walking with his wife, found her greeted by another man and made himself scarce so that they could talk the more freely. Another story concerned the Frankish knight who went to a public bath in a Moslem town during some period of truce and discovered for the first time that depilation was one of the services provided. He was so delighted to have his pubic hair removed that he summoned his wife so that the attendant could give her the same treatment which, to his grave embarrassment, he did. Then there was the Frankish merchant of Nablus who came home one day to find a strange man in bed with his wife. 'What', he asked, 'are you doing there?' The man claimed he was tired and needed a rest. 'But why in my wife's bed?' persisted the merchant. The man replied that it was her bed, when all was said and done, and he could not very well turn her out of it. 'If you do it again,' said the husband after a little reflection, 'you and I would have a quarrel.' There may be a connection between this story and the historical fact that the wife of a Nablus draper was the mistress of Heraclius, Patriarch of Jerusalem, and was known far and wide as Madame la Patriarchesse.

The stories are related as fact by Usamah in his memoirs but they sound more like comic fictions designed to enliven the conversation over the cakes and snow-cooled sherbert at some Damascus party; no doubt, though, they reflect a popular view of Frankish *mores* and are all the funnier because the Franks were usually thought of as tall, thin, beardless men with cropped heads and—another sign of a nature lacking ardour—blue or grey eyes, the result of eating pork. They were men with only the most primitive ideas of medicine and law. Insanity, they believed, could be caused by a devil in the head and this devil could be exorcized by carving a cross in the skull. Usamah knew that Frankish justice was not all trial by combat and ordeal. The many Moslems living under Frankish jurisdiction were subject to one of the Cours de la Fonde set up in each of the chief towns for the benefit of the native communities. Oaths could be taken on the Koran and the fairness of the courts was recognized. There was a right of appeal to the Cours des Bourgeois (courts for the non-noble Franks) which had twelve jurors chosen by the local Frankish magnate who himself, being noble, was a member of the highest court of the land, the High Court. But there was less emphasis than in Islam on the equality of all men before the law. There was a legal hierarchy in the Crusader states because it was held that a man was always to be judged by his peers; in theory a Frankish merchant who thought himself wronged by a knight could raise the matter in the Cours des Bourgeois but in practice it would have been difficult for him to get a verdict against his social superior. We hear of no Frankish king or prince say, as Nur al-Din would, 'I am but the servant of the law.'

The Europeans had been in the Holy Land long enough for two generations to have grown up there, but the stock was constantly being replenished by new arrivals, not only by men who came on organized Crusades and stayed behind when the others had returned; there was a constant flow of individual adventurers, younger sons with ambitions that could not be realized in Europe, pilgrims who stayed on, and men directly recruited to the increasingly important Military Orders, the Templars and the Hospitallers; they were monks in armour and particularly feared and hated by the Moslems because of their dedication and their fighting qualities.

The new arrivals from Europe were horrified by the extent to which their predecessors had gone native. The newcomers were often hawkish men on the make and bigoted, the residents much more pragmatic. The difference between the two kinds of Frank was clearly perceived by the invaluable Usamah. As a young man he had fought against the Franks and killed a good few of them in the raids and ambushes that, much more that the set battle, characterized warfare between the two sides. During periods of truce Usamah, like other Moslems, freely entered Frankish territory, even Jerusalem itself where he had Frankish friends, Templar knights among them. A Templar fresh from Europe caught Usamah at prayer. 'A devil of a man,' said Usamah, 'whose face changed colour and whose body trembled' at the sight of Usamah praying in the direction of Mecca. He tried to force Usamah to pray due east and would have attacked him but for the intervention of other Templars, old hands, who said to Usamah, 'He's a newcomer and does not understand our ways.' Another knight was so well disposed towards Usamah that he called him brother and offered to take Usamah's young son back to his own country 'where he can see the knights and learn wisdom and chivalry. When he returns he will be a wise man.' So much for Frankish naivety. Usamah was horrified at the thought of his son being brought up among ignorant barbarians and made the excuse that the boy's grandmother could not bear to be parted from him. 'Always do what your mother says,' commented the knight gravely. The conversation must have been in Arabic because Usamah knew no other language and he speaks of being on terms of 'intimate fellowship' with this 'reverend knight' who was possibly a cleric of some kind. This is an unconscious tribute to Frankish intellectual vitality.

The King of Jerusalem held Jerusalem, Galilee and the coast from Ascalon up to Acre; also certain territories to the east of the Dead Sea dominated by the fortress of Kerak in Moab. His was by no means a rich kingdom, poorer than the other two Frankish principalities to the north, Tripoli and Antioch, and the King was frequently short of money and men. Through his territory passed important trade routes from the Moslem east to the Mediterranean ports, particularly Acre which was the only port safe in all weathers, and much of the kingdom's income came from taxes on this trade. Antioch, now a shadow of what it had been in earlier times, was nevertheless a great city, but its princes were technically the subordinates of the Byzantine Emperor, and, though this did not mean a great deal in practice, the Principality often put its own interests first and did not work together with the other Crusading states. Tripoli, too, could act independently and did so particularly in relation to Moslem Syria. The whole system was feudal—that is to say, princes and counts held territory and strongholds granted by the king and, in return for these fiefs, owed him allegiance and military service; the system was more rigid than the one operating in the Moslem territories. Frankish magnates seem actually to have been in complete possession of their territories and they expected to pass them on to their sons.

The King in Jerusalem ruled more like a president than an absolute monarch. Medieval Europe was legalistic and the Franks in Palestine and Syria brought much of the system with them. The High Court consisted of those principal lords who had a direct feudal obligation to the king; he was there because they had elected him. At least, that is what the procedure had been in the early days of the kingdom but in practice the monarchy was now hereditary and the barons had the role merely of 'approving' the succession. The mortality of male infants was higher than of female and the barons' part in deciding whom a royal princess was to marry became important; if she had no brother then the king would be the man she married *ipso facto*, and everyone had an interest in ensuring he was capable. The current King of Jerusalem was Amalric, a big, fresh-faced man in his late twenties, the grandson of Baldwin II through his mother who had married a newcomer from Europe, Fulk of Anjou, and so made him king. Unusually for a Frank, Amalric had allowed his beard to grow, full and blond. He also had a loud laugh and a stammer which inclined him to taciturnity but he was a good soldier and statesman who certainly commanded the respect of the Syrians.

In the Seljuk tradition Nur al-Din maintained an intelligence network of paid informers within the Kingdom of Jerusalem and knew where the enemy's strengths and weaknesses lay. Amalric could call on up to 1,000 knights and perhaps 5,000 'sergeants' who were originally infantry but in course of time had become cavalry too. There was no reserve of local Christians to call on because under the Moslems they could not be soldiers and the tradition of fighting simply was not there. The offspring of Frankish sergeants and native Christian women were known as Turcopoles and made up a by no means negligible force of light cavalry. But Nur al-Din was well aware that the real military strength of the Franks was provided by the Templars and the Hospitallers who held the major castles and were landowners on a great scale. There were about a thousand knights belonging to the Military Orders in the Kingdom of Jerusalem. All these figures have to be multiplied by three to bring the County of Tripoli and the Principality of Antioch into the reckoning but it was by no means certain that these provinces would support the King in any particular action; they were capable of arriving at a separate truce with Nur al-Din if it suited them. The Frankish forces were small compared with what the Moslems, if united, could bring into the field. What they lacked in numbers they made up for by the strength of their fortifications and castles. The scale of their prodigious military architecture, great castles commanding the main lines of communication and some of them, like Krak les Chevaliers, stocked to withstand a siege lasting years, was evidence of the defensive ideas that now dominated Frankish military thinking. Towards Egypt, it is true, there were aggressive intentions, but even here Amalric thought in terms of a great raid that would produce plunder and the payment of tribute by the Fatimid Caliph rather than displacing him. Moslem military thinking, on the other hand, was essentially offensive; so they did not build castles and when Nur al-Din thought of Egypt he thought of annexation.

The affairs of Egypt were much discussed in Nur al-Din's Council. They were well informed because in spite of the division between the Fatimid Caliphate and orthodox Islam, merchants, travellers, pilgrims and adventurers (like Usamah who gives in his memoirs a vivid account of his stay in Cairo) were able to move freely between Egypt and Syria. The news they brought only confirmed the country's bad reputation. It was rich and food shortages were less common than in drought-prone Syria and Palestine but it was not a country that produced good native soldiers. The peasant population had heard of no better soil than their own black alluvium and no more reliable source of water than their own Nile. So they had no appetite for foreign adventures and the forces were manned by Nubians, by Sudanese, by men from the Maghreb (North-West Africa), by Armenians and by *mamluks* bought in the slave markets of Damascus, Aleppo and Mosul. They formed an old-fashioned, inefficient army but a useful navy. The regime itself was degenerate. In the absence of a firm and respected central authority it was a country of conspiracies, plots and counter-plots. Mob violence was liable to break out and be put down with much loss of life. Men of position who lost it lost their heads as well, entirely as a matter of routine, and their houses were handed over for plunder by all and sundry. No one in any kind of authority trusted anyone else, not even members of the same family.

The Egyptian situation was of particular concern in Aleppo and

[44]

Damascus because of changes on the international scene. For at least 150 years the Fatimid claim to suzerainty over all Moslems had made Egypt the natural ally of Byzantium which, for different reasons, was also hostile to the Seljuks and the Sunni regime in Baghdad they underpinned. But now there were developments. Because of the sorry state of Egypt Byzantium began thinking in terms of recovering what had once been its own imperial territory and this threat was all the greater because the Emperor was surprisingly pro-Latin and thought about getting the help of the mailed knights of the Kingdom of Jerusalem to help him. If Amalric and the Byzantine Emperor joined in an attack on Egypt and succeeded in turning it into a Christian power base all Islam would be threatened. Damascus, Aleppo, even the Holy Cities in the Hedjaz and the important trade routes with the Far East through Yemen and Aden would have to withstand attacks made all the more dangerous because of the strategic advantages presented by Egypt's geographical position and by the manpower her gold could buy. Or so it seemed to Nur al-Din's advisers, Saladin's uncle Shirkuh prominent among them.

Between 1164 and 1169 there were three Syrian invasions of Egypt, the first prompted by an appeal for help by the leader of one side in a war between rival factions. This was Shawer, a vizier of Arab descent who had been driven from office by a rival, Dirgam, and kept his head on his shoulders by escaping to Damascus where he promised Nur al-Din a third of the Egyptian revenue as annual tribute if his return to power could be arranged. Furthermore, he would pay for the actual invasion. This was the moment chosen by Amalric to march on Cairo, and Nur al-Din felt forced to move.

His expeditionary force was commanded by his leading general, Shirkuh, with Saladin (now 26 years old) as his uncle's adjutant—quartermaster-general would be the modern equivalent. For some distance the Syrian army followed the Mecca caravan route south from Damascus, avoiding as much as possible the Crusader castles of Kerak in Moab and Shaubak (called Mont Réal by the Franks) which had been built precisely to interrupt communications. And then Shirkuh struck west from the neighbourhood of Aila (present-day Aqaba) across Sinai to the isthmus of Suez. The army consisted in the main of Turks, many of them recruited from the Turkoman tribes, and there were *mamluks* of varied northern origin, together with a strong contingent of Arabs and, most significantly, Kurds who were thought to be particularly reliable.

From a distance it would not have been easy to tell them from a Frankish force because their steel helmets and coats of mail were much the same, flashing in the sun when they were not masked by white surcoats. One difference was the great number of baggage camels; the Franks did not use them to anything like the same extent. Because of the danger of attack the horsemen rode fully armed, lances bedecked with black ostrich feathers and at the ready. The banners and standards were black; some of them bore sacred texts. A flying corps of scouts ranged the ground ahead and on either flank. For most of the march they crossed a hard desert of rock and shingle out of which spectacular mountains rose jaggedly into the clear sky. Spearmen, javelin-throwers and axemen would be carried two at a time, one on each side of a camel in paniers, in addition to baggage. Some just ran to keep up with the horses and now and again were allowed to beg a lift, one foot in the stirrup. Others rode tandem. March discipline was maintained by the beating of drums, and drums gave the signal for breaking camp. This was in the very early morning to avoid the heat which even at this time of year, April, could be intolerable, particularly if the early summer wind—the *khamseen*—was blowing, when dust turned the sun to orange and the way ahead was obscured.

Amalric had already retired from Egypt, frustrated by flooding deliberately brought about by breaking down dams to hinder his progress, so Shirkuh had little trouble in restoring the deposed Shawer to his vizierate. Shawer then repudiated the bargain he had made with Nur al-Din and Shirkuh seized the walled city of Bilbeis as a bargaining point, but found that Shawer, the man he had come in to help, had now sent money to Amalric with a special present for the Hospitallers as an inducement to come and get rid of the Syrians. Shawer was indulging in that dangerous political game of trying to play off adversaries for his own advantage. Amalric and the Hospitallers came and did their best but, as often happened in these confrontations, arrived at an accommodation with Shirkuh because he had news of fighting back home; Nur al-Din had taken advantage of his absence to attack in Palestine. The Frankish and Syrian armies marched out of Egypt and across the Sinai desert almost within shouting distance of one another.

The Battles for Egypt

Shirkuh had agreed to leave because the joint Frankish–Egyptian forces were too much for him, but once back in Damascus he did not rest until another invasion was launched. He reported to Nur al-Din that there were 'no men in Egypt' and the country was ripe for a Syrian take-over. Nur al-Din was cautious because he did not want to split his armies between Syria and Egypt, making both parts vulnerable, but such was Shirkuh's determination that he even wrote to the Caliph in Baghdad to persuade him that an attack on Egypt would be a Holy War against the heretical Fatimids, an argument that weighed with Nur al-Din too. Early in 1167 Shirkuh, with Saladin at his side, was authorized to move. The army was nearly overwhelmed by a sandstorm of terrifying force and when the Syrians arrived in the neighbourhood of Cairo they found Amalric and his army already there, having been offered an enormous fee, 400,000 gold dinars in all (two dinars were slightly more than the weight of a British sovereign), to defend Egypt for the Caliph. Such an agreement was too important for negotiation by the Vizier Shawer alone and the Fatimid Caliph himself had been prevailed upon to receive a Frankish delegation.

This indicated some desperation in Cairo. Caliphs lived lives of the greatest seclusion. Even the Abbasid Caliph in Baghdad appeared only once a year in public; this was during Ramadan when, riding a mule, he went to lead prayers in the cathedral mosque wearing a black veil, a sign of the way worldly pomp would be converted into darkness on the day of death. When urged by his courtiers to show some favour to pilgrims who had come to pay their respects all he was prepared to do was put one corner of his ample sleeve out of a window for them to kiss. If this was the remoteness of a mere man how much greater was the seclusion of his rival, the Fatimid Caliph who still, in spite of some falling away from earlier times, trailed clouds of holiness.

The streets of the city entered by Amalric's delegation were, in contrast to Jerusalem and Damascus, wide and straight, some of them lamplit at night and lined with substantial houses having courtyards and north-facing vents on the roof to catch the cooler northern breezes. Here were the Twin Palaces (fortresses really) connected by an underground passage and housing some 30,000 people, including 12,000 servants and a guard of 1,000 *mamluk* cavalry and black infantry. This was the administrative capital and parts of the walls and three main gates of the city, built in the Byzantine style by Armenian brothers from Edessa, still remain.

The business capital Fustat was some 3 kilometres to the south, on the other side of extensive pleasure gardens that were under water during the annual Nile flood. Here were bazaars with produce from as far afield as the Baltic (amber), equatorial Africa (ivory), India and China (spices and precious stones) and West Africa (gold dust). This city of perhaps 250,000 people was above flood level and from a distance it 'looked like a mountain' with houses of anything up to fourteen storeys.

Amalric's delegation to Cairo was led by Hugh of Caesarea, who spoke Arabic, and Geoffrey Fulcher, Commander of the Templars in Jerusalem. They were led, both hands held, through a warren of corridors and antechambers in the Great East Palace crowded with noisy attendants. At the entrance to each successive chamber were black guards holding naked swords and then, just as the Franks expected to be ushered into the Caliph's presence, they found themselves in an open courtyard with marble fishponds and exotic birds. Beyond the courtyard was a range of ostentatious buildings with gilded ceilings. The Caliph's zoo was here, with animals the Franks could not put a name to. The Chief Eunuch now conducted them through even more dark and winding passages into what apparently was the Throne Room itself for here the Vizier Shawer, who had been one of the company, prostrated himself before huge embroidered curtains with hangings of gold leaf and pearls which were then drawn back to reveal a swarthy youth of about 16 years with the beginnings of a beard, the Caliph—and last of the Fatimids as it turned out—al-Adid.

Hugh of Caesarea wanted to shake the Caliph's hand, without gloves, but he was told it was an impiety even to make the request. Hugh said: 'Unless you offer your hand bared we shall be obliged to think that on your part there is some reservation or lack of sincerity.' The boy Caliph shrugged and, to the horror of his courtiers, bared his hand and allowed Hugh to take it. So the alliance between Fatimid Egypt and the Latin Kingdom was made.

Leaving a regiment of Franks in Cairo, to the scandal of the population who could not understand why infidels should be granted so many liberties, and sending a force up the east bank of the Nile, Amalric and his army now set off on the west bank in pursuit of Shirkuh who had retired as far south as Ashmunein and here a typical Frankish–Moslem battle took place. The knights in chain-mail (the horses too, sometimes) and wearing iron caps with nasals, armed with heavy swords and lances longer than Moslem lances, were capable of launching an irresistible charge; in the face of such formidable opponents the traditional Moslem tactics were to avoid as far as possible receiving this charge with any substantial part of their army. The more lightly armed Moslem cavalry had a weapon the Frankish cavalry did not. All Frankish bowmen fought on foot but the Moslems had mounted archers who could harass a Frankish column on the march and then, if charged, scatter.

In battle the usual trick was a feigned retreat. The centre would apparently take flight, the knights would charge after them and then the right and left flank of the Moslem army would close round them 'like a halo' as one Arab writer put it. Drums and trumpets were used for signalling and, once the Franks had been out-manoeuvred, fighting at close quarters with lance, sword and club was joined to the accompaniment of intimidating howls and fierce cries. The Fatimid army which made up part of Amalric's force at this important battle did not have mounted archers; they were organized much more like a European or Byzantine army and Amalric, once the language difficulty was overcome, had no problem coordinating their tactics with his own.

At Ashmunein the Moslem centre was led by Saladin who, on his uncle's instructions, made the traditional feigned retreat between two hills. Shirkuh's Turkish horse closed in from the hills and the Frankish–Egyptian army crumbled. Amalric escaped only because, it was said, he was wearing a Fragment of the True Cross. Defeat for him in Upper Egypt was unfortunate but it was not the end of the war, he was still in the field, and when Shirkuh was unable to follow up his victory by attacking Cairo and made for Alexandria across the desert, between the western branch of the Nile and Wadi Natrun where the Christian monasteries bubbled in the heat haze, Amalric was after him with a sizeable army drawn from those not involved at Ashmunein.

Alexandria was a strongly fortified city (still with its ancient Pharos largely intact), but the Cairo government was not popular there and Shirkuh entered the place without opposition. The siege that followed reduced the city to near-starvation and Shirkuh, with most of the army, managed to slip away for a pillaging tour of Upper Egypt, leaving Saladin in command with 1,000 men. It was his first independent command and years later he said: 'What I went through in Alexandria I shall never forget.'

He hated Egypt. No doubt the climate had something to do with this but the main reason for his aversion lay in the untrustworthiness of the men, like Shawer, he had to negotiate with, the hostility of most Egyptians to the Syrians (whom they regarded indiscriminately as Turks) and the constant danger of being poisoned or stabbed in some unguarded moment. Alexandria was particularly dangerous because his forces were inadequate to withstand Amalric's siege and at the same time deal with city mobs who, once food ran out, were all for opening the gates. At his urging Shirkuh was forced to suggest peace to Amalric and since he too was in difficulties (Nur al-Din was attacking Tripoli) there was an accommodation once again. The siege of Alexandria was lifted and as part of the truce arrangements Saladin visited the Frankish camp. The customary honours were paid, as between army commanders. A Christian chronicler recorded that Saladin was knighted by a well-known Arabist in Amalric's army, Humphrey of Toron, who, if such a ceremony took place, would have been the man to perform it. The story is unlikely. But it was certainly the case that by his conduct on this second Egyptian campaign, successfully commanding troops in action and defending Alexandria, Saladin had for the first time demonstrated his qualities as a leader.

When he returned to Syria with Shirkuh, he was determined never to set foot in Egypt again but that is not how matters turned out. The following year, 1168, Amalric led an army into Egypt not, as on previous occasions, by invitation but as an invader. The Hospitallers had nearly bankrupted themselves on military expenditure, hiring knights, buying horses and equipment, all in the expectation of some rich prize, and they wanted a return on their investment; the securing of an Egyptian city in perpetuity—Bilbeis, for example. They put pressure on Amalric to embark on this adventure out of self-interest and, in retrospect, it can be seen as the beginning of a course of events that led to the destruction of the kingdom. Shawer tried to buy Amalric off, without success, then gave orders for the city of Bilbeis to resist. The Franks were surprised and exasperated by the vigour of this resistance. When eventually they broke into the city they plundered and massacred without mercy, slaying Christian Copts as well as Moslems. Cairo and the rest of Egypt were horrified by the reports; such was the Egyptian determination to resist that Shawer won support for a scorched earth policy, and the city of Fustat, which had no walls and could not be defended, was set on fire with the help of thousands of naphtha barrels and torches. The population was not so much evacuated as driven out by terror and despair. The great fire went on for two months. Hillocks of debris mark part of the site to this day.

The Caliph al-Adid had meanwhile appealed to Nur al-Din for help, sending a letter in his own handwriting and a lock of his wife's hair as a symbol of the straits to which he had been reduced. Nur al-Din was quick to respond. He would have gone to Egypt himself but he was having trouble with his Mesopotamian vassals and the greatly experienced Shirkuh was the obvious commander. It was assumed that Saladin, as on the two previous occasions, would also go, but when the moment of decision came Saladin refused. He had seen quite enough of Egypt and was not prepared to return there. The refusal is well attested and it is hard to believe it was merely because he feared for his own skin or disliked the country. Perhaps part of the explanation lay in a reluctance to serve once more under his uncle because of a suspicion concerning Shirkuh's real motives. Shirkuh was an ambitious man. When Nur al-Din had fallen seriously ill in 1159 and it was thought he might die, Shirkuh, in Damascus, was only dissuaded from attempting a *coup d'état* by the advice of his brother Ayyub who said it would be wiser to wait and see what would happen. Nur al-Din and Shirkuh drew back, content to wait for the next opportunity. Saladin may have known of a secret ambition to rule as an independent king of Egypt and decided he wanted no part in such an act of treachery to the prince, Nur al-Din, he genuinely admired.

Ironically, Nur al-Din himself was foremost in persuading Saladin to go, not indeed commanding him to go (emirs had to be persuaded, not commanded) but applying pressure, supplying him with money and horses for the campaign that Saladin had claimed, as a last desperate excuse, he could not afford. Shirkuh was quite capable of listening to all this with a smile on his face, even when he heard Saladin say: 'If the kingdom of Egypt were offered to me I would not go.' Ayyub had the last word. Whatever his father said had a self-evident rightness for Saladin. He pointed out that as a vassal of the Prince Saladin had duties which must be openly honoured. If Saladin feared the Egyptian expedition might end disloyally he should remember he had duties towards his uncle too and keep his mouth shut; in any case only God knew what would happen. Saladin was in a trap. When he eventually agreed to go, he confessed years later to the Cadi Beha al-Din who wrote his biography, 'I went as to my grave.' He had been forced to commit himself to Shirkuh in a way that aroused forebodings. Some such explanation is necessary to explain his determined resistance and it would be consistent with what followed.

The main contingent in the expeditionary force were 6,000 Turcomans each of whom was given 20 dinars by Nur al-Din. Shirkuh was given 200,000 dinars for the preliminary expenses of the campaign which turned out a complete success. The Syrians joined forces with the Egyptians and Amalric retired to Palestine without a fight. Shirkuh entered Cairo to be greeted by the enthusiastic citizens as their deliverer and the Caliph presented him with the gift traditional on such occasions, a robe of honour, in which Shirkuh displayed himself to his troops. The Vizier Shawer continued to intrigue. Having, with Shirkuh's help, got the Franks out he now wanted the Guzz (as the Turks were known) to go home too and, when Shirkuh gave every indication of staying, planned to have him murdered at a banquet. Or so it was rumoured. The fact was that the Vizier had enemies in the Caliph's palace and his fate was probably as much due to them as to any distrust by the Syrians. He maintained an appearance of cordiality by daily visits to the Syrian camp, riding out 'with drums, trumpets and banners' of the southern Zuweila gate of Cairo past a squalid huddle of tenements called El-Mansuriya where Nubian and Sudanese troops lived with their followers, a bluff of the Mokattam hills on the left and the great mosque of Ibn Tulun on the right, practically all that was left of the one-time city of Katai. Beyond the still smoking ruins of Fustat to the west, on the other side of the Nile (so broad at this point it might have been a lake) rose the Pyramids of Gizeh.

That particular day, 18 January 1169, Shirkuh was not in the camp but out visiting the tomb-mosque of the venerated Imam al-Shafiy who had been responsible for the school of law named after him and in which Shirkuh and Saladin had been educated. Saladin himself, or one of the Turkish guard immediately under his command, dragged Shawer from his horse and placed him under arrest. His guard, the drummers and the trumpeters galloped off. When the news was received back in Cairo the Caliph al-Adid decided to regard it as but the downfall of another vizier and, according to the usage of the time, asked for his head as evidence. The Caliph then proceeded to appoint Shirkuh in his place. Shirkuh's acceptance is evidence of Shirkuh's personal ambition; it had never been part of Nur al-Din's plans, for how could one of his own servants become the vizier of a foreign and heretical power? Nur al-Din was so angry that when he heard of it he confiscated all Shirkuh's feudal holdings in Syria.

If Nur al-Din, in his displeasure, summoned Ayyub for a discussion of his brother's conduct there is no record of the meeting, but events were moving quickly. Nine weeks later Shirkuh gorged himself so immoderately that he was taken ill and died; and once the Syrians had recovered from the shock there was great political activity in the camp to decide who should succeed him. No one, oddly enough, thought of sending to Nur al-Din to ask whom he nominated as the new Commander-in-Chief. It was assumed that the decision would be taken on the spot. The leaderless Syrian army was in danger of being attacked by the Fatimid forces who (now that Shawer was dead) were also leaderless, and the main concern at such a time must have been for the preservation of the army.

In the army there was a Kurdish faction and there was a Turkish faction, both determined that their particular man should succeed Shirkuh but both very much aware that the danger of their situation was such that a quick decision would have to be made. Senior among the Kurdish contenders was Saladin's maternal uncle, Shihab al-Din Mahmud al-Harimi; prominent among the Turks was the emir Ayn al-Dawlah al-Yaruqi. Either would have been competent but Shirkuh's dying nomination had been Saladin and intensive lobbying on Saladin's behalf took place. It was conducted with great skill by the Kurdish jurist Aisa al-Hakkari who had been Shirkuh's Cadi of the Army. He was able to point out to Shihab al-Din that Shirkuh's own Kurdish regiment was in favour of Saladin, that he himself would not have general support if it came to a demonstration, least of all from the Turks who might prefer their own man. So would it not be wise to throw in his lot with his sister's son? Shihab al-Din agreed. Al-Hakkari then played upon the jealousies between the Turkish emirs, putting Saladin forward as a compromise candidate. As senior officer present Shihab al-Din now recommended his nephew Saladin to the Caliph.

He had no business to do so. The command of Nur al-Din's forces was a matter either for the emirs themselves or for Nur al-Din. But the danger of fighting between the Fatimid troops and the Syrians was so great that Shihab al-Din urged on the Caliph the appointment of a Commander-in-Chief of all the armed forces in the country, and al-Adid, who had no authority over the Syrian army, behaved as though he had. He gave Saladin command of his own Egyptian troops and confirmed him in his command over the Syrians. The Chief Secretary of the dead Shawer—the Cadi al-Fadel who came to play a great part in Saladin's life—was instructed to compose a diploma running to ninety-eight folios making the appointment and granting him the title of al-Malik al-Nasir (king strong to save). Ayn al-Dawlah said, 'I shall never serve Yusuf.' He and some of the other Turkish emirs refused to acknowledge the appointment and went back to Syria where Nur al-Din listened to their story with some annoyance and confiscated Saladin's Syrian *iqtas*, his fiefs, as he had confiscated his uncle's.

Saladin now found himself, at the age of 30, on the same road where with great foreboding he had seen his uncle set out. He may have mentioned his doubts to Aisa al-Hakkari who would have quoted the Koran to good effect. 'Perhaps you hate a thing but it is better for you; perhaps you love a thing although it is worse for you; but God knows and you do not.' Nothing happens in this world but by the Will of God; it is impious to question or challenge. The doctrine of predestination is as strong in Islam as it was later to be in Calvinism, so the very unexpectedness of his advance to the highest power could have been enough to convince Saladin that God had picked him out. In a fatalistic society it is hard to know where proper initiative ends and impious ambition begins but, like the Prophet Mohammed himself who initially doubted, even resisted the idea he was a Messenger of God, Saladin saw himself as doing no more than surrender to God's purpose.

4

The Transfer of Power

An over-successful general often arouses the suspicion of the master back home, and Saladin was no exception. Nur al-Din, for all his virtues, listened to the mischief-makers and his suspicions hardened into wary hostility. He had many virtues. He governed in the light of the Koran, lived austerely, and had little money of his own. When his wife complained that she had no money even to buy clothes, he allotted to her from his private property three shops that would bring in about 20 dinars a year. She objected that this was not much and he replied, 'I have no more. Of all the wealth I have at my disposal I am but the custodian for the Moslem community, and I do not intend to deceive them over this and cast myself into hell-fire for your sake.'

The threat of hell-fire was real to Nur al-Din. He levied only those taxes authorized in the Koran and by the Traditions and when his Commander-in-Chief, Shirkuh, had argued against his suspension of the *mukus* (uncanonical taxes) on the grounds that the military budget would suffer, commented: 'If we have to make war at such a price I would rather not make war at all.' It was Nur al-Din's belief that the prayers of holy men were a better guarantee of victory than an extra battalion; he was not prepared to divert funds from Sufi convents for the recruitment of mercenaries. In the presence of a scholar or man of religion he was known to rise to his feet and invite him to sit next to him. He set up institutions to ensure the rule of Sharia, such as a new Court of Appeal over which he presided in person to deal with administrative injustices and, another innovation, a college specializing in the teaching of Hadith, the Traditions of the Prophet. After a severe illness in 1159 his already austere nature became even more devout, so much so that a poet, Ibn al-Qaysarani, described him as being engaged in two Holy Wars, one against the Franks and another in his own soul against the forces of evil. Nur al-Din was the first Moslem ruler to see that the Holy War against the Franks could only be successful if Moslem states were united in the effort (his own resources were not enough) and that this unity must be based on acceptance of the basic Sunni ideology. Hence the severity with which he cracked down on deviations from orthodoxy, whether it was the major deviation of Shiism or the theosophical speculations then popular among intellectuals in Aleppo.

Such was the man who, next to his own father, Saladin respected more than any other and yet could not help antagonizing. Egypt was a country that needed firm government if it was not to destroy him. Stability could be achieved only if freed from the remote control of Syria, and in particular from the regular payments of large sums of money which Nur al-Din expected. Even if Saladin was not personally ambitious the appearance of ambition was forced upon him. Just at what point the independence of Egypt and the elimination of opposition shaded into calculations of personal advantage to Saladin would require the fine judgement he expected to be made on him in the life to come; but one thing is sure, he never ceased to follow Nur al-Din's example and took nothing for himself.

He very soon had an army mutiny on his hands. In order to strengthen Syrian control of the country Saladin had been phasing out the Fatimid commanders; this involved the transfer of their estates to Syrian emirs who held them on the Seljuk pattern, which was new to Egypt, as *iqtas*. Great resentment, quite naturally, was caused and the black troops, between 30,000 and 50,000 of them, were in particular worked upon. They were not negroes but Nubians with their own language, quite different from the indigenous Egyptian, or Coptic, and quite different from Arabic. They were, and are, a proud and independent people who volunteered for military service and sent back to their native territories for brides. Contemporary Arab writers indicate that they were often a threat to government; they were now set to get rid of Saladin and his Turks even if it meant bringing back Amalric and his knights. A eunuch, Moutamen al-Khilafa, tried to send a message to Amalric sewn up in a sandal but the very newness of the sandal, carried by a man in ragged clothes, attracted attention, the message was discovered and Moutamen lost his head. The Nubians demonstrated violently in the great square of Cairo between the Twin Palaces.

The Transfer of Power

Thousands of them struggled to get to grips with the Syrians who were dangerously outnumbered. After two days of uncertainty the Syrians began driving the Nubians down the main street. Saladin gave orders for the Nubian cantonment of El-Mansuriya outside the walls to be set on fire, and the Nubians rushed to the Zuweila gate to save their families only to find it shut. They agreed to surrender if they were given a safe conduct out of Cairo. After the remnants of the Cairo garrison had been shepherded across the Nile to Gizeh the Syrian troops attacked them again, this time so mercilessly that only a few escaped to Upper Egypt where the rebellion flickered on.

The 'white' troops in the Fatimid army—Arab, Turkoman, Armenian, *mamluks* of various racial origin—presented nothing like the problem of the Nubians because they lacked their tribal cohesion and loyalty to one another. Provided they received their pay regularly and were given opportunities to loot and plunder they were ready to serve the strong man of the day. Even so, Saladin began a systematic replacement of their senior command by men of his own choosing, in particular his brothers Turanshah, Tughtigin and al-Adil who joined him from Syria, followed later by their father Ayyub who received the unprecedented honour of having the Caliph al-Adid ride out to meet him. Saladin offered to surrender the vizierate to his father but Ayyub told him not to play with his luck. 'God would not have chosen you for this great position if you had not been fitted for it.' In spite of his displeasure with Saladin no difficulty was placed in the way of the Ayyubid departure from Syria by Nur al-Din; he trusted, in these early days, their family loyalty to his own princely house, particularly if the deeply respected Ayyub was there to give sobering advice. There was no immediate alternative to giving Saladin his head if he was to establish order in this turbulent country; he needed lieutenants he could trust and no Turkish emir came into that category. Nur al-Din was realistic enough to see this.

As bad luck had it, the mutiny of the Nubian troops was followed almost immediately by a joint Frankish-Byzantine attack on the Egyptian port of Damietta, and Saladin had to send a strong relieving force under his nephew, Taqi al-Din. He himself could not leave a still murmuring Cairo to go off and deal with the invasion in person. In spite of Nur al-Din's suspicions of Saladin's ambition he was quick to respond to an appeal for reinforcements, but what really saved Damietta were the strength of its defences, disagreement between the Byzantines and the Franks, and bad weather which delayed the 220 ships of the Emperor Manuel's fleet and turned Amalric's camp into a quagmire. An attack by Amalric was only to be expected, but the intervention of the Byzantine fleet, the most powerful in the Mediterranean, was a new development; at the same time as he was reorganizing the army Saladin now saw the need for an expansion of the already large Fatimid fleet which, manned by sailors from the Maghreb, had already successfully interrupted the sea routes between Europe and the Latin Kingdom, but would be needed to fight off the galleys of the traditional Egyptian ally now turned enemy, Byzantium. Within nine months he had dealt with a major mutiny in Cairo, brought in new men to reorganize the army and the government, and had now seen off a dangerous land-sea attack; all this was firm evidence of the organizational powers, the shrewdness and general unflappability that, more than mere skill as general in the field, lay behind his eventual successes.

Nur al-Din now asked Saladin to put an end to the Fatimid Caliphate and substitute the name of the Abbasid Caliph al-Mustadi for that of al-Adid in Friday prayers throughout Egypt. Saladin hesitated. He told Nur al-Din that the change would spark off more rebellions, but to Nur al-Din it seemed more than ever important to make a quick move for religious and political uniformity. Once this was achieved the Frankish states would be so many nuts for the cracking between the pincers of a Moslem world owing allegiance to Baghdad. Did Saladin not understand that this was what Shirkuh and he had been sent into Egypt to achieve? The Byzantine galleys at Damietta were significant. They showed that the Emperor's notorious and misguided liking for the Latins, so different from his predecessors, had led to a military alliance that would certainly go into action again, perhaps in Egypt, perhaps in northern Syria. So long as al-Adid held court in the Cairo palace he would be a focal point for dissent, and in the Holy War Nur al-Din could not afford dissent that might lead to more secret deals with the King of Jerusalem. Moreover, it was an affront to God that the Fatimid heresy should be countenanced. Nur al-Din addressed Saladin not by the title that al-Adid had given him but wrote to 'the Emir, Commander-in-Chief, and to the other emirs'. That was all Saladin would be when al-Adid was out of the way. Even before the arrival of Nur al-Din's instructions, prayers had been said for the Abbasid Caliph in Alexandria and one of the minor Cairo mosques. On Friday, 10 September 1171, a visiting prayer-leader from Mosul was authorized to omit al-Adid's name from the bidding prayer in the chief mosque and the following Friday that of the Abbasid Caliph al-Mustadi was pronounced. Saladin had moved cautiously, testing the ground. The swarthy youth who had shaken hands with Hugh of Caesarea knew nothing of this latest momentous development because he had already fallen ill and by 12 September he was dead. His immediate family and their relations were placed under house arrest, the males separate from the females, so that the line would in due course conveniently die out. To Baghdad Saladin sent the Fatimid regalia and insignia of office, to Nur al-Din he sent ceremonial attire and money, though there was not much of this because Shawer had spent vast sums trying to buy off Amalric and the treasury was empty. Nur al-Din was greatly disappointed. In celebration the Caliph al-Mustadi gave orders for Baghdad to be illuminated, for robes of honour and the black war flags of the Abbasids to be sent to Nur al-Din and Saladin; and, significantly emphasizing his appreciation of the formal position, to Nur al-Din he sent two swords, one to represent his rule over Syria, the other over Egypt.

The Fatimid palaces were stripped of their treasures. The jewels, the rich furnishings, the embroidered curtains, the hangings of gold leaf and pearls, presumably even the exotic birds and animals observed by Hugh of Caesarea and Geoffrey Fulcher were auctioned off and the money fed into the public treasury for the payment of troops and the financing of a great programme of building. The library of 120,000 manuscript volumes was disposed of in regular sales that were still being held five years later. Saladin did not take up residence in the Great Palace, as might have been expected, but handed it over to the army. His brother al-Adil moved into the Western Palace with his harem but even he had no great taste for luxury and they camped rather than dwelt in the ostentatious quarters. Saladin and his retinue remained in the Vizier's house where they were already established. In course of time the Twin Palaces decayed. One observer noted that no wood was taken in for fuel and no rubbish thrown out. Furniture was broken up to fire the

ovens and the refuse heaps grew month by month. An unlikely
supporter of the Fatimids was a poet from Yemen called Omara
(unlikely because he was Sunni) who addressed a 'censurer of his
love for the sons of Fatima', asking him, whatever his opinion might
be of the older order that had passed away (and it had been good to
Omara) at least to be sufficiently understanding to 'join in my tears
over the desolate halls of the Twin Palaces'.

Every Friday the preacher, now dressed in Abbasid black, struck
the steps of the pulpit in the Chief Mosque with his sword scabbard
as he climbed to take up position at the top between two black
banners and invoke the name of the Caliph of Baghdad, al-Mustadi.
All was quiet. The pro-Fatimid demonstrations had not material-
ized. 'Not so much as two goats butted,' wrote one witness, and
Saladin was master of Egypt.

The Fatimid version of the Ismaili cult was a court religion that made
little impact on the population at large. Its overthrow did not stir up
any strong religious feeling because most people carried on as they
did before under the tolerant but remote Fatimid Caliph. What
concerned the officers of the old regime was the way they were being
pauperized by Saladin's economic changes; and there was popular
antipathy to what looked like a Turkish army of occupation. The
country had suffered much from a succession of foreign rulers and
xenophobia was never far below the surface. The combination of
discontent among the displaced Fatimid officials and a dislike of alien
Turks and their ways led to more conspiracies.

No medieval Moslem ruler could feel secure without a personal
guard he could trust. Saladin established a guard of white *mamluks*
known as the *Halka*, each of whom had a fairly small fief which, to
provide a stake in the country, could be passed on to a son. These
men were the professional core of the army; they took up position
with Saladin at the centre of the battle line. When not campaigning
they supervised the harvest, though as this came much earlier in
Egypt than Palestine they were free to raid Frankish territory by
February when the Palestinian wheat was merely greening the
ground. Saladin's principal commanders had large estates, usually
scattered in different parts of the country to avoid, rather like the
Norman settlement after 1066 in England, the possibility that one of
these emirs might get ideas above his station. They had their own

mamluks and, together with members of Saladin's own family, provided the two wings of the army. As in England, resistance to these changes was dealt with severely but there was no trouble that interfered with agricultural production; grain prices were remarkably stable throughout this period, 100 kilograms of wheat selling for a dinar at a time when a journeyman in one of the big cities received about 2 dinars a month. We do not know what pension a displaced official might receive but it would not have been anything like the 4,000 dinars a year they had on average been receiving under al-Adid, and there would have been subversive talk in the villages to which they had been forced to retire.

Saladin made an early start on abolishing the non-Islamic taxes (the *mukus*) and replacing them with an alms tax (*zakat*) on goods and property which came within the religious canon. Originally the *zakat* was for charitable purposes but Saladin, without violating religious principles, was able to use part for the army and navy. One of the earliest pieces of evidence for the success with which Saladin had reorganized the army and strengthened the navy had been the surprise attack he launched before the death of al-Adid in that sensitive area between the Dead Sea and the Gulf of Aqaba. All communication with Syria had to pass this way and the Franks held not only the strong castles of Kerak and Shaubak there but also the port of Aila and its castle, which was on an island. Saladin's attack was intended to clear the way for a large caravan that was bringing his family from Syria. A fleet of galleys was built in the yards at Bulaq, near Cairo, and transported in sections (a skill practised from Pharaonic times) to the Gulf of Suez where they were reassembled and used for the transport of marines. These galleys usually had three lateen masts but the main means of propulsion was seventy or so men who, with another 200 soldiers on board, could drive the galley along at up to 7 knots. Aila was taken, the first Frankish strongpoint to fall into Saladin's hands, and he was able to return to Cairo well pleased with the performance of his new style forces.

A critical reporter of Saladin's career was the contemporary historian al-Athir who wrote in Mosul, the one-time stronghold of the *atabeg* Zengi, father of Nur al-Din. Not unnaturally al-Athir was a propagandist for the Zengi family and hostile to Saladin who came to displace them. The excuse given by Saladin for not joining forces with Nur al-Din for an attack on Shaubak (Mont Réal) in 1171, that he had insurrections in Egypt to deal with, was not accepted by al-Athir, perhaps with reason. Saladin with his army was already in the neighbourhood of the Crusader castle when he heard of Nur al-Din's approach. His response to the news was to strike camp and return to Egypt immediately. There was always the chance that once in Nur al-Din's presence he would be relieved of his command, ostensibly for failing to provide greater quantities of Egyptian gold. According to al-Athir the same thing happened two years later when Saladin moved up to besiege Kerak; on Nur al-Din's deciding to move down from Damascus to join him Saladin gave the excuse that his father Ayyub was seriously ill. But al-Athir is wrong about the facts. There seems little doubt that Saladin was not attacking the castle direct but taking punitive measures against the Beduin of the area because of the assistance they had given to the Franks as guides. In any case Nur al-Din was not in Damascus, he was away on a campaign in the north (against his co-religionist, the Seljuk Sultan who ruled in Anatolia) and would have known nothing of Saladin's expedition until it was over.

Although Nur al-Din would clearly have liked to call Saladin to heel, al-Athir exaggerated Saladin's anxieties. He said that Saladin, fearing an attack from Syria, looked around for remoter countries he could escape to, such as Nubia and the Sudan, even Yemen. It is true that he sent out many expeditions but with the object not of preparing for flight but of acquiring wealth for the defence of Egypt. The conquest of Yemen was particularly important from this point of view. From here and the Hadramaut came frankincense and myrrh. Aden itself was the great market for India, Zanzibar, Abyssinia, Oman and even remoter countries; whoever controlled it controlled the taxation of the most flourishing international trading centre of the age. The poet Omara described with enthusiasm the wealth of his homeland, adding that an invasion could well be regarded as an act of Holy War because in Yemen there were so many Fatimid sympathizers and Ismailis. Saladin might have paused to consider what Omara, who had prospered under the Fatimids, expected to gain from this, but if he did he was not prevented from despatching his brother Turanshah to invade the country. Travelling via Mecca and increasing his forces as he marched south Turanshah approached Yemen, the Arabia Felix of the Romans, with such strength that his success was never in doubt. There were other expeditions to other parts. One of the emirs of Saladin's nephew, Taqi al-Din, led one as far west as Tunisia which could provide timber for shipbuilding and sailors for the fleet. Nur al-Din, when he heard of it, was so far from being displeased that he wrote to the Caliph claiming the credit for himself of planting Abbasid banners in the homeland of the Fatimids.

Nevertheless the anti-Saladin Turkish emirs in Aleppo and Damascus, particularly those who had left Cairo in disgust on Saladin's appointment to the vizierate, would encourage Nur al-Din to dismiss the upstart. News was received in Cairo that there was such displeasure in Syria over the small sums and presents sent by Saladin that an official was being dispatched to audit the finances of Egypt. There were discussions in Cairo about the possibility of Nur al-Din coming himself. Al-Athir said a formal council of war was held at which Taqi al-Din said they must fight. Ayyub is reported as saying, 'No, if Nur al-Din came we would kiss the ground at his feet.' To Saladin Ayyub said, 'If he ordered us to take your life we should do it. . . . We are all his *mamluks* and slaves and he may do with us as he likes.' So much for the public discussion. Only when they were alone did Ayyub warn his son against dangerous talk in public which might get back to Nur al-Din. The truth was that Ayyub would fight Nur al-Din if he tried to take so much as a sugar cane from his son, but the wise course was to send a conciliatory message to Damascus, saying, 'You may send but a courtier on a camel to lead me back to Syria with a turban cloth about my neck and not one of my people would resist him.' It sounds improbable. Who, one wonders, would have reported such a conversation to al-Athir? Saladin's own account of the supposed council of war, as given years later to his Cadi of the Army, Beha al-Din, was that 'we heard Nur al-Din might attack us. Everyone thought we should resist him but I held to the opposite opinion and argued, "Nothing of this kind must ever be said." '

Al-Athir was probably nearer the mark when he wrote that in 1174 the poet Omara played a leading part in a conspiracy on an international scale. The attack on Yemen had been suggested by him as a means of drawing off substantial forces. 'I've got rid of his brother, Turanshah, to the Yemen,' Omara was heard to boast, in preparation for a rising of the Nubians in Upper Egypt, the part of the country for which Turanshah had been primarily responsible.

The Transfer of Power

This was planned to coincide with an attack by Amalric towards Bilbeis and an attack on Alexandria by the fleet of the Norman King of Sicily, Roger II. Even with modern means of communication the organization of such an audacious scheme, involving collaboration from bases many hundred of miles apart, would be difficult. The Sicilian fleet was huge. Two hundred galleys were intended to transport some 50,000 men, including 1,500 knights and 500 more lightly armed cavalry. There were eighty freighters to carry the horses and equipment. And while this great force was being assembled for the hazardous 2,000-kilometre voyage knights were checking their equipment in Jerusalem and Nubians were sharpening their swords and feathering their arrows in the province of Aswan.

The scheme was betrayed to Saladin's intelligence service by a prominent member of the *ulema* who was originally one of the conspirators himself; all he asked by way of reward was the confiscated property of the men with whom he had plotted, and this he was granted. Saladin was warned of the attack from Sicily by no less a person than the Emperor Manuel, which may seem surprising in view of his own naval attack on Alexandria a few years previous; but in spite of his fraternal relations with the Franks of Palestine the Emperor had no love for the Normans of Italy who had taken Corfu from him and plundered Greece. He did not wish to see his enemies in possession of Alexandria. In the event the naval attack miscarried, Amalric made no move and the Egyptian conspirators, Omara among them, were publicly crucified. Even so, it is not entirely certain there was a conspiracy or, if there was one, it could well have been the work of *agents provocateurs*. It provided Saladin with an excuse to rid the country of trouble-makers, as at the time of the attack on Damietta in 1169 when, following the mutiny of the black troops, a number of Egyptian leaders who had nothing to do with it were executed. Saladin was quite capable of this kind of ruthlessness. The country was dangerous for the ruling foreigners and he was determined to be master.

By this time Saladin was without the benefit of his father's advice; Ayyub had been thrown from his horse and fatally injured. Saladin would have naturally turned to him because the quite unexpected news came from Damascus that Nur al-Din too, at the age of 59, was dead. His heir was his 11-year-old son, al-Salih, a notably intelligent child but clearly not able to rule in his own right and the object, therefore, of much attention by rival strong men at the court. Whoever secured the person of al-Salih could claim to be his *atabeg* and the effective ruler of the Zengid empire. Within two months of Nur al-Din's death news came from Jerusalem of the death of Amalric at the age of 38 from dysentery, to be succeeded by his son Baldwin, a boy of 13. Both Syria and the Latin Kingdom were rocked and weakened by these two deaths and Saladin, whose position had been by no means assured, was now by virtue of his control of Egypt, the Hedjaz, Yemen and sections of the North African seaboard as far as Tunisia, the most powerful figure in Islam and perhaps second only to the Byzantine Emperor himself in the whole of the Near East. The very ease with which he had gained Egypt persuaded Saladin, he later told Beha al-Din, that it would be his destiny to recover the Sahil (Palestine) from the Franks, and the events of 1174 would have convinced him that God had revealed the means.

A short time before his death Nur al-Din rode through the orchards of the Damascus Ghuta talking with some companions of the uncertainties of life, how impossible it was to know the future. Only God knew. When he fell ill with a quinsy he said that his chief fear for the future was what Saladin would do to his family after he was gone, and he made the emirs swear loyalty to al-Salih. There were many differences between Islam and Latin Christendom, including the Kingdom of Jerusalem, in what was held to constitute legitimate government. In Europe at this time the fiction still existed that the king was elected by his peers. Christian canon law ruled out the achievement of sovereignty by conquest; William the Conqueror became King of England not because he won the Battle of Hastings but because he had a right to the throne, approved by the Pope, established by prior agreement with the Anglo-Saxon magnates, notably Harold himself, and by inheritance through his wife from Alfred the Great. Because Kingship was held to be also, in some respects, a priestly office, flagrant usurpation could be punished by excommunication. In Islam not only was there no equivalent to the threat of excommunication but there was clear provision for usurpation, indeed a readiness in Moslem jurisprudence to give unconditional assent to the right of the stronger.

[65]

The Transfer of Power

All that a Moslem ruler required once he had seized power was a diploma from the Caliph confirming him in his office, and this diploma was rarely refused. 'Governorship by usurpation' as Moslem jurists called it was not limited to the office of vizier in Fatimid Egypt, and the doctrine made the demise of princely power both uncertain and divisive. When the news reached Egypt that Nur al-Din had named al-Salih to succeed him, Saladin immediately acknowledged the boy as his suzerain and caused his name to be mentioned in the Friday prayer and placed on the coinage. But when the inevitable squabble broke out in Syria over the Regency he wrote to say that no one had a better claim to the guardianship of al-Salih than himself and he would come and deal with the usurpers as they merited—which, he implied, was severely. Nur al-Din's kingdom was coming apart. His nephew Saif al-Din of Mosul had taken Edessa and other cities for himself. The claim to the Regency by the emir Ibn al-Muqaddam in Damascus (backed by al-Salih's mother) was challenged by the governor of Aleppo, Gumeshtekin, on the grounds that Aleppo had been Nur al-Din's capital city.

Many long letters were sent from Cairo not only to Damascus and to Aleppo but, more important from Saladin's point of view, to Baghdad, putting his case with great eloquence. They were composed by the Cadi al-Fadel who was now, in effect, Saladin's Minister of Propaganda. When Gumeshtekin won the argument over al-Salih and the boy, with his mother, went to Aleppo (after some of his father's emirs had been arrested in case they made trouble), al-Fadel emerged from long briefings by Saladin to write even more powerful letters. In reply to those Syrian emirs who deplored Saladin's threat to intervene, appealing to his loyalty to the house of Zengi, al-Fadel wrote:

> In the interests of Islam and its people we put first and foremost whatever will combine their forces and unite them in one purpose; in the interests of the House of Atabeg Zengi we put first and foremost what will safeguard its root and branch. Loyalty can only be the consequence of loyalty. We are in one valley and those who think ill of us are in another.

When Saladin did intervene, al-Fadel wrote to Baghdad describing the achievements of Saladin since his assumption of power in Egypt, defending the take-over of Yemen and arguing that 'in the

[66]

empire of Nur al-Din was confusion of spirit, disorder and anarchy. In each strong place a chief had established himself, each country had its pretender. The chief emirs of Nur al-Din were thrown in prison, tortured and their goods confiscated.' As for al-Salih: 'We shall protect the heir presumptive and, in truth, this care is more properly ours than of those who use his name to eat up the world and behind an appearance of devoted service are working only in their own interests.'

Saladin's intervention was prompted by the imminence of war between Aleppo and Damascus where Ibn al-Muqaddam was in a state of such alarm that he wrote saying the citizens would welcome his presence. With a force of a mere 700 Turkish cavalry, his brother Tughtigin and the indispensable al-Fadel, Saladin set off with all speed, making across Sinai and then following the old caravan route fringing the Arabian desert, to enter Damascus in triumph towards the end of October. He went not to the Citadel but to his father's old house, saying that he was no more than al-Salih's *mamluk*. When he did enter the Citadel, however, his undoubted popularity with the citizens of Damascus was increased by the generosity with which he made gifts from al-Salih's treasury.

Saladin might not have gone to Damascus with such confidence if Amalric had been alive and capable of marching into Egypt; the defence of that country was always to be one of Saladin's prime concerns. It would be too much to say that Frankish power in Palestine, like that of the Zengids in Syria and Mesopotamia, was on the point of breaking up, but the removal of Amalric from the scene undoubtedly diminished the threat the Latin Kingdom presented to the Moslems. Amalric's son, Baldwin, had been accepted as king by the barons but ever since the boy's tutor, William of Tyre, had noticed he felt no pain when his arm was pinched in play it was known that he was a leper and that his life would be short. Their thoughts must have turned to the possibility of electing someone else, but he was the only remaining prince of the royal house. Here, as in Syria, there was a squabble about the Regency, and when it was decided that Raymond of Tripoli should take on the responsibility there were further disputes between two factions, one led by Raymond who stood for achieving some kind of accommodation with the Moslems and another led by Reynald of Chatillon and Joscelin de Courtenay who were all for aggression. These dissensions were made worse by personal animosities. The nobility were all related to each other and the rivalry had the bitterness of a family quarrel, particularly among the powerful queens or ex-queens, who hated each other. The death of Amalric meant that the Latin Kingdom was so weakly led and so disunited that no important military initiatives were possible for some time. Information about all this leaked to Saladin who felt free to go his own way.

Moslem armies were reluctant to campaign in the winter. Saladin's insistence, once he had received reinforcements from Egypt, on moving into North Syria that December shows how determined he was. He was able to take the smaller towns of Homs and Hamah without much difficulty, but Aleppo was the real objective. Although it was not far (about 100 kilometres) from Antioch, the first great Eastern city to be taken by the First Crusade, its defences were so strong that it never fell to the Franks. In flat, tawny northern Syria the citadel of Aleppo could be seen three days' march away, seeming to grow out of a great hump of rock in the middle of the town which itself was protected by great walls. A Moslem pilgrim from Spain, Ibn Jubayr, said the citadel was like a round table with sides of hewn stone; all around were massively built houses 'with large markets arranged in long adjacent rows . . . all roofed with wood so that their occupants could enjoy ample shade.' But that was in the summer. Winter could be severe and when Saladin took up position in front of it snow lay on the ground. This was the city where he had been closest to Nur al-Din and now that he had returned in this totally unforeseen way the son of his old master appeared before the population to entreat them not to surrender. Gumeshtekin, a eunuch and one of Nur al-Din's most trusted veterans, had found little difficulty in convincing al-Salih that Saladin was a ruthless man who intended to steal his heritage. There were many Shiites in Aleppo. Nur al-Din had given them a hard time but now, in an effort to win support for al-Salih, they were once more allowed to use the Shiite formula in prayer. In addition to this truckling to heterodox opinion Gumeshtekin was so desperate that he even called in the Franks to create a diversion by attacking Homs. He hired Assassins to do away with Saladin, and al-Salih appealed to his cousin of Mosul, Saif al-Din, for assistance.

For the time being Saladin had to withdraw from Aleppo but in April he rather luckily defeated the joint forces of Mosul and Aleppo at the battle of the Horns of Hamah—the name given to some prominent hills overlooking the Orontes—and so became master of Syria. Aleppo was, by agreement, left in the hands of al-Salih on condition the army of Aleppo collaborated with Saladin against the Franks. And it was to Hamah, this town 80 kilometres down the road from Aleppo to Damascus that the envoys of the Caliph, responding to al-Fadel's argument and to Saladin's military successes, brought the diploma and robes of investiture for the government of all Syria (except Aleppo), Egypt and Yemen.

In this way Saladin came to sit in the chair of his one-time master, quite clear in his own mind that he had pre-empted an attack upon himself, the only man capable of holding Nur al-Din's dominions together. He had done his best to fulfil his obligations to al-Salih but his efforts had been rejected. He was, therefore, absolved from all further duty to the Zengi family. In his conduct and zeal for the Holy War he was more like Nur al-Din than any of them, so he had a moral claim to be considered his heir. Needless to say, none of this was accepted in Aleppo or Mosul.

❧ 5 ❧

Consolidation in Egypt

The Assassins hired to kill Saladin on his campaign in North Syria were members of that famous and feared Brotherhood, so called because it was thought that the taking of hashish was part of their training. Kemal al-Din, who wrote a *Chronicle of Aleppo*, was born two years before Saladin died and was able to draw on first-hand information from people who knew the Sultan and from oral traditions in wide circulation. On the evidence of his elder brother he recorded a strange story about Saladin and the Assassins. This Ismaili sect had been established at the end of the eleventh century when a certain Hasan-i-Sabbah gained control of a remote castle in north-west Persia known as Alamut (the eagle's nest) because of its position on top of an unclimbable crag. This became the mother convent of the Batiniya, men of the *batin* (the inner meaning of texts), and from here emissaries were sent out to murder prominent men of the orthodox persuasion as a way of hastening the millennium. Their first victim was Nizam al-Mulk, chief minister of the two most powerful Seljuk sultans. They also killed two Caliphs. The Batiniya had a particular detestation of Turks whom they regarded not as human beings but *jinn*, or evil spirits. Because he proscribed the Shiite formulae used in prayers, Nur al-Din was given the dramatic warning of a poisoned dagger on his pillow, for the Batiniya were extremist Shiites. By this time they had established themselves at a number of strongholds in Lebanon and their current leader, Sinan, held the castle of Masyaf which was in a strong, almost inaccessible mountain-top position. To the Crusaders he was the Old Man of the Mountain. Even without the prompting of Gumeshtekin when his city of Aleppo, with al-Salih in it, was under siege, Sinan would have regarded Saladin as a prime target. He had put an end to the Fatimid Ismaili caliphate, which the Batiniya were committed to restoring under a descendant of an earlier deposed Fatimid caliph Nizar, who was regarded by them as the last authoritative Imam of the Moslems. Knowing the fanaticism of Sinan's followers and the skill with which they infiltrated even the personal retinue of their intended victims, Saladin took the threat of assassination very seriously indeed.

Kemal al-Din said that Sinan sent a messenger to Saladin asking for a private interview. Saladin had the man searched and, finding he was unarmed, dismissed most of the men in attendance but kept a few armed *mamluks* to act as his guard. He then asked Sinan's emissary to deliver his message, only to get the reply: 'My master ordered me not to deliver the message unless in private.'

Saladin reduced his guard to two but even then the Batiniya would not deliver the message, saying that his master's conditions had not been met.

'These two do not leave me,' Saladin said.

The messenger was insistent but Saladin said he regarded them as his own sons. 'They and I are as one.' There was no confidence he was not prepared to share with them.

At this the messenger turned to the two *mamluks* and said: 'If I ordered you in the name of my master to kill this Sultan would you do so?'

They drew their swords and said, 'Command us as you wish.'

Kemal al-Din said that the Batiniya, having demonstrated with the skill of a magician that the very men Saladin had identified as the most trustworthy were in fact his potential murderers, then left taking the two *mamluks* with him. Thereafter, Kemal said, Saladin was inclined to make peace with Sinan but (and this was the usual formula for not guaranteeing the absolute truth of an anecdote) 'God knows best.'

Saladin's relationship with Sinan did, in fact, develop in a strange way that has never been adequately explained. The first attempt on his life was made outside Aleppo by a number of Assassins (Moslem chroniclers call them Fidai, 'devoted ones') who penetrated his camp and were only cut down when they had entered the tent where he was sleeping. A second attempt nearly succeeded because the Fidai (as in Kemal's story) had managed to get themselves enrolled in his bodyguard. He received a dagger-thrust to the head but was saved by his helmet; another thrust to his throat did not penetrate his chain-mail. The rest of the guard was alerted and the Fidai killed. As

[71]

a result Saladin decided to attack Masyaf and put an end to Sinan and all his works, but he did not succeed.

The Batiniya version of what happened is that when Saladin marched on Masyaf he was reduced to a state of superstitious dread by Sinan's magical powers and his soldiers paralyzed by an inexplicable force—all this in spite of powdered chalk and flour being scattered round Saladin's tent. Sinan manifested himself in the tent to deposit a threatening note with a poisoned dagger thrust through it, and scones still hot from the oven, in the shape of a Batiniya symbol. Sinan's footprints were seen outside the tent, but pointing only outwards.

Behind this legendary story we may discern the possibility that there was a meeting between Saladin and Sinan at which a deal of some kind was struck, because it is certainly the case that after the siege of Masyaf was lifted Saladin never had any more trouble from the Batiniya. They liked to surround their activities with an aura of irresistible magic in which they were helped by the credulity of even the orthodox like Kemal al-Din. Although a belief in magic was frowned upon by orthodox Moslem opinion nevertheless there was wide popular acceptance of magicians and demons. Saladin may not have been immune to such beliefs. He may not, either, have been persuaded that Sinan would honour whatever agreement they had arrived at because from now on he slept, for extra protection, in a raised wooden cabin within the tent.

Unlike Nur al-Din, a dignified man whose council meetings were conducted with restraint and in whose presence no man raised his voice, Saladin seemed unconcerned about the respect that was due to him, even lacking in dignity. One of his council meetings was so noisy that a distinguished doctor of the sacred law withdrew and Saladin sent after him to apologize and promise that greater decorum would be observed in future. Men were not intimidated by him. They felt free to speak their minds in his presence, some with great candour. He even put up with insolence and threats. One of the Turkish emirs who had left Cairo when he became Vizier said to him: 'The swords that captured Egypt for you are still in our hands and the spears with which you seized the Twin Palaces of the Fatimids are ready on our shoulders and the men who once resigned your service will now force you to leave Syria. Your arrogance has overreached itself.' Saladin took no offence. The jealousy of the Turkish emirs and the continuing hostility of the Zengi family, particularly Nur al-Din's nephew, Saif al-Din, the Prince of Mosul, were perfectly understandable. He did not go in for hard words himself. Speak softly and carry a cudgel is a motto that would have served for his escutcheon if profane texts had been permitted. He did not hesitate to use the cudgel when it was necessary and usually with such speed that his adversaries were taken by surprise.

Saif al-Din, who now took it into his head to attack Saladin, was a greedy and rather foolish man, but at the battle of Tell al-Sultan which was fought on 21 April 1176, some distance south of Aleppo, it was Saladin who was taken by surprise. If Saif al-Din had pressed his advantage all would have been lost but he declined to inconvenience himself over the destruction of one he called 'this upstart'. He said, 'Tomorrow will do.' Saladin himself led the charge that routed Saif al-Din who barely escaped with his life. His camp, when Saladin seized it, was said by one chronicler 'to be more like a tavern, with all its wines, guitars, lute bands and singing girls'. Saladin urged his troops to reflect on the evidence of such imfamy, praying that they might be preserved from anything like it. Nevertheless, in his usual way he had the booty distributed in line with the approved usages of war, that is, divided up according to rank under supervision, one-fifth being allocated to replenish the war chest. Cages of birds, parrots, doves and nightingales were sent after Saif al-Din with the suggestion that they suited him better than war. For himself Saladin kept nothing. Saladin's famous generosity was an important factor in ensuring loyalty; it was welcomed for the material advantages it brought but also regarded admiringly as evidence of greatness of character.

Feeling, after this victory, that Syria was now safe Saladin decided to return to Egypt. If he had been a close imitator of Nur al-Din he would probably have stayed in Syria, viewed by so many as the centre of power, and governed Egypt through one of his brothers, Turanshah, say, but that was not how he saw the new strategic realities of the Damascus–Cairo axis. Its economic strength lay in Egypt, the defence of that country was always the priority, and it was there that he went. Another man who understood where Saladin's strength lay was William of Tyre, the contemporary

[73]

Frankish historian of the Latin Kingdom. Through Egypt came gold (the Nubian mines were almost exhausted by this time and the main source of gold was the country known to the Arabs as Ghana, right away on the other side of Africa, between the Senegal river and the Falema in the present-day country of Mali) and William saw how Saladin could use it. All the provinces of his empire, he wrote, furnished him with 'numberless companies of horsemen and fighters, men thirsty for gold since it is an easy matter for men possessing it to draw men to them'. Everyone understood the power of money. Nizam al-Mulk, author of a treatise on statecraft, *Rules for Kings*, and victim of the Assassins, had written: 'Countries are held by men and men by gold.'

Before leaving Damascus Saladin took as one of his wives Ismat al-Din who was a widow of Nur al-Din (not the mother of al-Salih) and daughter of the last independent ruler of the city, Muin al-Din. From the earliest days of Islam it had been accepted that the conquest of a state was consummated by possession of the former monarch's wife or daughter, and the 'upstart' would have seen the taking of his former suzerain's widow in this light; the marriage provided a certain status, perhaps a degree of legitimacy in the eyes of Syrians, not quite expressed in the Caliph's diploma. He left Turanshah, back from his conquest of Yemen, as Governor of Damascus with full powers and, after an absence of two years, himself returned to Cairo.

At just this time, September 1176, news came of the disastrous defeat of the Byzantine Emperor Manuel by the Seljuk Sultan of Iconium, Kilij Arslan, at the Battle of Myriocephalum. This was good news for Saladin. If the Emperor had won he and the Crusading States would have been in a strong position to mount a joint offensive against him, but as a result of the battle (which the Emperor himself compared to the disaster of Manzikert 105 years earlier) Byzantium was put out of the military reckoning for a long time to come and Saladin's position was made all the stronger.

These were the years, from 1176 onwards, when Saladin established himself in folk memory as the great builder; work he in fact had nothing to do with, like the Bahr el Yusif, the great irrigation canal in Upper Egypt dating from Pharaonic times, was ascribed to him in years to come. He did inaugurate a tremendous programme of public works and there is no doubt that the amount of money spread around in this way was a stimulus to the economy. He had already made a start on new fortifications in and around Cairo. Although cities had been fortified in Egypt from time immemorial the idea of having an inner stronghold which could be defended even if the city itself was taken, as in Syria and Palestine, had not developed. Nowadays, from as far off as Sakkara, 32 kilometres to the south-west on the other side of the Nile, the great mass of the Citadel can be picked out on its outlier from the Mokattam hills, but at the time Saladin recognized the strategic importance of the site it was not built on at all. He envisaged an impregnable fortress with a wall that would reach out in the north and link with the walls of Fatimid Cairo. Another wall would extend to the south and west to enclose Fustat, now being repopulated, as far as the Nile opposite Roda Island. Ibn Jubayr, en route from Spain to Mecca, saw European prisoners of war 'whose numbers were beyond computation' doing forced labour, sawing marble, cutting huge stones—some of them transported from the smaller pyramids—and digging ditches. The work was directed by the white eunuch Karakush, who had served Shirkuh and was now Saladin's right-hand man. One reason why the hill had not been built on defensively was the lack of a water supply. Karakush was responsible for a well 86 metres deep, the Well of the Winding Stairs, still called 'Joseph's Well' after the Sultan Joseph by which name Saladin was now popularly known.

At the same time as these military works were being planned, building and reconstruction for ideological reasons went on apace. Colleges modelled on those in Baghdad and Damascus were founded among the ruins of Fustat in 1170 with the object of producing the Sunni administrators and secretaries the new order required; students were provided with not only free education but generous living allowances as well. The teaching mosque of Al-Azhar which had been founded by a Fatimid Caliph in AD 970 as a centre of Ismaili scholars and missionaries was purged of its heresy and re-established for the teaching of the four main schools of Islamic law.

In spite of heavy military expenditure there was a perceptible rise in the standard of living; this reconciled people more than anything else to a regime they had at first distrusted. We can only speculate about the thoughts of ordinary people. Popular entertainment offers hints. The repertoire of professional story-tellers, who gave street-corner performances to the accompaniment of drum and lute, provided one source of fun and excitement. We can read these stories in the collection known as *The Thousand Nights and a Night*. Some of the tales are ancient, coming from India, Persia and Iraq, but many of them have Egyptian settings and were current in Saladin's time without necessarily having been set down on paper. A certain al-Qurti, a contemporary of Saladin, referred specifically to them. The Cairo stories are of a kind unlikely to interest Saladin in the slightest (they would have been much more to Saif al-Din's taste) but many of them do express values and attitudes of mind that must have been widespread.

Authority is seen as oppressive and unpredictable. Neither merit nor hard work can achieve success and happiness; these depend entirely on the will of God and He acts in a mysterious way, revealing hidden treasure to one and condemning another to death. The main characters are merchants and their servants, trading in cloth and spices, bakers, barbers, dyers, metalworkers, fishermen, peasants, living sometimes in squalor but all quoting the Koran piously, performing their ritual ablutions and repairing to the mosque on Fridays. And these made up the audience. They were the kind of people who saw Saladin with his bodyguard, with yellow silk over their breastplates, ride out to inspect the work being done on the fortifications.

The colloquial Arabic of the story-tellers was despised by the learned who cultivated an archaic and elaborate literary style, men like Ibn al-Khallal who presided over Saladin's secretariat in Cairo and was described, by Imad al-Din, as 'the pupil of Egypt's eye, combining all the noble qualities of his country'. Such men were moved to tears by literary elegance. Poetry was a passion. A sermon was responded to as a great work of art, with rapt attention, usually in silence and with the kind of concentration that would allow a listener to repeat whole passages from what he had heard. Sometimes the preacher's eloquence was such that his listeners could not restrain themselves. Ibn Jubayr reported on a sermon by saying that 'Hearts were struck with longing, spirits melted with ardour and the sobs of weeping resounded.' This was in Baghdad but the phenomenon was widespread in the Moslem world. The distinction between colloquial Arabic, which varies from country to country, and literary or classical Arabic has continued to the present day.

Consolidation in Egypt

Arabic had been the official language in Egypt for 300 years but the substantial Christian, or Coptic, population still spoke their own language, which had evolved from the language of ancient Egypt, and wrote it using the Greek alphabet plus seven additional characters from the Egyptian demotic script. (The last Coptic speaker died in the eighteenth century and the language is now used only in church services.) The Copts are Monophysites, believers in the single nature of Christ both human and divine, and as such regarded as heretics by both Greek and Latin Christianity. Under Islam Christians, like Jews, were tolerated (because they had a scripture) provided they paid the appropriate taxes or tribute and lived in a proper state of humiliation; the general tax on Christians was known as *kharaj* and there was a poll-tax on all able-bodied males who were then debarred from military service. In the nature of things most Copts were peasants but a significant number of the educated classes had clerical and administrative abilities that allowed them to play an important role in the running of the state. But they were always at the mercy of a ruler's idiosyncracies. Under the tolerant Fatimids they had been spared the requirement of wearing a distinctive dress and a blind eye was turned on them when found riding a horse. With Saladin these disabilities were imposed again and, as in Damascus, Christians wore black turbans and heavy crosses.

Jews, too, paid their general tribute and poll-tax, and they never appeared in public except in a distinctive dress. They much preferred Moslem to Christian rule and had migrated in considerable numbers out of the Frankish kingdom. Alexandria had a Jewish community of 3,000 at this time, as large as the Damascus community. In the Cairo area there were 2,000 Jews with two synagogues and a rabbi who was recognized by the authorities as the legitimate president of the community. It was to Cairo that the Rabbi Moses, better known as Maimonides, came from his native Spain where, as in Morocco where he spent some time under the ruling Berber dynasty, the Almohades, Jews had to observe the Islamic way of life and hide their true religion. Not so in Cairo. Maimonides went first of all to Palestine but found the condition of the Jews there under the Franks so wretched that he soon moved on to Egypt, in 1163, and it was here that he wrote his *Guide for the Perplexed*, which is a learned and deeply felt attempt to harmonize biblical teaching with the

[77]

philosophy of Aristotle, the inescapable philosopher for Jews, Arabs and Christians alike in the Middle Ages.

Like many other philosophers in medieval Islam (notably Avicenna who died 100 years before he was born) Maimonides was a physician. He made no great contribution to medical science (Avicenna's *Canon of Medicine* was his authority, as it was for Europe in translation until the seventeenth century) but he was sufficiently eminent to be given an appointment at Saladin's court as a consultant. It is tempting to imagine the philosopher and Saladin exchanging views on the limitations of human knowledge and evil considered as a consequence of free will. He married the sister of a certain Ibn al-Mali who was employed in Saladin's secretariat, which means that Ibn al-Mali, working in this sensitive area, was a Jew. Maimonides subsequently became physician to Saladin's son. His brother David was a jeweller who traded with India and lost his life in a shipwreck.

David's fate reminds us of the scale of intercontinental trade under medieval Islam. The annual pilgrimage from all parts of the Moslem world was a powerful stimulus to trade; Mecca was the most important Islamic fair and clearing-house. 'There are no goods in the whole world', wrote Ibn Jubayr, 'which thanks to the confluence of pilgrims are not to be found in Mecca.' The Nubian port of Aidib, on the other side of the Red Sea from Jiddah, was the place through which much trade flowed into Egypt and when Ibn Jubayr was there he reported caravans, too many to count, bearing the merchandise of India:

> You will find loads of pepper, cinnamon and the like thrown unguarded by the side of the road. They are left like this through the sickness of the camels that bear them, or for some other reason, and remain there in their place until their owners remove them, secure from all risk despite the great number of men of all kinds who pass them by.

When a merchant did not actually accompany his goods on one of these great trading missions, many months in duration sometimes, but sent his spices, aromatics or whatever in the charge of some middleman, there was an accountancy difficulty. In the absence of a banking system that could have provided international letters of credit there was reluctance to send gold, silver or copper coin for fear of robbery. International trade was made possible by the rendering of mutual services. A merchant in Aden would have an agreement with another merchant in Cairo by which each was the agent of the other with no money passing. 'You do for me at your end what I do for you in my place here.' This system of mutual aid and profit seemed to work and must have been based on some calculation of the amount of work involved because there was a current saying: 'Be friends with one another but keep good accounts.' The association worked best when it was within the family. A twelfth-century merchant called Abu'l-Abbas al-Hijazi, who had spent many years in China, lost all but one of his twelve ships in the Indian Ocean and then re-established his fortunes by getting a cargo of porcelain and aloe wood from his base in Yemen to Egypt. He had seven sons, we are told, and posted them to seven different commercial centres, including Cairo, and so established a trading network.

The greatest trading family of all were the Karimis of Aden who dominated trade from the Far East and East Africa into the Red Sea. They had their agencies everywhere and were much supported by Saladin because of the wealth their activities generated. A special *funduq* (a kind of trading post in which people from overseas lived and traded, rather like those of the Hanseatic merchants in Northern Europe) was built for the Karimi traders. Cairo had other *funduqs*, including one specializing in oil from Syria, another for fruit, and one for amber. Saladin's policy normally was to exclude Western merchants from Cairo. The Pisans once traded there but as a punishment for their association with the Crusaders they were now limited to Alexandria. On all this trade Saladin was able to impose a tax of something like 25 per cent of the value of the goods in transit and he could do it with a good conscience; it was all quite canonical. Slave traders, who operated mainly from the Black Sea area, paid less tax because it was recognized that a good supply of *mamluks* was necessary for the defence of Islam.

The Fatimid Caliphs had been the largest merchants of all within their realm, owning *funduqs*, shops, property; their officials were all active in business with some of the advantage enjoyed by the Caliph himself to buy and sell at prices determined not so much by the market as by their own sense of what was right and proper. Saladin followed this example, but unlike the Fatimids he put the profits not into luxurious living but into the public purse for use in what he judged to be the public interest. Major enterprises like the building of the Citadel and the new walls were financed by earmarking the revenue of a given area or resource. South-west of Cairo is the Fayoum, an oasis providing grapes, olives, emmer wheat, sugar cane, figs, apricots, beans and lettuce. The taxes from this rich province were allocated by Saladin for the expansion of the navy; so was the tax on nitre which came from a valley in the desert to the west of the Canopic branch of the Nile (incidentally, a great and surviving centre of Coptic monasticism); nitre and alum were exported in great quantities to northern Italy where the textile trade largely depended on them. In modern terms it could be said that under Saladin the Egyptian economy became much more productive than under the Fatimids and, in spite of the high proportion of resources allocated to defence, there was little inflation until the time of the Third Crusade. The price of wheat remained remarkably stable for years.

This consolidation of Saladin's power in Egypt was greatly helped by a truce with the Franks. No general peace could ever be agreed between Moslem and Frank; the fighting of the Holy War was a religious duty to Moslems and all they were entitled to was a respite. Sometimes there was an unacknowledged truce as in 1170 when there were devastating earthquakes and everyone was more concerned with repairing shattered homes and fortresses than fighting. But formal truces, accompanied by solemn oaths taken on the Koran and Bible, or a Fragment of the True Cross, were agreed when both parties saw an advantage to be gained, as after the death of Amalric when Saladin was still struggling to stamp his authority on Syria. When a truce was broken it was usually by the Franks who took the Christian view that an oath sworn to an infidel was no oath at all.

It so happened that in 1177 a new figure from Europe, Count Philip of Flanders, appeared in Palestine with a sizeable army, eager (it was wrongly thought by King Baldwin the Leper and his lords) to fight. It was part of any truce agreement that when someone as important as Philip of Flanders appeared on the scene from Europe the truce was suspended, to be renewed on his departure, a rule of the game that was understood and accepted by the Moslems. Count Philip, as it turned out, had no wish to invade Egypt as was expected of him but he did consent to campaign against certain towns in Syria,

Consolidation in Egypt

Hamah for one; no sooner was he on the march than Saladin felt free to raid southern Palestine, even threaten Jerusalem itself, as a means of drawing off Frankish forces from Syria. It was not too soon. Any prolonged period of military inactivity against the Franks was dangerous for Saladin because it gave rise to talk in Syria and Mesopotamia that his zeal for the Holy War was a pretence. The time had come for Saladin to achieve a dramatic success that would once and for all establish his credentials as the champion of Moslem orthodoxy. As it turned out he suffered a humiliating reverse.

He led a force from his new remodelled army up the old military road of the Pharaohs across Sinai and crossed the so-called River of Egypt, the traditional frontier, on 18 November. It was a cavalry force made up of Saladin's elite regiment of guards, a considerably larger number of *mamluks*, regular soldiers, and the largest contingent consisting of Arab, Berber, Egyptian and Nubian horsemen raised by Saladin's feudal tenants. The speed with which Saladin took this force into Palestine shows it could not have been transporting heavy siege equipment. They were on a *razzia*, the time-honoured Moslem raid for plunder, and were on Gaza almost before the garrison—they were Templars—were aware of what was happening. Saladin ignored the place and pressed on to Ascalon, the one-time Fatimid base which the Franks had taken in 1144. William of Tyre described the city as being 'in the form of a semi-circle, the chord or diameter extending along the shore'. Its defences consisted of a wall of solid masonry with towers and gates and, outside these, substantial earthworks. It had no port or safe harbourage and was dangerous to approach by sea except in calm weather.

The 16-year-old King Baldwin, active in spite of his leprous condition, had hurried down from Jerusalem with all the forces he could muster and taken up his position in the city, strengthened by the presence of the True Cross which was in the care of the Bishop of Bethlehem. Things now went seriously wrong for Saladin. The Egyptian army began to plunder the countryside, including the towns of Ramleh and Lydda, right up into the hills towards Jerusalem itself, and there was a breakdown in discipline.

King Baldwin called up the Templars from Gaza to join him and made a desperate sortie from Ascalon. His smallish force of knights surprised Saladin and his regiment of guards in a wadi near Mont Gisard, a castle south-east of Ramleh, and charged them down.

[81]

Consolidation in Egypt

Imad al-Din, Saladin's Syrian secretary, wrote: 'Suddenly the Franks appeared, squadrons of them surging to the attack, nimble as wolves, barking like dogs, a mass of knights on fire for battle.' Saladin himself, after vainly trying to re-form his force in some kind of battle order, described how he was attacked by 'three knights with lances pointed at his chest'. He would have been killed but for a vigorous counter-attack by three of his guards who cut the Franks down. He managed to escape under cover of night but his small party would have been lost if his vizier, the elegant stylist al-Fadel, had not had the foresight to hire camels and guides from the local Beduin who brought them, after many days and nights, sometimes across shifting sands and by little known routes, safely back to the River of Egypt.

Most of the Egyptian army were killed or taken prisoner. The remnant that did escape only did so by abandoning their equipment and running, to be preyed upon by the Beduin who did not mind whom they plundered, Christian or Moslem. King Baldwin could be forgiven for thinking he had disposed of the Egyptian threat for years. As for Saladin, his main thought was to let it be known throughout Egypt and as quickly as possible that he was alive and well. His use of carrier pigeons for this communiqué is the first we hear of these birds in Egypt. He had been defeated but he had not suffered a major setback. Within three months he was back again on the attack, campaigning against the Franks in Syria, showing not only his personal resilience but the effectiveness of the measures he had taken to build up the strength of Egypt and its armed forces. He assured the Caliph in Baghdad that within a year he would attack Jerusalem itself.

6

The Diploma for Aleppo

Philip of Flanders went back to Europe in 1178 and so the truce was on again, but the Franks broke it, attacked the Syrian town of Hamah and were defeated. Saladin was so provoked by what he regarded as a breach of faith that the Franks taken prisoner were executed. This was the moment when King Baldwin, against his better judgement, was strong-armed by the Templars into rebuilding a fort at Jacob's Ford on the Jordan, so called because it was here that Jacob had wrestled with the angel. It commanded the plain of Banias which produced wheat, cotton and rice; by good custom and usage the fertile plain had become a demilitarized area where Moslem and Christian could pass freely. A large oak, the Tree of Measure, marked a theoretical boundary, but shepherds and their flocks ignored it. The fort would make this boundary rigid, besides providing the Franks with a strong point within striking distance of Damascus, and Saladin regarded it as such a threat that he tried to buy Baldwin off, first with 60,000 pieces of gold, then with 100,000. He was unable to move militarily because, much to his annoyance, he was unexpectedly tied down by a family dispute. Difficulties created by ambitious members of his own family were to be recurrent from now on.

His brother Turanshah had turned out to be a failure as Governor of Damascus. He was one of those dashing officers who fall into dissipation when not actually campaigning; he was even known to be in communication with al-Salih in Aleppo which Saladin had to take as evidence of incipient disloyalty. He owed a great deal to Turanshah's support and hesitated before removing him. (He was replaced by Saladin's very capable nephew, Farrukshah, a man he trusted more completely than any of his other relations and who wrote competent poetry into the bargain.) Turanshah demanded Baalbek in compensation for the loss of Damascus. This involved displacing the resident governor, Ibn al-Muqaddam, who objected so strongly that Saladin had to threaten force. A satisfactory conclusion was reached in the end, but Saladin was kept so busy that the fort at Jacob's Ford went up without interruption.

But from now on luck was on Saladin's side. In April 1179 he sent Farrukshah out on a reconnaissance with the Damascus army of 1,000 horsemen. He surprised a force of Franks under the leadership of King Baldwin himself in the wild country near the gorge of the Litani river where it was possible for hostile forces to be in close proximity without being aware of the fact. The King himself would have been taken prisoner but for the gallantry of Humphrey of Toron, whose acquaintance Saladin had made at Alexandria: he was wounded and died shortly after at his castle of Hunin. 'A man,' said al-Athir, 'whose name was a proverb for bravery and skill in war.' Saladin respected Humphrey's honourable bearing and honesty, but as he was Constable of the Kingdom (that is, Commander-in-Chief of the army), Seneschal, Master of Ceremonies and Treasurer, his loss to the Franks was a blow which Saladin could only welcome.

That summer food was so short that Saladin sent raiders into southern Lebanon to plunder and harvest what grain they could. A Frankish force under Baldwin and Count Raymond of Tripoli came up to attack, moving through a strategic valley where they hoped to escape detection by Saladin, but their progress caused sheep to scatter on the hillside and this was noticed by his scouts. Baldwin, rocking in his saddle from physical weakness, had an initial success against a detachment of cavalry commanded by Farrukshah but when he came on Saladin's main army the Franks were so over-confident that the knights under the Master of the Templars, Odo of Saint-Amand, rushed ahead of the infantry, only to find the Moslems scattering to avoid combat. Saladin was able to rally them and make his counter-attack at a moment when the Franks were at such disadvantage that they were routed: he took some distinguished prisoners. Over 270 knights were paraded before his tent, among them the Templar Odo who was largely responsible for the disaster. He refused Saladin's offer to exchange him for one of his own senior officers who was locked up in a Jerusalem dungeon, saying a Templar would ransom himself only with his belt and dagger (in fact he was outraged that Saladin should think one of his own emirs his equal), so was dispatched to prison in Damascus where he died the following year. Baldwin and Raymond of Tripoli had managed to get away to the castle of Beaufort.

For the first time Saladin was now able to put together a major force drawing on both Syria and Egypt. They mustered near Damascus. There were regiments from Hamah, Baalbek and Homs, troops from Nubia, Turkoman mercenaries, Beduin auxiliaries, specialists from the north with sapping and mining experience, all intended for the too long delayed attack on the fort at Jacob's Ford. Most troops wore padded clothes to serve as some kind of protection against arrows and sword-thrusts, but such was the summer heat, the sun blazing back from limestone and basalt, that they risked removing these clothes to work at making screens out of vine poles and leather. These were intended to protect the sappers as they dug under a part of the wall of the fort. The idea was to make a great cavity and fill it with wood which would then be fired, thus cracking the masonry and causing the wall to collapse.

Saladin was alert for the arrival of a relieving force but the Franks had been too badly mauled. After a siege of five days the wall over the mine gave way and the Moslems stormed in to release the prisoners and take 700 Franks captive. On his orders Moslem apostates were killed and so were the crossbowmen who were regarded as particularly dangerous adversaries. The object was not merely to take the fort but to eliminate it and Saladin himself stayed on the scene, the air rank with the stench of bodies and smoke from the burning timber that was being used to fire and break up the masonry, until nothing was left but heaps of blackened stone. These victories were celebrated throughout Saladin's territories and were seen by his partisans in Baghdad and the Zengid cities of Aleppo and Mosul as evidence that God had decided he was indeed the champion of Islam and the only leader of the Holy War.

Set battles between large armies operating from prepared positions, as in Europe, were less common than might be supposed during the Crusading period. Time and again we read of important clashes coming about by accident, as in 1179, presumably because of the difficulty of knowing just where the enemy was in this hilly country. Fighting usually resulted from raids on what was supposed to be the enemy's weak point. Forces were comparatively small. It was difficult to get a large army together and maintain it in the field for any length of time; troops lived off the land and most of the region was arid. Famine was common. Moslem troops in particular, who had harvested the crops in hostile territory, would rarely want to stay under arms for longer than nine months at a time. The Frankish tactics tended to be defensive, maintaining a position in a fortified city or castle. If, as so often happened, the besiegers grew tired, ran out of supplies, or got so cold and wet that they went home, this, for the defenders, was as good as a battle fought and won. The side with its forces intact at the beginning of winter while the enemy had faded away had in a real sense gained the advantage, and these were usually the Franks.

Saladin's great strength as a field commander was his ability to retrieve a bad situation by quick thinking and coolness. A better general might not have allowed the bad situation to arise in the first place but once the Frankish knights had charged he was a brilliant exploiter of the greater flexibility his light cavalry were capable of. He was the master of the rally and counter-attack. Many of the men under his command were as certain they would be instantly transported to Paradise if killed in battle with the polytheists as they were of the hell-fire that awaited the slaughtered enemy; these convictions gave a ferocious edge to the Moslem attack. Their dash and impetuosity caused them to consider the slower moving, disciplined Frankish knights as sometimes over-cautious.

In spite of treaty obligations Zengi's grandsons, al-Salih in Aleppo and Saif al-Din in Mosul, showed not the slightest enthusiasm for providing Saladin with troops to fight the Franks. On the contrary, they had negotiated with the Franks on how best to bring Saladin down. It was all complicated by rivalry between Aleppo and Mosul; even if Saladin succeeded in persuading al-Salih to honour his obligations this would have the effect of increasing Mosul's suspicions and hostility. For the next few years this Mesopotamian problem occupied Saladin even more than his dealings with the Franks with whom he agreed a truce in 1180. The Franks needed it because of Baldwin's deteriorating condition, and the dynastic squabbling this sparked off. Saladin needed it because of food shortages and an inability to mobilize the manpower of his supposed allies to the north and east.

Mosul was particularly unhelpful. It occupies a splendid site on the west bank of the Tigris, opposite the ancient site of Nineveh which was obliterated by sand. Outside its walls were wide fields of wheat, brilliantly green in the springtime, orchards and rolling uplands inhabited by gaunt shepherds and their flocks. It dominated the Jezireh to the west, the 'island' between the Tigris and the Euphrates. To the north were the foothills of the snowy ranges of the Diyar Bekr and Greater Armenia. This was Kurdish country in the main but with a great admixture of Persian, Turkoman and other tribesmen. Here were cities under petty princes feuding with each other and yet able to export tribesmen and soldiers to fight for a season as mercenaries, perhaps for the Prince of Mosul, or the Seljuk Sultan who ruled from Konia in Anatolia, or even the Caliph al-Mustadi in Baghdad who was more preoccupied with the Seljuk *atabeg* in Persia, away to the east, than he was with any *jihad* against the Franks. When winter set in these warriors from the mountains went home with whatever pay or, more important, plunder they had picked up in the richer lands to the south and west.

In the Caliph's entourage there were those who supported and intrigued on behalf of Zengi's grandsons and there were those, more influential after his victories in 1179, who did the same for Saladin. He never ceased to bombard Baghdad with letters claiming that his achievements had all been made in the name of the Caliph and asking that his authority should be more widely recognized. 'Is there among all the leaders of Islam another whose extension of power is a source of grief and affliction to the infidels?' The truthful answer was no. But even when the Caliph al-Mustadi died in 1180 and was succeeded by the able and more energetic al-Nasir not much was done in Baghdad to strengthen Saladin's arm. With the recent history of the Caliphate in mind, who could blame al-Nasir for looking to the east? That was where trouble came from, not from Palestine. Less than fifty years previously the Sultan had come out of Persia, confiscated the then Caliph's property, looted 10 million dinars worth of goods and so much gold and silver coin that 170 mules were needed to carry the chests away.

Succeeding Caliphs had been stronger, largely because of the way the secular power of the Sultans in Persia disintegrated, and al-Nasir in particular proved himself to be a figure of consequence. His two enemies were the Ismailis, who challenged his spiritual authority, and a new force rising in eastern Persia, the Shahs of Khwarizm who saw themselves replacing the Seljuks. In the Babylonian tradition al-Nasir had himself represented on the gates of Baghdad tearing

[87]

apart the jaws of two dragons, probably the Ismaili Imam and the Khwarizm Shah. But it might be the Persian *atabeg*; anyway, a threatening force out there in the east. Al-Nasir's ambition was to re-establish the theocratic welfare state of earliest Islam. He abolished the non-canonical taxes, opened soup kitchens, and tried to harness the energies of a radical movement that had been gathering strength in the cities for some years, the Futuwwa, young men with anti-establishment ideas who claimed to be full of religious enthusiasm; they were ready to riot and go in for all sorts of revolutionary activities in the name of the pure doctrines of Islam. They were organized in societies. It sounds more like Shia than Sunni (orthodox) Islam and so in fact it was. Al-Nasir had Shiite leanings. He joined one of these societies himself and tried to organize the whole movement as an order of chivalry. All his princes and emirs were expected to become members of the order, the Caliph's way of ensuring the establishment of a new theocracy in the provinces, and no exception was made for Saladin. Not that he would have wished it. Perhaps he saw these enthusiasts becoming in time a Moslem equivalent of the Templars and Hospitallers.

What Saladin was trying to obtain from Baghdad was a diploma recognizing his authority over Mosul but this was never granted; if he was to intervene successfully in the affairs of the Jezireh it would have to be by other means. An opportunity came when one of the independent princes there appealed to Saladin for help against the Seljuk Sultan of Konia who was threatening him. The situation arose out of a harem quarrel.

Rather surprisingly for so powerful a ruler, the Seljuk Sultan of Konia, Kilij Arslan, had given one of his daughters in marriage to the Emir of the city of Hisn Kaifa, so far up the Tigris that it was only about 80 kilometres south of Lake Van in present-day eastern Turkey. This Emir was another Nur al-Din, one of the Ortoqid Turkish ruling clan (so called because of their descent from a certain Ortoq) who had evolved in a comparatively short time from predatory tribesmen into the rulers of important cities which continued as cultural centres with teaching mosques and libraries; the library of the neighbouring city of Amid was one of the largest in the Moslem world and certainly larger than any in the West. That Nur al-Din should have appealed to Saladin is interesting. He was nominally in the Mosul sphere of influence and his appeal for help should have gone there but, in the first place, he thought Saladin's help would be more effective and, secondly, he wanted to break away from Mosul anyway.

Nur al-Din's marriage was not happy. He took up with a singing girl and his wife complained to Kilij Arslan who was so enraged at his daughter's displacement by a girl of no standing that he organized a punitive expedition and prepared to move. Kilij Arslan had given Saladin cause for some displeasure by trying to take a city from him in northern Syria (indeed, there had been a fierce battle in which Taqi al-Din had routed Kilij Arslan's army) so he had a number of reasons for marching up to the frontier and issuing an ultimatum. 'Abandon this expedition against my Ortoqid ally or by my faith I will march into your capital and seize all your dominions.' This Kilij Arslan, it must be remembered, was the man who only four years previously had destroyed at Myriocephalum one of the greatest armies ever commanded by a Byzantine emperor. Saladin's threat sounds like a bluff. His objective was not military but to gain the credit of as much conciliation in Nur al-Din's favour as he could manage. Kilij Arslan's ambassador reproved him:

Is it not shameful for a prince such as you . . . of whom men hear he has made peace with the Franks [Baldwin IV], who has taken away what was of advantage to Moslems, who has brought together troops of different countries, and all for a wretched singing girl? What will be your excuse before God, the Caliph, the kings of Islam and all these people?

Saladin was impressed by the moral argument and when he met Kilij Arslan an alliance was agreed. Nur al-Din was told to give up his singing girl, which he did. The effect of this intervention was felt most strongly in Mosul from where complaints about Saladin's interference were sent to Baghdad. There, they were studied with sympathy.

The truce with Baldwin IV was for two years and can be taken as evidence that Saladin had made a decision about priorities. Mosul and the Jezireh first, Jerusalem second. He wrote to the Caliph, 'This little Jezireh is the lever which will set in motion the great Jezireh (that is, Mesopotamia, Syria and Egypt); it is the point of division and the centre of resistance and once it is set in place in the chain of alliances, the whole armed might of Islam will be coordinated to

The Diploma for Aleppo

engage the forces of unbelief.' The style is al-Fadel's. The letter soared into hyperbole. Once Saladin had Mosul there was no limit to what he could add to the Caliph's dominions. He would capture Jerusalem, Constantinople, Georgia and the lands of the Almohades in the west 'until the Abbasid caliphate has wiped the world clean, turning the churches into mosques'. The Caliph would not have believed a word of it—Saladin would not have expected him to—but it was the kind of exaggeration the diplomatic exchanges of the time sometimes seemed to require.

Saif al-Din of Mosul, wine drinker, patron of singing girls and collector of exotic birds, died in June 1180, and was succeeded by his brother Izz al-Din, a not dissimilar character. He calmly asked Saladin to recognize his authority over the cities of the Jezireh and was peremptorily refused. The cities, Saladin said, had been seized unlawfully on the death of Nur al-Din in 1174, had now been granted to him by the Caliph (which was true) and Mosul's enjoyment of their revenues was entirely conditional on the sending of troops to serve in the Holy War. Izz al-Din said that for the life of him he did not see the matter that way at all.

For Saladin it was a time of uncertainty and frustration. He was a man of restless energy, never wishing to put off until tomorrow what should be attempted today. But in his dealings with al-Salih and Izz al-Din he had constantly in mind the necessity to win them over. He wanted their military support, not their possessions. So he had to proceed cautiously. He was popularly supposed to take little sleep or relaxation. 'His saddle', to use one of his favourite expressions, 'was his council chamber,' and some of the expeditions he now threw himself into look like the gesturing of a man who wanted outlet for his energies—the short campaign towards the Amanus mountains in north-west Syria, for example, because the Armenian Ruben who ruled there had been plundering Turkoman tribes. Al-Fadel viewed this with some amazement. Never very happy away from the Nile he could not understand how this adventuring in the north could extend his master's power.

Al-Salih died unexpectedly in Aleppo on 4 December 1181 at the age of 19 after refusing, as being contrary to Koranic teaching, a glass of wine which his doctors thought might do him good. He was a devout youth of great promise who never faltered in his hostility to

The Diploma for Aleppo

Saladin and when he knew he was dying from some intestinal complaint he nominated his cousin, Izz al-Din, as his successor. Izz al-Din did not care to undertake the responsibility and invited his brother Imad al-Din, ruler of Sinjar, to take over, which he did in the early summer of 1182. Saladin was in Egypt at the time and his first thought was to prevent the forces of Mosul joining those of Aleppo in what he expected to be an attack on his own territories. He instructed Farrukshah, back in Syria, and Taqi al-Din (Saladin's nephew, the one who had been all for defying Nur al-Din and had campaigned west to Tunis) to prevent Izz al-Din from crossing the Euphrates. This they were unable to do because, almost as though there was collusion between the Zengi brothers and the Franks, the Lord of Kerak in Moab, Reynald of Chatillon, had reconnoitred into the desert and Farrukshah had to deal with him. Taqi al-Din was tied down by a pro-Zengid rising in the city of Hamah. As a consequence Saladin decided to go back to Syria himself to safeguard his interests. This was May 1182. The evening before his departure he sat with some companions and remarked on the pleasant breeze and the scent of flowers. A tutor to one of his sons quoted, without thinking what he was doing, from an old love poem: 'Enjoy while you can the perfume of the ox-eyed flowers of Nejd. After tonight there will be no more flowers.' Saladin was disturbed because he took the words as an omen. After that night he did not, in fact, see Cairo again.

He was still away in the north, campaigning against his Zengid enemies, when news came that the truce between him and Baldwin had been sensationally broken by that same Reynald of Chatillon who had ventured into the desert some months before. Now he planned to invade the Hedjaz itself, plunder shipping in the Red Sea and, it was rumoured, remove the Prophet's body from Medina.

How disgraceful it was, Saladin pointed out to the Caliph in a letter drafted by al-Fadel, that at the very time his forces were defending the city of the Prophet, Medina, from the polytheists, Aleppo was being unlawfully seized by the Prince of Mosul—unlawfully because the previous Caliph had issued him, Saladin, with the diploma for Aleppo. This was not true and everyone knew it, but Saladin was so disturbed by the new instability in the north of Syria that he wrote some very angry letters indeed to Baghdad. If the Caliph were to authorize the dishonest handing over of Aleppo why not all Syria and Egypt as well? It was a rebuke to the Commander of the Faithful and it testifies not only to the strength of Saladin's feelings but also to his position. It did not lie within the Caliph's power to give the diplomas for Syria and Egypt to anyone but Saladin.

Reynald of Chatillon was a man for whom Saladin came to form a deep loathing. He had originally come crusading from France with Louis VII in 1148 and had taken part in the abortive attack on Damascus. Having no prospects back home he stayed on to carve out a position in the Holy Land and made his first great step by turning the head of the widow Constance, Princess of Antioch, one of the greatest ladies in the Frankish east, marrying her and so becoming Lord of that great city. He was a capable and fearless soldier, but brutal, bigoted and (to use an expression that would have pleased Saladin) pig-headed. He was the egregious example of those newly arrived Franks who despised the old hands for having 'gone native'. Because the Greek Emperor Manuel refused to hand over a subsidy to which he thought he was entitled Reynald, helped by Armenian forces under their Count Thoros, invaded the imperial territory of Cyprus after torturing the Patriarch of Antioch for the necessary funds. Christian, albeit Orthodox, Cyprus was plundered and devastated in a way that shocked the rest of the Frankish east. On a raid into northern Syria for cattle and horses Reynald was taken prisoner and spent sixteen years in an Aleppo jail from where no one, not even his wife, made any attempt to ransom him. Along with others he was released by the al-Salih regime out of gratitude to the Franks for frustrating Saladin's siege of that city. Constance of Antioch now being dead, he married another heiress–widow, Stephanie, and so became master of her great castle Kerak in Moab from where he raided the caravan routes to Egypt and Mecca. From its walls he could look some 1,200 metres down to the blue waters of the Dead Sea and, on the other side, to Bethlehem and Jerusalem on the Judaean hills. A truce meant nothing to him.

Reynald raided piratically down the Red Sea on ships transported overland from Ascalon in sections and launched in the Gulf of Akaba. The expedition was a failure. He sacked the Egyptian Red Sea port of Aidab through which so much of the trade from Yemen and the Far East passed. But when he was preparing to land on the Arabian coast prior to marching on Medina (to destroy the tomb of the 'accursed camel driver') an Egyptian squadron under the

The Diploma for Aleppo

Armenian admiral Lulu arrived. In the fighting on shore that followed most of the raiders were killed but Ibn Jubayr saw some of them as prisoners in Alexandria, mounted backwards on camels. They were subsequently killed too, at Saladin's special insistence, in spite of their having been promised their lives. He said their attack was 'an unparalleled enormity in the history of Islam' and if they were given quarter 'a rent would be caused amongst the faithful that can never be mended'. Reynald himself managed to escape but his sacrilege sent a thrill of horror throughout Islam That Saladin's navy had defeated him brought special glory to the Sultan and showed what a force he now was, not only by land but by sea.

From the beginning of Saladin's ascendancy after the death of Nur al-Din men of talent wanted to work for him. Never were their political gifts needed more than now, when diplomacy and military manoeuvring went hand in hand. They were, in the main, products of the colleges, notably those established by Nizam al-Mulk (and therefore called Nizamiya) to train men for administrative and judicial posts. These high-flying civil servants went wherever their talents could command office. A man of outstanding ability could have offers from Nisapur, Mosul, Aleppo, Damascus and Cairo. Imad al-Din was a Persian who graduated from the Nizamiya in Baghdad, became a protégé of Saladin's father Ayyub and was appointed Nur al-Din's Head of State Correspondence in Aleppo where he wrote with great elegance in Persian and Arabic. Under Saladin he became President of the Council of State and Chancellor of the Syrian kingdom.

His Egyptian equivalent, al-Fadel, lacked Imad-al-Din's virtuosity but he was a poet and a great exponent of poetic prose in the letters he wrote on Saladin's behalf. Born in Ascalon, he came of an old Arab family and was devoted to Egypt. On arriving at the Euphrates with Saladin he wrote some verses which can be translated: 'Bear from me a message to the Nile; tell it I could never quench my thirst with water from the Euphrates. Ask my heart if I say the truth.'

Between them these two men conducted Saladin's propaganda with Baghdad. The Zengids in Mosul and Aleppo, they claimed, were hand in glove with the Assassins and the Franks. The previous Caliph's diploma granted all Syria, except Aleppo, to Saladin but, they argued, this had been out of respect to al-Salih personally and now that he was dead the exception no longer applied. In Baghdad this claim was thought too weak to be taken seriously. Before attempting to assert his authority over Aleppo by force, Saladin fought a sanguinary battle with the Franks in Galilee and ordered up the Egyptian fleet to attack Beyrout while he made an assault from the land. The marines poured arrows so thickly into the town that the inhabitants could do nothing but keep their heads down, but Saladin, lacking the necessary siege machinery, was forced to withdraw. He marched on Aleppo to dispossess Imad al-Din and exercise the rights he claimed over the city and then received a quite unexpected invitation from one of the Mesopotamian emirs to cross the Euphrates, assuring him of a cordial welcome. This was Geukburi, governor of the dusty, wind-swept city of Harran, an adherent of the Zengids who had come to the conclusion that Saladin provided the only answer to the unsettled, almost anarchic, conditions in the area. He was a fearless soldier, ostentatiously generous and a great music lover.

At this crossing of the Euphrates al-Fadel wrote those lines saying how much he preferred the Nile. In the long letter he now wrote to the Caliph in Saladin's name he compared the limpid waves of the Euphrates with the pure and sublime intelligences that graced the Caliph's court, and the sweetness of its water with the deeds of the Caliph himself. At the same time he did not fail to point out that 'the men of Mosul are tied to the Franks by a pact that holds them body and soul.' They were also, in desperation, trying to get support from another enemy of the Caliph, al-Pahlawan, the *atabeg* of the Seljuk Sultan in Persia. Would it not be sensible for the Commander of the Faithful to issue Saladin with the diploma for Mosul and put an end to this subversion? No answer.

Saladin took over much of Mesopotamia without great difficulty but Mosul was a different proposition. Ibn Jubayr described the high, immensely thick walls capped with 'towers set so closely together they almost touch'. Within the walls were chambers that provided 'a safe refuge for the warriors. . . . At the highest point of the town is a great fortress with stones compactly set. . . . The Tigris flows east of the town, touching its walls whose towers rise from the waters.' Over the years Saladin made three attempts on the place. At one time a compromise seemed possible and the Caliph sent a delegation to mediate. Its leader, the Sheikh of Sheikhs, approved one idea put forward, that Izz al-Din should be left in possession of the city but his vassals in the key cities of Irbil, Tikrit and elsewhere should be allowed to choose between Izz al-Din and Saladin for their master. Izz al-Din's envoy turned this down so rudely that the Sheikh of Sheikhs withdrew to Baghdad in a rage and there was even more bad feeling in the area than before.

A wild plan was put to Saladin of diverting the Tigris and so depriving Mosul of its supply of water, but this came to nothing and Saladin turned on Sinjar, 80 kilometres away, which was held by Izz al-Din's brother. He was helped in this enterprise by Nur al-Din of Hisn Kaifa, he who had been in trouble with his father-in-law over a singing girl; he was promised as a reward the Ortoqid city of Amid on the upper Tigris right up in the mountains of Diyar Bekr. Sinjar surrendered after a fifteen-day siege and the garrison was evacuated to Mosul. Saladin regarded it as within his competence to offer Amid to Nur al-Din because the Caliph, who did not favour the Ortoqids, had been prevailed upon to grant him a diploma for the place. So this city with black basalt walls, an iron gate and an easily defensible site on a sharp bend in the river was taken after eight days' siege in May 1183. Al-Fadel took away a selection of books from the famous library on seventy camels but the rest of the wealth of this city was handed over intact to Nur al-Din. The defeated governor was treated with the courtesy that had now become customary with Saladin. He extracted no advantage for himself from the capture and his reputation for disinterested generosity was boosted even among those who previously had been sceptical.

Reports had been coming in of Frankish incursions into Syria. Saladin took them calmly. 'Whilst they knock down villages we are taking cities; when we come back we shall have all the more strength to fight them.' But this was not a view that impressed all his followers, especially those with families back in Syria and *mamluks* from Egypt who wondered at so much effort being expended in the north when the real danger to their security lay much nearer home. After pointing out to the Caliph that success had been achieved at Amid because of the diploma and that the gates of Mosul could have been opened with the same key Saladin returned to Syria in the early summer to invest Aleppo.

There was sharp fighting during which Saladin's youngest

[95]

The Diploma for Aleppo

brother Bori was wounded and later died. Saladin had no heart for a real assault. There were too many of Nur al-Din's old guard in the city, men he respected because of their record as fighters in the Holy War. The ruler, Imad al-Din, for his part had no appetite for hard fighting. He was not popular in Aleppo, hankered for a return to his original city of Sinjar and this, being in Saladin's possession as a result of his recent campaign, he was willing to grant. An agreement was made, part of which involved Nur al-Din's giving support in the war against the Franks, and at long last Saladin's yellow banner waved over the citadel. The possession of Aleppo was of enormous political and strategic importance. It was the commanding military city of North Syria, the base of the great exemplar Nur al-Din, and when Saladin returned in power to this scene where he had spent so much of his youth it was, in his view, an especially significant sign of divine favour. But the loss of Bori, of whom he was fond, was no less hard to bear.

7

Mosul Won Over and the Truce Ends

At the age of 45 Saladin was now the most powerful figure in the Moslem world and could call for men and supplies from an area extending between the Tigris in the east and the borders of Tunis in the west. He was respected not only for his military strength but also for his fairness and generosity. If there were abuses he was credited with knowing nothing about them; the rapacity of the customs officials at Alexandria, for example, of whom Ibn Jubayr said, 'There is no doubt that this is one of the matters concealed from the great Sultan. If he heard of it, from what is related of his justice and leanings to pity, he would end it.' (Tax was exacted even on pilgrims' personal provisions and other goods were confiscated.) It was a time when everyone assumed honorific titles. Theoretically only the Caliph could confer them but it became a commonplace for rulers 'to embellish themselves with titles taken from religion [din]. Not one of them', said Ibn Jubayr, 'is known by a cognomen that fits him, or is described by an epithet of which he is worthy. Not one save Saladin [Salah al-Din means Honouring of Religion] Lord of Syria, the Hedjaz, Yemen, and Egypt, and famous for his virtue and justness.'

Damascus was now Saladin's permanent base. Like Nur al-Din before him, he presided every Tuesday and Thursday at the Hall of Justice 'for the redress of wrongs, to exact recompense from the oppressor, to give justice and to listen to the words of his subjects with his own ears, without any intermediary'. If there was a dispute in which he himself had an interest he surrendered his place to the Cadi, as over the ownership of a certain slave, when Saladin left his state couch and sat at the side of the plaintiff. After the case had been decided in his favour he sent the disappointed plaintiff away with gifts of clothes and money. Because of the Moslem tradition that all subjects had reasonable access to the ruler he was exposed not only in formal sessions but on less public occasions. He was preparing to take a nap one afternoon when a *mamluk* insisted on presenting a petition and would not be put off even when Saladin said he was without his inkstand. The *mamluk* told him there was a big inkstand behind him in the tent. 'By God! He is right,' said Saladin, turning to see, and without more ado he signed the petition.

He had the ability of a highly practical man to seize the essentials of a complex issue and make a decision accordingly. He enjoyed religious discussion but he had no mastery of the technical terms, so used homely language which was much to the purpose. He was not even certain he had a complete grasp of doctrine or, if he had, felt he needed constant reminding of what was required for salvation; he regularly used a handbook of religious instruction specially prepared for him.

But he was rarely in the city for any length of time because he was so busy claiming back the various gains the Franks had made during his absence in Mesopotamia. There was one battle and it ended inconclusively. A particularly strong Frankish army, 1,300 knights and 15,000 infrantry, advanced to al-Fulah, just west of the Jordan. There were disagreements among the leadership with the result that the main force was not committed, but Saladin never attacked a fully prepared Frankish army if he could help it. He went off and, within a period of some months, conducted two sieges of Reynald of Chatillon's Kerak in Moab. For the second of these attacks Saladin was able to mobilize the largest army yet, with contingents from Aleppo, Egypt and Mesopotamia, prominent among them being the forces of Nur al-Din of Hisn Kaifa who wanted to show gratitude for what Saladin had done for him at Amid and conducted himself with such distinction that Saladin gave him a robe of honour.

The castle had been built at about the time Saladin was born. It was on a plateau cut off from surrounding high ground by deep ravines and isolated from the town itself, also fortified, by a fosse. Together with Shaubak some 100 kilometres to the south, Kerak, when held by such a man as Reynald, made it impossible for caravans to travel between Egypt and Syria without strong military escort. Reynald's recent attack on the Hedjaz was another reason for assaulting the castle. But it is evident that Saladin had a number of objectives in mind. Each of the sieges coincided with important movements of

[98]

men and equipment between the two centres of his power. In 1183 he switched his brother al-Adil from Cairo to the newly acquired Aleppo and his nephew Taqi al-Din from Syria to Cairo. Their respective forces made rendezvous at Kerak. If the castle fell, so much the better. If not, at least the caravans would pass without interruption.

There was a further reason. An important gathering of Frankish leaders took place at Kerak that winter and it would be agreeable to give them a jolt. The occasion was the marriage of the 11-year-old Isabella (King Baldwin IV's half-sister) to the 17-year-old Humphrey of Toron IV, who was heir to the castle, and the town was full of musicians, jugglers and dancers. Even Queen Maria Comnena, widow of King Amalric and now married into the Ibelin family, was there—a remarkable fact in itself because she and the ebullient lord of the castle, Reynald of Chatillon, heartily disliked each other. The wedding had been favoured by the King as a possible means of reconciling two hostile factions in his realm, the Ibelins who were Levantine Franks and Reynald of Chatillon's faction who supported a newcomer called Guy de Lusignan and were hawkish Europeans. Both groups were strongly represented in the castle. The atmosphere was electric.

The dynastic squabbles in the Latin Kingdom were studied by Saladin with as much interest as he studied the pedigrees of horses on which he was a great authority. 'He was well acquainted with the pedigrees of the old Arabs . . . he had the pedigrees of their horses at his fingers' ends, and was master of all curious and strange lore.' So wrote one who knew him well, Beha al-Din, who became his Cadi of the Army. The pedigrees of the ruling Franks could scarcely be of less interest, particularly if he remembered the advice of Nizam al-Mulk in his *Rules of Kings* (an influential eleventh-century treatise that anticipated Machiavelli) that a successful ruler needed confidential information about his enemies, 'whether the king is a homosexual so that his weakness can be played on'.

King Baldwin the Leper was expected to die soon. His heir was his nephew, another Baldwin, who was not a robust child either, and there was bound to be a quarrel over the Regency. The young bridegroom at the marriage in Kerak was the grandson of the Humphrey of Toron whom Saladin had known and admired. As he was marrying a royal princess it was not impossible that in course of time he might become king. His mother, the Lady Stephanie, sent out to Saladin some of the dishes prepared for the wedding feast and he, not to be outdone in gallantry, asked which part of the castle housed the young couple and gave orders that it was not to be bombarded. The effectiveness of this pre-gunpowder artillery should not be underestimated. A mangon, which was a huge sling worked by torsion, was capable of hurling, rather inaccurately, rocks big enough to demolish a building. The more accurate trebuchet depended on counterpoise for its kick and could hurl missiles as big as a millstone. At Kerak Saladin had trebuchets capable of knocking out towers and crushing the roofs of buildings, so he was offering a real respite.

His men forced their way into the town and even managed to fill up the fosse with debris but the castle itself, where the wedding celebrations went on without interruption, held out. At night a beacon fire was seen away across the Dead Sea, up in the Judaean hills on the Mount of Olives, signalling that relief was on the way. Saladin struck camp and withdrew to Damascus.

He did not keep up the pressure on the Franks, even after the death of Baldwin IV by when the personal animosities among the Frankish barons had become so great that civil war was a possibility. Raymond of Tripoli, who spoke Arabic and was well informed about Moslem history and institutions, became Regent for the 8-year-old Baldwin V and found himself at odds with the dead king's sister, Sibylla, and her husband Guy of Lusignan, an indecisive and churlish man. The Latin Kingdon was going through a crisis because not only was it divided by this internal feud but no reinforcements for the Franks had come from Europe and the country was starving as a result of the failure of the winter rains. Surely now, from the Moslem point of view, was the moment for a drive on the real centres of Frankish power—not hilltop Jerusalem which had no military significance but the great commercial centres of Acre, Tyre and Sidon. Saladin might have starved the Franks into some humiliating arrangement; however this was the time he not only agreed to a four-year truce (urged by Raymond of Tripoli) but even to supply wheat and barley from the Hauran, the rich agricultural lands west of Damascus.

Those who view Saladin as a mere adventurer see this as the time when his real nature was unmistakably revealed. He was hostile to any other Moslem, such as Kilij-Arslan, who might aspire to being champion of Islam and marched against him, rather than against the Latin Kingdom. Any rival for power in what he regarded as his own legitimate sphere of influence, all the territories of Nur al-Din, was branded as an enemy of the Faith. And so intent was he on bringing these rivals to heel that the territories under his control, particularly Egypt, were bled white to pay for the campaigns. Al-Fadel, in spite of his loyalty to Saladin, took this view and for a while there was a distinct coolness between the two men.

But in Saladin's judgement northern Iraq and the adjacent territories were the seat of real power. So long as the area remained politically unsettled and hostile he had no alternative but to assert himself there. News came that Izz al-Din in Mosul had switched loyalties from the Caliph and accepted the suzerainty of al-Pahlawan, the Persian *atabeg*, in return for 3,000 Azerbaijani horsemen to attack Saladin's ally, the Governor of Irbil. Saladin again marched across the Euphrates but, once more, the defences of Mosul were too strong and after sitting in front of them with his army for some time in the heat of the summer of 1185 he unexpectedly struck camp, and leaving part of his army behind, marched north into Armenia.

This Armenian expedition seemed to confirm al-Fadel's worst fears. But Saladin had his reasons. A number of the key princes in the Upper Tigris, allies of Saladin, had died, and he was anxious to restore his position in this Diyar Bekr area. One of these princes was the ruler of Khilat on Lake Van, and the city was being threatened by al-Pahlawan of Persia who had sent the 3,000 Azerbaijani horsemen. Saladin, having asked the Caliph for a diploma granting him sovereignty over Armenia, went to the rescue accompanied by Uncle Shirkuh's son, Nasr al-Din, and the fighting jurist, Aisa al-Hakkari, who had played such a part in Saladin's succession to Shirkuh's position all those years ago in Cairo. Aisa wore the ordinary military uniform with the yellow surcoat belted over his body armour and on his head the big lawyer's turban, perhaps with a white covering with ends that were allowed to fall over the shoulder, like a *puggree*. He may have looked strange but no one dared to say so. He was a man with a reputation for blunt speaking, even to Saladin who tolerated him because of past services and present shrewdness.

Mosul Won Over and the Truce Ends

The way led up broad valleys enclosed by mountains so high that they were snow-capped even at this time of year, mountains with ragged peaks and long ascending slopes where flocks of sheep wandered under the eye of Kurdish horsemen. In the cultivated areas the barley was ripe to harvest. In the rich pockets of alluvium grew grapes, beans and vegetables. This was the world from which Saladin's father and his grandfather before him had emerged to seek power and fortune in the lowlands. It is tempting to think of Saladin conversing in his rusty Kurdish with men from the mountains who, in their independent way, had walked into his camp to ask what his intentions were. Men in his force who came from the Nile delta might have looked up at the snow fields, heard the howl of some strange mountain animal, and wondered too. Saladin secured a friendly succession at Amid (Nur al-Din who had distinguished himself at Kerak was one of the recent dead) and other places but he turned back from the road to Khilat when he learned that the new ruler there, Bektimur, had been recognized by the threatening al-Pahlawan and had married his daughter. Saladin never expressed any regret for this atavistic trip into the kind of country that was more congenial to him than the Nile valley. He had also, he hoped, 'supervised Diyar Bekr and the interests of its orphan princes', to quote the diploma that came from Baghdad (no mention of Armenia) and stabilized that part of his frontier. But Mosul was still defiant.

A key figure in the negotiations there was Beha al-Din, a native of Mosul and a chief agent for Izz al-Din, who went to Baghdad to ask for the Caliph's intercession. He had already been on a mission to Damascus where Saladin was so impressed by his bearing that he offered him the headship of a college in Cairo which Beha al-Din refused. Otherwise it might appear he had accepted an inducement to influence the negotiations in Saladin's favour. He was seven years younger than Saladin and, like Imad al-Din, a product of the Nizamiya college in Baghdad. He did not enter Saladin's service until 1188 but in the biographical study he subsequently wrote of his new master first-hand witness is provided of the desperation that his master of Mosul, Izz al-Din, felt when he learned that neither the Caliph nor the Persian *atabeg* were prepared to help him against Saladin. From Izz al-Din's point of view it was providential, said Beha al-Din, that Saladin fell seriously ill.

Mosul Won Over and the Truce Ends

On 25 December 1185 Saladin struck camp at Mosul and left for Harran to seek the hospitality of Geukburi, not riding in a litter as his condition would have justified, but on horseback so that the army could see that he was still in command. With singular directness al-Fadel wrote to say that his illness was God's punishment for fighting fellow-Moslems, but the illness was more serious than al-Fadel supposed. When Beha al-Din arrived from Mosul at the end of February with instructions to secure peace on the best possible terms he found that everyone had expected Saladin to die.

The illness revealed what rivalries and ambitions there were among members of his family. At such a time they took thought how to protect their own interests in the event of his death. Of Saladin's brothers Turanshah and Farrukshah had died recently, and only two were surviving—Tughtigin who was in faraway Yemen ruling in Saladin's name and al-Adil, his junior by seven years, who was now the ruler of Aleppo. He was a fine soldier and the kind of large-minded diplomat and negotiator who won the respect even of his enemies. In the crisis brought on by the illness Saladin wanted his support and advice more than anyone else's. The 200-kilometre journey from Aleppo to Harran could be made in two days in good weather and when necessity drove, but this was the middle of winter when the desert tracks were treacherous because of the snow that turned to slush in the midday sun and froze again at night. Al-Adil brought his own physician with him, not knowing whether Saladin would still be alive on his arrival.

Saladin had already tried to force his emirs to swear loyalty to his sons, who were many. He had something like seventeen by his several wives. Al-Afdal, the eldest, then 15 years old, was the nominal ruler of Egypt under the guardianship of Saladin's nephew, the ambitious Taqi al-Din, and it would be the rights of al-Afdal that Saladin would be most anxious to have recognized. But there were other important sons, al-Aziz, aged 14, al-Zaher, 13, and al-Safir who was the same age. However, a certain member of the Ayyubid clan did not recognize these rights and had no intention of swearing loyalty to the boys. Just as when Nur al-Din had been ill in 1159 and Shirkuh had planned a *coup d'état*, so his son now plotted to do the same. He was Nasir al-Din who had as his *iqta* the city of Homs. He had accompanied his cousin Saladin into Armenia but now that he expected Saladin to die he returned precipitately to Homs and there

[103]

entered treacherous negotiations with the Aleppo militia (behind al-Adil's back) and with leading citizens of Damascus, aiming to become master of all Syria.

There was a possibility of history repeating itself in yet another way. Taqi al-Din, down in Cairo, would not have been content with a secondary role; fifteen years earlier he had been ready to fight Nur al-Din himself for the possession of Egypt and was likely to usurp any powers in that country that descended to his own protégé, the 15-year-old al-Afdal. If Saladin had any illusion that his relations would sink their differences in devotion to the Holy War his long fever at Harran would have taught him otherwise. Even the blood tie was not strong. The legitimacy of the House of Ayyub was of too recent growth to make it inevitable that the succession passed from father to son without challenge. On his sick bed Saladin's thoughts must have wandered to al-Salih who had been 12 when his father died, never to inherit the kingdom. His own al-Afdal, should God so decide, might be another al-Salih. In discussion with al-Adil Saladin came to the conclusion the time had come for a realistic accommodation with Mosul.

Izz al-Din in Mosul was of the same opinion. Beha al-Din wrote: 'When the news of the Sultan's illness was received in Mosul we saw that it was an opportunity not to be neglected, for we knew how readily that prince lent his ear to an appeal, and how tender-hearted he was; so I was commanded to go to him. . . . Make every endeavour, my instructions ran, to obtain favourable conditions quickly.' What came out of this was an agreement by Saladin to recognize Izz al-Din's position in Mosul, even restoring certain territories in return for an acknowledgement of Saladin's suzerainty. The oath to observe this treaty was taken not only by Saladin himself but by his brother as well which might indicate some agreement between the two about al-Adil's succeeding to effective power in the event of Saladin's immediate death, with guarantees for the succession of al-Afdal. Suzerainty over Mosul meant, for Saladin, the right to call on its armed forces for the Holy War and now that this had been achieved his name was invoked in the Friday bidding prayer in place of the Seljuk Sultan of Persia, Izz al-Din's previous overlord. Saladin's name appeared on the Mosul coinage. He was now ruler of all the former possessions of Nur al-Din and the Zengids. Al-Fadil, who had written, 'May God turn the swords of

Saladin from shedding the blood of other Moslems', could have felt his prayer had been answered. Secure in the knowledge of support from the great recruiting ground of Mesopotamia and Diyar Bekr Saladin could now turn to what would prove the greatest struggle of his life, the war for Palestine.

News came almost immediately of the unexpected death of the would-be usurper in Syria, Nasir al-Din. Like his father Shirkuh he enjoyed his food and wine and, it was now said, 'like father, like son', he expired after over-indulgence. The Mosul chronicler al-Athir characteristically hinted he might have been poisoned by one of Saladin's emissaries, in which case the spectacle of al-Adil sitting in public under a canopy to receive condolences for this family bereavement, which he did, would have been notably hypocritical and much relished by those who cynically thought they knew the realities of power. But a surreptitious poisoning does not square with the rest of Saladin's conduct. He did not appear for the condolences because he was still too ill. The removal of Nasir al-Din from the scene did mean, though, the disappearance of a man who could have been dangerous to Saladin's sons.

When he was fit enough to return to Syria Saladin confirmed Nasir al-Din's 12-year-old son in his father's possessions, though he was shocked to find that Nasir al-Din had made himself rich by the imposition of non-canonical taxes. Everything was inventoried and, in Saladin's presence, divided between the widow, son and daughter. Saladin returned to Damascus like a man risen from the dead and the immediate crisis had passed.

The illness had concentrated Saladin's mind on the succession. Like any other ruler who had come to power through his own efforts he wanted to establish a dynasty. It was evident, though, that those in the best position to take over were not his sons but his brother al-Adil and his nephew Taqi al-Din. The point was made to him by an old friend called Suleiman ibn Djandar, an emir of Aleppo who was, said al-Athir, 'wise, wily and perspicacious'. Out riding one day Suleiman referred to Saladin's illness. 'How do you think your last wishes would have been carried out and your orders respected? Perhaps you thought you were off hunting and when you came back everything would be the same as before. By God, are you not ashamed that a bird knows better than you what is in its best interest?'

[105]

Mosul Won Over and the Truce Ends

Saladin was surprised. 'How is that?'

'When the bird wants to build a nest for its young it goes to the top of a tree for a safe place. But you, you have left your children in the plain and given the fortresses to others. Aleppo is in the hands of your brother. Your son is in Egypt with Taqi al-Din who will kick him out as soon as it serves his purpose.' And so on, giving other instances where Saladin's sons were badly placed compared with their uncles or cousins.

'You are right,' said Saladin after a silence. 'But don't talk in this way to anyone else.' He would have to move everyone around.

Taqi al-Din, when recalled from Egypt, was so angry that he threatened to go off to Cyrenaica and set about conquering Tripolitania and Tunisia for himself; but reason prevailed, he did as he was told and was given the city of Hamah as compensation. His charge, Saladin's eldest son al-Afdal, had already returned to Damascus with the expectation of eventually succeeding his father there. So that left two other important sons with no obvious power bases to succeed to, al-Aziz who was 14 and al-Zaher who was a year younger. Saladin decided to hand Egypt over to al-Aziz and Aleppo, which he regarded as the military linchpin of his empire, to the precocious al-Zaher of whom he was particularly fond. Party to these arrangements was al-Adil, who was asked to be al-Aziz's *atabeg* in Cairo and was by no means reluctant to exchange northern Syria for Egypt, a country which he knew well and was attached to. He understood the dynastic considerations. Whatever long-term ambitions he may have had on his own account the immediate task was to establish a trusting relationship with his two nephews.

He made a point of speaking to them together, the two brothers sitting on either side of him. To al-Aziz he said: 'My lord, the Sultan, has commanded me to enter your service, and to set out with you for Egypt. I know that there are a great number of wicked people, some of whom will come to you, and will abuse me, and counsel you not to trust me. If you intend to listen to them, tell me now, so that I may not go with you into Egypt.'

Al-Aziz replied: 'I shall not listen to them. How could I?'

Al-Adil then turned to al-Zaher. 'I know quite well that your brother might listen to men who devise mischief and that, if he did cause me that grief, I could not rely upon anyone but you.'

Al-Zaher said: 'Bless you! All will go well.'

This was candid talk and the boys may not have realized the full implications. He was ready to fall in with Saladin's great family plan but not at the expense of finding himself thrust out by some Egyptian conspiracy. He wanted an assurance that Aleppo would be a place where he could look for a welcome. If he was thinking of a possibility that might arise after Saladin's death it is interesting that he left Saladin's eldest son, al-Afdal, then 15 years of age, out of his reckoning. Perhaps he trusted al-Afdal even less than he trusted al-Aziz. But al-Zaher, now to be Prince of Aleppo, bore himself in such a way that, although only 13 years old, he gave promise of being a man whose word could be relied upon.

The Greek Emperor Manuel had died of a fever and the new Emperor was a man who knew the Moslem East well. He was Andronicus Comnenus, a Byzantine Don Juan. In his early life he had been in trouble at the Court for his sexual adventures, and lived for some time in Palestine; he abducted Baldwin III's young widow, Queen Theodora, and took refuge with her at the court of Nur al-Din where they were received with honour. He went to Baghdad and was received by the Caliph. After this he moved on and flourished as a robber baron under Moslem protection on the borders of the imperial province of Paphlagonia. He came to power on a wave of anti-Latin feeling (the substantial immigrant Latin population of Constantinople was massacred in 1183) and reversed Manuel's policy of friendship with the Latin Kingdom. Instead he wanted an alliance with Saladin whom he saw as the rising, if not the risen, power in the East; they had enemies in common, the Latins of Europe with their Frankish kingdom in the Holy Land, and the Normans of Sicily. Kilij-Arslan, Sultan of Konia, was also ready to take advantage of any slip either the Emperor or Saladin might make.

Andronicus knew enough about Moslem politics to realize that Saladin would be quite ready to play off the Orthodox against the Latin Christians but he had characteristic Byzantine illusions about the strength of his position and the esteem in which the Empire was held. He was living in the past. The embassy he sent to Saladin proposed that they should divide Palestine between them with Saladin taking Jerusalem for which he must do homage to Andronicus 'because he was the Emperor'. Saladin must have thought this ridiculous. Andronicus was not in a position even to recover Cyprus which was in revolt and he was having trouble with his own aristocracy, witness the number of them taking temporary refuge in Aleppo and Damascus (not in the Latin Kingdom, it will be noted). Plainly he envisaged Saladin doing most of the fighting for the recovery of Palestine. He did not understand how much Saladin's authority in the Moslem world depended on his identification with Sunni Islam and that this would be compromised by the acceptance of any secondary role, still less the paying of homage to that traditional ancient enemy, the Greek emperor. Saladin was prepared to do a deal if it was plainly to the advantage of the Moslems but the Champion of Islam could not afford to give the impression he was being used. This particular proposed alliance came to nothing anyway because Andronicus' melodramatic career was ended by an insurrection in Constantinople. But the idea was revived by his successor, Isaac Angelus, who had been one of those aristocratic exiles, with his brother Alexius, at Saladin's court.

The Greek Emperor was badly in need of allies. The fleet he sent to recover Cyprus was defeated by the Greek rebel who held the island, Isaac Comnenus, and the Sicilian admiral Margaritus sent there by the Norman King William II, who was threatening Constantinople itself. To help him Isaac asked for his brother Alexius' return from Saladin's court, a request that Saladin made no difficulty about granting, but it is indicative of the deep suspicion with which the Greek Emperor was regarded by the Franks that Alexius was arrested when passing through the Latin Kingdom and thrown into prison in Acre. Isaac Angelus sent a letter to Saladin urging him to attack the city and secure his brother's release which shows an almost comic unawareness that Saladin might have other reasons for wanting to take Acre from the Franks but, for the moment, was unable to act. It may say something about the Empire's finances that when Alexius did manage to get away to Constantinople he had no money to pay for his passage on a Genoese ship and was still being dunned for it years later.

Limited though his powers were to help them it was to the Emperor that the Orthodox Christians of the East, whether under Moslem or Latin rule, looked for support. Ever since the taking of Jerusalem by the First Crusade in 1099 they had lost the guardianship of the Holy Places and their rite was for a time proscribed in the

Church of the Holy Sepulchre. Their most sacred possession, a Relic of the True Cross which in happier times had been taken in procession through the streets, was hidden. The 'acting' Latin Patriarch in 1099, Arnulf, had used torture to recover it, so it passed out of Orthodox guardianship. The Greek patriarchate was abolished and Orthodox bishops were replaced by Latin bishops. The Emperor did his best to negotiate the return of the status the Orthodox Christians had enjoyed under the Moslems but so far as the Latins were concerned they remained second-class Christians. Of all the minorities in the Latin Kingdom they were the most likely to collaborate with any move Saladin might make to invade. What they looked for was the return of the Latin Churches to the Orthodox rite and in the negotiations that went on between Saladin and the Emperor from time to time this was always one of the stipulations. Saladin's link with the community was through Joseph Batit, an Orthodox Christian born in Jerusalem, who now lived in Damascus and was given very friendly treatment there. When the time came for Saladin's attack on Jerusalem, Batit said the Orthodox community would be ready to betray the city, if the opportunity arose, by opening the gates.

Joseph Batit was the kind of agent, or paid informer, typical of the time. Intelligence gatherers were everywhere. Saladin had his paid informers in Baghdad as well as the main centres of Frankish power, Jerusalem, Acre and Tripoli. In the Frankish state of Antioch, no less a person than Sibylla, wife of the ruler Bohemond, was in his pay. She passed on information about troop movements. In the handling of propaganda, notably by al-Fadel, and in the way agents and informers were used to check on the activities of dissidents the Saladin state was prevented from resembling later police states by the comparative crudity of its methods, the inefficiency with which they were carried out and, above all, by the obligation Saladin always felt to conciliate, not to impose his will but (as he put it later to one of his sons) to win 'the hearts of men by gentleness and kindness'.

There was even a rumour that Raymond III, Count of Tripoli, and one of the greatest lords in the Frankish east, was in the pay of Saladin or at least had a private understanding with him. So long as the boy king Baldwin V lived Raymond III of Tripoli was Regent and there was a truce between Saladin and the Franks; but when the boy died a *coup d'état* directed against Raymond brought about the rule of the dead king's mother Sibylla and her new husband, Guy of Lusignan. Of all the Frankish leaders Raymond of Tripoli was certainly the one with whom Saladin treated most easily. His family had been established in Syria since his great-grandfather had come on the First Crusade. During an eight-year imprisonment by Nur al-Din in Aleppo (he had been taken at the surrender of Banias in 1164) he had learned Arabic and become so well informed about Islam that Saladin's secretary, Imad al-Din, formed the impression that he would be ready to turn Moslem but for the fear of being thought ridiculous by the rest of the Franks. He was popularly supposed in Damascus to be Saladin's vassal. Al-Athir wrote that Raymond 'began a correspondence with Saladin, established a cordial relationship with him and turned to him for help in achieving his ambition to rule the Franks. Saladin and the Moslems were pleased and Saladin promised to help him. . . . He guaranteed to make him King of the Franks.' Imad al-Din's testimony was that 'Raymond whipped up the Sultan's determination to attack them [Guy of Lusignan and Sibylla] that he might return the kingdom to him.' In fact, Raymond wanted to see on the throne Humphrey of Toron IV, the boy whose wedding Saladin had in a sense attended at Kerak. From Saladin's point of view it was good policy to send Raymond flattering and sympathetic communications, saying how intolerable it was for such a prince to be the inferior of King Guy, a newcomer from France who did not understand the East and was plainly a man of little account. There was some truth in this. Raymond was bitterly opposed to the new set-up in Jerusalem which he regarded as highly irregular (Sibylla, daughter of King Amalric, had actually crowned her non-royal husband Guy herself) and Guy handled the matter so clumsily, showing no respect for Raymond's seniority or regard for his past services, that he actually threatened to invade Raymond's territory. He was only deterred when at Raymond's request Saladin sent troops to reinforce him at Tiberias and promised more. This looked like treason.

The Latin Kingdom was on the brink of civil war and it was very much in the interest of Guy and his supporters that the four-year truce with Saladin which Raymond of Tripoli had agreed as Regent in 1184 should run its full term. Guy and Sibylla needed the time to consolidate their position which they hoped to do by isolating

Raymond and other hostile barons who supported him. Guy might even have to fight them and he could not fight Saladin as well. Yet this was the moment Reynald of Chatillon chose to sally out from Kerak and capture a particularly rich caravan on its way to Damascus, kill the escorting troops and carry off the merchants and their goods back to his castle. He rejected Saladin's request for their release. King Guy was so concerned at this breach of the truce and the consequences for his deeply divided kingdom that he asked Reynald to meet Saladin's demand. Reynald's response was: 'They trusted in Mohammed that he should deliver them. Then let him deliver them,' which shows that Reynald shared the common Frankish illusion that Moslems worshipped Mohammed as a god. Saladin went in person to ensure the safety of a later caravan from Mecca in which his own sister was travelling and made a vow that he would kill Reynald with his own hands. This marked the end of the truce. Reynald's act triggered a series of events that led within a matter of months to his own death and the loss of Jerusalem. Saladin, judging that the moment had come to commit his forces fully, issued the call to Holy War throughout his empire and made another vow, to take the Holy City by storm.

The invasion of Palestine would take time to organize and he wanted to strike an immediate blow. He had troops in Raymond's own town of Tiberias (which was a breach of the truce too) and he now thought to extend this Moslem presence by raiding into Galilee. He asked his ally Raymond for permission to do this, hoping perhaps to drive a wedge between Raymond and King Guy. Raymond was a somewhat cold, calculating man. In spite of his anger with Guy, Sibylla and their faction (which included the Master of the Temple, Gerard of Rideford, as well as Reynald of Chatillon) he sat in his castle at Tiberias considering Saladin's request. He hesitated to make the final treasonable breach with Jerusalem especially as he knew that a delegation led by Balian of Ibelin (another Frank known and admired by Saladin) was on its way to mend relations.

Eventually Raymond agreed to Saladin's plan provided the force (which was nominally commanded by Saladin's young son al-Afdal but in fact by the Geukburi who had invited Saladin into Mesopotamia) remained in Galilee only during the hours of daylight of a single day. There was to be no plundering. Raymond then sent

out warnings to all knights in his territory not to interfere with the
Moslems, but from that moment on things went badly wrong. His
messengers reached Balian's delegation when they were resting in
the small castle of Faba. Balian himself was not there. He had
stopped to hear Mass in Sabat. The Master of the Templars and the
Master of the Hospitallers who were in the delegation took fire at the
news of Saladin's invasion, as they saw it, and set about mustering
local support to repel it. They raised about 130 knights and 300 or so
foot, no match for the much greater number of horsemen Geukburi
had under his command (7,000 according to al-Athir, but this is
incredible) and when the Franks impetuously attacked them near
Nazareth (at the Springs of Cresson) they met with disaster.
Geukburi kept his word about riding back over the frontier before
nightfall but Raymond, to his great dismay, saw that many of the
mamluks had severed heads on the points of their lances. Among
them was that of the Master of the Hospitallers.

If Saladin had meant to compromise Raymond and so cause even
greater divisions among his enemies the plan did not work.
Raymond was so appalled by what had happened that he went to
Jerusalem to do what previously he had refused, pay homage. King
Guy received him well. The Kingdom was in no state for further
dissensions and the Franks now busied themselves in preparation for
the revenge they intended taking on the Moslems. King Guy
ordered a general mobilization.

The Moslems too were mobilizing. The army that now gathered
at Ashtara in the ochre, sun-dazed, open uplands of the Hauran in the
early summer of 1187 received its largest contingent from the north
and east, those parts of the Zengid territories Saladin had been at
such pains to recruit. From the cities of the Jezireh, from Mosul and
Diyar Bekr came 5,000 horsemen. A somewhat smaller force
travelled up from Egypt. Then there was the Damascus militia and
the Aleppo militia, say 1,000 men each. Saladin had a personal guard
of 1,000 *mamluks*. There were about 12,000 horsemen in all and as
many again foot soldiers, auxiliaries and hired Beduin and quite a
number of Fidai and Sufi volunteers fanatically in search of the
martyr's reward. The tented camp was vast. It was the largest and
best-trained army Saladin had ever commanded but it would have
been unrealistic to suppose he could invade the Latin Kingdom and
invest Jerusalem or Acre with any certainty of success; even allowing

for the tension between its rival factions the Franks were capable of putting a formidable force into the field. In set battle, fighting from prepared positions, they were well-nigh invincible and Saladin knew it.

But in the Latin Kingdom there was concern. Some of the older knights remembered the good old days when Fulke was king in Jerusalem, when there was reasonable harmony in the Kingdom and the Moslems were disunited. William of Tyre had written:

> In former times almost every [Moslem] city had its own ruler. . . . To contend in battle against adversaries of widely differing and frequently conflicting ideas, adversaries who distrusted each other, involved less peril. . . . But now, God has so willed it, all the kingdoms adjacent to us have been brought under one man. . . . This Saladin, a man of humble antecedents and lowly station, now holds under his control all these kingdoms,

a man, he went on to say, 'who was wise in counsel, valiant in war and generous beyond measure'. Saladin's reputation was as high in the Latin Kingdom as it was in Moslem lands and the fact that he had succeeded in uniting so many conflicting interests by conciliation rather than intimidation made him, as an enemy, seem all the more formidable. Whereas once it had been the Moslems who were divided, now it was the turn of the Franks. King Guy was not respected by the native Franks and Raymond, in spite of his change of heart, was not trusted—even hated by Gerard of Rideford, Master of the Templars, who nursed an old personal grudge.

As news came through of the size of the army Saladin had gathered in the Hauran the minds of the Franks were powerfully concentrated. Nothing short of complete unity and total mobilization would, it seemed obvious, prevent Saladin making a drive for Acre. The traditional place of muster was at Saffariya, a small town in the hills just north-west of Nazareth with a good supply of water from wells and a stream; and here King Guy was able to mobilize 1,200 knights, about 2,000 Turcopoles and 10,000 infantry. It was the greatest army the Latin Kingdom had ever raised, including practically every knight available, lay knights as well as the Templars and Hospitallers. In that high summer of 1187 Reynald of Chatillon was there with as many knights as he could safely draw off from Kerak. Raymond of Tripoli, in whose territory they all were, still distrusted by Reynald and the Master of the Temple, commanded his own division. The Relic of the True Cross was in the charge of the Bishop of Acre as a guarantee of victory. The Patriarch of Jerusalem, who should have performed this duty, had sent his excuses.

It was evident that if there was a decisive battle the losers would lose more than a battle. Too much of the strength on either side was committed, too many leaders. But would there be a battle? Both sides were capable of holding on to a favourable position, Saladin at Ashtara and Guy at Saffariya, rather than commit forces when the terrain was not to their advantage. And this hilly limestone country, where it was possible to light on great tracts totally without water and where the two armies were divided from one another by the torrid Jordan valley, 230 metres below sea level at this point, offered many traps. The Jordan valley, with temperatures of over 100°F was no place for prolonged effort. Men in chain-mail or padded coats might, without water, sweat their lives away in a matter of hours. An army could be trapped between the hills and Lake Galilee. There were lesser valleys ideal for the kind of ambush the light Moslem cavalry delighted in. There were many reasons for caution but both armies were now driven by forces that made them forget caution. Jealousy between rivals in the Frankish army led one leader to want to outdo the other. For the Moslems it was a time of religious fervour. The accumulation of strength, the intensity of emotion on both sides had reached such proportions that events, if not out of control, took on a momentum of their own and both commanders made surprising decisions. Saladin in particular took a chance.

❧ 8 ❧

Hattin and the Taking of Jerusalem

Tiberias occupied a narrow strip of ground between Lake Galilee and the hills, a hot, airless place in summer. Back in 1122 Zengi himself had led an expedition against it; he chased a troop of Franks back into their own city and rattled his lance against the gate only to find his men had not followed. For this early exploit he became known as Zengi the Syrian and now Saladin decided to outdo Zengi not just by chipping at the gate but by sacking the town. He had set out on a Friday at the time of prayer in all the mosques, his favourite time for attacking the enemy because of the spiritual support which he believed came from the simultaneous witness of all the faithful. The town fell but the castle held out. Raymond of Tripoli's wife, the Countess Eschiva, was there with a small garrison and she sent to King Guy for help, as no doubt Saladin had planned and hoped. Only by getting the Frankish army to attack while he occupied a strong position could Saladin hope to defeat them decisively. But the position he now took up was not particularly strong, It was even dangerous.

The Moslem army advanced out of the valley and up to the plateau where it took up position south of the small village of Hattin and a rocky double hill known as the Horns of Hattin. The right was commanded by Taqi al-Din, the left by Geukburi, the centre, with his son al-Afdal, by Saladin himself. Imad al-Din describing the army in the field said it was 'like a cloud heavy with rain'. Saladin 'marshalled his gallant knights. They swept like a cloud over the face of the earth, making the dust fly up to the Pleiades and sending the crows, to escape the dust, flying as far as Vega.' But it was a position from which the army could not fall back; behind was the steep descent down to the lake and once the Franks started to drive them down it there would be total disaster. It was almost as though Saladin wanted to present as tempting a target as possible. But he also knew that between Guy's camp at Suffuriya 25 kilometres away and Hattin there was no water whatsoever.

There was a row in the Frankish high command about what to do. Raymond of Tripoli argued that it would be fatal to go to the relief of his wife. Even if the castle fell she would be honourably treated by Saladin and certainly released. So why risk the army? To march across the Galilean uplands in the height of summer would expose them to attack at the moment of exhaustion, perhaps without water, while the Moslems were fresh and provided with water. At first his argument carried the day but during the night, surprisingly, Guy reversed the decision after listening to Gerard of Rideford and Reynald of Chatillon. They would march for Tiberias in the morning. Events turned out as Raymond had foretold.

On the road to Tiberias the Frankish army suffered badly from the dazing heat, lack of water and harassment from the Moslem horse-archers who shot their arrows in an arc, hoping to find the enemy's unprotected face or some weak point in his armour. They also aimed at the horses' legs and bellies. The job of the infantry was to mask the cavalry by receiving some of these arrows in their padded jackets and by withstanding Moslem charges with grounded pikes or with shafts from their powerful crossbows. Moslem tactics when dealing with a Frankish army on the march was to make the main effort against the rear of the column and on 3 July this was done so effectively that the Templars and Balian of Ibelin in the rearguard sent a message to King Guy saying they could not carry on. The order was given to halt. Raymond of Tripoli rode back from the van, shouting angrily: 'The war is over. We are dead men. The kingdom is lost.' He foresaw that the Moslem success in stopping the march would decide the outcome of the battle.

Guy's army camped round a well that, as Saladin knew from his reconnoitring scouts, was dry. The Franks were so hemmed in that 'a cat could not have escaped through the Moslem lines' and as the hours of darkness passed they heard repeated cries of '*Allah akbar. Allah il Allah*. God is great. God is great. There is no god but God.' It was a time, Imad al-Din wrote, when 'the Angel of Hell watched and the Angel of Paradise rejoiced', the one in anticipation of damned Frankish souls, the other of blessed Moslem martyrs. The following day the Franks were destroyed more by heat exhaustion and dehydration than by any feat of arms on Saladin's part, but defeat it was nonetheless, and total. The armies met 3 kilometres south-west of Hattin. The sun came up to glint on the rocky hill and blind the Franks with its brilliance. Time was on Saladin's side. The longer he waited the fiercer the sun grew and the greater the enemy's suffering. His 'volunteers for the Holy War', the Fidai, set fire to the sere grass and scrub and the flames were fanned by a west wind; heat and smoke added to the misery. Saladin had pushed out the two wings of his army in the beginning of an encircling movement. After discharging a hail of arrows the Moslems charged. The hand-to-hand fighting was merciless. The Frankish infantry out of sheer exhaustion could do little to protect the cavalry and many of them, crazed by thirst, tried to make for the lake. But it was hopeless. They were forced to one side and took no further part in the battle. Saladin was amazed to receive five Frankish knights (Raymond of Tripoli's men) who in despair urged him to attack these infantry. 'They cannot help themselves. They are dead men.' These knights deserted and, to save their lives, made the Moslem affirmation of faith. Among the Moslems the confidence grew. They were fresh, well-equipped, had no lack of arrows and seventy camels stood by laden with fresh supplies.

In spite of exhaustion such was the determination of the Frankish knights that the outcome was far from certain. After repelling a charge they made an attack on Saladin's position in the well-founded belief that, if he were disposed of, his army would disintegrate. So much depended on his personal authority. Raymond of Tripoli charged the wing commanded by Taqi al-Din who ordered his ranks to open, the classic Turkish tactic, and Raymond and his heavy brigade thundered helplessly through and out of the battle. (He died in Tripoli some weeks later—from shame, some said.) But there were other more successful charges.

Years later, al-Afdal recalled what as a boy of 15 he had seen:

I was at my father's side during the battle, the first that I saw with my own eyes. The Frankish king had retreated to the hill with his own band and from there he led a furious charge against the Moslems facing him, forcing them back upon my father. I saw that he was ashen pale and distraught, and he tugged at his beard as he went forward, crying: 'Away with the Devil's lie'. The Moslems turned to the counter-attack and drove the Franks back up the hill.

When I saw the Franks retreating before the Moslems I cried out for joy: 'We have beaten them!' But they returned to the charge with redoubled ardour and drove our army back towards my father. His response was the same as before, and the Franks retired back to the hill. Again I cried: 'We have beaten them!' but my father turned to me and said: 'Be silent; we shall not have beaten them until that tent falls!' As he spoke the royal tent fell and the Sultan dismounted and prostrated himself in thanks to God, weeping for joy.

The main casualties were the horses. Imad al-Din noted that the Frankish knight, so long as his horse was safe and sound, could not be downed. 'Clothed from head to foot with a coat of mail that makes him resemble a block of iron, he is not affected by repeated blows, but as soon as his horse is killed the knight is thrown over and captured. Although they numbered thousands there were no horses or mounts in the booty. . . . It was necessary that his mount fall under blows of lance and sabre for the knight to lose his saddle.' After the battle there were more dead horses than dead knights. The custodian of the True Cross, the Bishop of Acre, was killed and the Relic taken; Imad seemed to think it was quite literally the Christian God.

The battle over, the Frankish leaders were paraded before Saladin. King Guy was given water to drink but when the King tried to pass the cup to Reynald of Chatillon Saladin intervened, dissociating himself from a gesture that according to tradition would have made Reynald's life safe. Reynald was invited to become a Moslem. When he refused Saladin, to fulfil his oath, struck at him with his sword, possibly killing him, but more probably as a signal for members of his bodyguard to cut off his head. Guy expected the same treatment but Saladin reassured him. 'Kings do not kill each other. It is not the custom. But he had gone beyond the limit.' He then authorized the murder of 200 Templars and Hospitallers (having bought each one from his captor for 50 dinars) by the 'divines, jurists and members of the Moslem mystical orders', some of whom, reported Imad al-Din who was there, 'slashed and cut cleanly, and were thanked for it; some who refused and failed to act, and were excused; some who made fools of themselves, and others took their places.' He saw men

[118]

who laughed as they killed the knights of the warrior orders. The killing of prisoners by 'men of piety' was not uncommon and thought a worthy act by some, though al-Fadel wrote on another occasion, 'to kill a prisoner with his hands tied is a foul action. Men's souls must always be naturally inclined to find it disgusting.' There is no evidence to show that Saladin did. Imad al-Din said he watched 'with a glad face'.

It is significant that only Hospitallers and Templars were singled out for this treatment. These fighting, often fanatical monks were held in special detestation by Saladin. They were men of whom St Bernard had said: 'They never dress gaily and wash but seldom. Shaggy by reason of their uncombed hair, they are begrimed with dust and swarthy from the weight of their armour and the heat of the sun.' That is how they must have looked after Hattin. They could not be ransomed for large sums of money (it was against their rule); because of their uncompromising natures they were useless and therefore of no value as slaves; and they represented the crack fighting force in the Frankish army, so in any exchange of prisoners the advantage would be to the Latin Kingdom. They were given the choice, death or conversion to Islam; the great majority chose martyrdom but those who did not were later reported to have made good Moslems. The Master of the Temple was spared, in deference to his rank. A much greater number of ordinary Frankish soldiers were taken into slavery and in the Damascus market they became cheap. One, it was recorded, was bought for a pair of sandals.

Saladin's victory was so complete that the Latin Kingdom could no longer put a fighting force into the field and cities were without organized defence. Jerusalem itself had only two knights left. So in the months that followed Saladin fairly easily took over the great cities of Palestine. They surrendered because he offered generous terms which were scrupulously observed—lives spared, citizens allowed to depart with their goods—often to the dismay of his followers who looked for plunder. The richest prize was Acre, 'the Constantinople of Syria', as one Arab chronicler called it, which fell without any resistance and the stores left behind by the fleeing Italian merchants (Saladin had hoped they would stay and continue to trade) were distributed among the troops. After a brief resistance, in which two of his emirs were killed, Ascalon surrendered in exchange for the persons of King Guy and the Master of the Temple.

Exceptionally, Jaffa was taken by storm (al-Adil came up from Egypt to make the attack) and its population killed or taken into slavery. Everywhere else the take-over was more civilized. Jerusalem itself surrendered after a siege of two weeks on 2 October when, in contrast to the massacre of the inhabitants eighty-eight years earlier after the First Crusade had taken the city by storm, Saladin behaved with singular magnanimity.

At first he wanted to spare the city a siege by making use of a military convention of the time. When a city seemed doomed the besiegers would sometimes offer to withhold the assault, even to supply the inhabitants with food, for a limited period. If at the end of that time no relieving army appeared the city would be surrendered unconditionally. The commander of the garrison, Balian of Ibelin, refused this offer and warned Saladin that any attempt to take the city by assault would cause the Christians to sack the Moslem Holy Places, destroy the wealth and possessions of the city, murder 5,000 Moslem prisoners and slaughter 'our own sons and our women' so that there would be nothing left to loot and no one to enslave before the remaining men sallied out to attack Saladin's forces, determined to sell their lives dearly. Balian, it might be noted, a survivor of Hattin, was in the city only because he had been allowed there on parole by Saladin to remove his wife! (He apologized to Saladin, explaining that the citizens had prevented him from leaving, by force.)

Saladin had vowed to take the city by assault, but faced with this determination he now said that he was prepared, if the city were surrendered, to treat it as though actually won by force of arms. The population could then be regarded as prisoners of war, who might ransom themselves. This was the eventual agreement. The Moslems took over Jerusalem in an orderly, disciplined way with no looting or violence. The evacuation of the Christian population went on for forty days. Ransom was fixed at 10 dinars a man, 5 for a woman and 1 for a child. Thousands who could not find the money were released at the urgings of al-Adil, Geukburi and others. Saladin himself 'made his alms' by releasing all the old people who could not pay. Many thousands were left who ended up as slaves but there is no doubt that the taking of Jerusalem was effected in a way remarkably humane for the period. It was estimated that 220,000 dinars were raised in ransom money.

Hattin and the Taking of Jerusalem

Saladin's generosity was regarded not only by Moslems but by the less bigoted Christians as extraordinary. According to the usages of the time the payment of a ransom entitled a citizen to freedom and a certain amount of his personal property but the richer citizens took away goods by the cartload, notably the Patriarch Heraclius with Madame la Patriarchesse in his train who, having paid 15 dinars for both, then left with his ecclesiastical treasure, 'all that stood above the Sepulchre', chalices, monstrances, gold plate, with carpets and a great amount of money of his own, all loaded into wagons drawn by mules. The Moslems were scandalized. If realized, this wealth (the Church property was worth 200,000 dinars, it was said) could have ransomed many of the poor. Although he realized the Patriarch was behaving disgracefully towards his fellow-Christians and in breach of the spirit of the surrender Saladin refused to stop him, saying: 'I prefer to make them obey the letter of the treaty, so that they are then unable to accuse the Believers of breaking their word, but will tell others of the benefits we have bestowed on them.'

By granting easy terms he hoped to avoid the lengthy business of sitting down before a succession of fortified towns; the important thing was to gain possession of as many of the Frankish strong points as possible even if it did mean refugees and their possessions going to swell the resources of such remaining Frankish cities as Tyre. Who could tell? Perhaps the influx of refugees would be more of a burden than a benefit. Lack of food and accommodation would go to sharpen the rivalries and feuds among the Franks that Saladin knew to exist and was keen to foster. More serious was the lack of plunder for his troops. For the time being they put up with this deprivation out of religious enthusiasm.

Saladin saw it as particularly significant that his triumphant entry into Jerusalem was on the anniversary of the very day, Friday, 2 October (the twenty-seventh day of Rahab in the Moslem calendar) when the Prophet according to Tradition was brought to the Haram al-Sherif in his sleep and mounted from the Sacred Rock to Heaven and the presence of God himself. Saladin's ride through the narrow streets up to the higher level of the Temple area where this event took place, quite literally to his fundamentalist mind, was to initiate the religious purification of the city which was 'the first of the two qibla, the second of the two houses of God, the third of the sacred zones'. From his early success in Egypt Saladin had claimed to be

[121]

under Divine Guidance; his presence now in the Holy Place was final proof. That same day secretary Imad al-Din wrote no less than seventy letters proclaiming the news to all parts of Islam and to the Emperor in Constantinople.

The Sacred Rock had been covered with marble (too many Christian pilgrims had been chipping pieces off for souvenirs and the marble was for protection) but this was now removed. The large golden cross over the Dome of the Rock was thrown down. The Templars had lived in the al-Aqsa Mosque, having added living quarters and stables. A start was made on dismantling these Christian accretions and the following Friday an immense congregation of soldiers and members of the *ulema* gathered there to pray with Saladin. It was a great service of thanksgiving. The chief Cadi of Aleppo, Muhyi al-Din ibn al-Zaki, dressed in black and standing between two black banners, according to Abbasid usage, preached the sermon with such eloquence, said al-Fadel, that 'the stars left their places, not to shoot upon the wicked, but to rejoice together.' They were in the place where God's revelation came down and where all mankind must gather on the Day of Resurrection and of Judgement. Almighty God was asked to prolong the reign of the champion of the Faith and Defender of the Holy Land, Saladin. 'Grant, O God, that his empire may spread over all the earth.'

The *minbar*, or pulpit that now stands in the al-Aqsa Mosque was probably not the one used by Muhyi ibn al-Zaki on this occasion though Nur al-Din had ordered its construction for the mosque in Aleppo twenty years earlier; there would not have been time to transport it and perhaps an unwillingness on Saladin's part to invoke the spirit of his great predecessor. As time went by and Saladin's success became more and more evident there was even a readiness to disparage Nur al-Din. 'For nearly a century,' he wrote to the Caliph al-Nasir, 'this city was in the hands of unbelievers and polluted by polytheism . . . and yet the wish to reconquer the city did not come to previous sovereigns, until the moment God chose me and called me to take it.' No one would have known better than Imad al-Din who composed this letter in his master's name that this was untrue, as the making of the Aleppo *minbar* demonstrated, for Imad had served Nur al-Din and it was well known that the idea of Jerusalem itself being the great object of the Holy War had grown and hardened during his reign. But an edginess had developed in the relationship between Saladin and the Caliph and the propaganda became shriller than necessary. Instead of being elated by Saladin's success the Caliph was envious of it and possibly apprehensive. There were mischief makers at his court who said that Saladin now planned to turn on the Abbasids as he had turned on the Fatimids. So the Caliph's letters were petulant. Instead of congratulations there were questions. Saladin was accused of granting political asylum to dissidents from Baghdad and encouraging subversive activities on the borders of the Caliph's own lands. He was challenged over the title of al-Nasir which was the Caliph's prerogative. And as to the jubilation over the capture of Jerusalem, 'had she not been conquered by the Caliph, under the banners of the Caliph?'

Much angered, Saladin rebutted the accusations. Addressing the Caliph's envoy, he said that the title had been granted to him by al-Nasir's predecessor (in fact it had been granted by the last of the Fatimid Caliphs) and 'as for the claim of the Caliph that I conquered Jerusalem with his army and under his banners—where were they at the time? By God! I conquered Jerusalem with my own troops and under my own banners.' However, he said that 'the Caliph is too great to allow such harsh words to be written' and a letter, composed by Imad al-Din, was sent to allay the Caliph's jealousy and anxiety. He was assured that Saladin's sole purpose was 'to complete the conquests for the Commander of the Faithful'. No reference was made to Saladin's alleged trouble-making in Iraq.

Some of his more zealous advisers argued that the Holy Sepulchre and the other Christian sites in Jerusalem should be destroyed. 'Plough the soil up,' said one of the learned doctors. Jesus and his Virgin Mother were revered by Moslems and the better informed had a clear idea of Christian doctrine. 'Here [in Jerusalem] they say,' wrote al-Athir, 'the Messiah was crucified, the sacrificial victim slain, divinity made incarnate, humanity deified.' But the claim was rejected. Jesus was an authentic prophet but he was not God, nor was he crucified; only a likeness of him, not the man himself, hung upon the Cross, and all relics such as those of the True Cross, the Empty Tomb and other places holy to Christians were an idolatrous perversion of the message from God that Jesus really gave. The Holy Sepulchre was called in Arabic al-Qiyama, the Church of the Resurrection, but it was commonly referred to as al-Qumama, the dung-heap. It would be no irreverence to the person of Jesus for these sites to be destroyed. Such was Moslem belief. The matter was debated. The majority view was that the destruction, though perhaps praiseworthy, would serve no real purpose. The site itself was the object of Christian pilgrimage, not the buildings. Desecration, as the Christians saw it, would only increase their fanatical idolatry. So the Holy Sepulchre was spared. Its destruction would have been short-sighted from another point of view. It was every bit as holy to Eastern Christians as it was to the Latins and there was political advantage in not outraging them, either their protector the Greek Emperor in Constantinople or the Orthodox communities in the cities of Islam. It was said that some of them regretted the peaceful handing over of Jerusalem. They would have preferred the city to be taken by assault so that they could have given themselves the pleasure of taking part in the general massacre of the Latins. But they would have been shocked and alienated by any sacrilege of the Holy Sepulchre.

Saladin sent an embassy to Constantinople with gifts to announce the taking of Jerusalem. They included an elephant, Turkish horses, saddles, bows, quivers and armour. Isaac Angelus was delighted with Saladin's victory at Hattin and his capture of Jerusalem. In due course he sent imperial robes and a gold crown (an inappropriate gift for a Moslem) with the patronizing and unrealistic message that in the Emperor's view Saladin was now worthy to be a king and would remain so 'with my assistance and God willing'. At the same time he asked that the Christian Holy Places should be handed over to the Greek Orthodox (Melkite) authorities; which was done in part and the Latin rite superseded.

The Emperor's message was that Greek Orthodox Christians and Moslems could quite happily coexist. To prove the point in Constantinople Isaac accepted a revival of Moslem worship in the already existing mosque there. Saladin sent off a *minbar* and, when that was captured by the Latins en route, a replacement was despatched, together with an imam, several muezzins and readers of the Koran, all for the spiritual welfare of the many Moslem merchants and travellers in the city. He also sent with this particular mission twenty Latin chargers, gems, a musk-ox, an ostrich and a supply of poisoned wine to be offered to any Crusaders in transit whom the Emperor might be entertaining. The Emperor's dealings with Saladin, particularly his permitting Moslem worship, was thought quite scandalous in the West but the alliance did not turn out well. Isaac came to realize that Saladin was unable to help him directly against the Latins and, for his part, Saladin saw that the Byzantine Empire, which had featured so large in the power politics of the East, was a shadow of what it had been and certainly incapable of interrupting any European response to the fall of Jerusalem. Al-Fadil wrote, for Saladin's benefit: 'We gain nothing from the Emperor's friendship and need fear nothing from his enmity.'

Certain castles continued to hold out against him but all the cities of Palestine and southern Lebanon were in Saladin's hands. All, that is, with the exception of Tyre and Tripoli. The ancient city of Tyre was on an island about 2 kilometres long and more or less parallel to the shore, but a causeway had been built, most recently by Alexander the Great, linking the island to the mainland. It was an easily defended stronghold. At the landward end of the causeway was a massive deterring gateway and on either side of the causeway enough depth of water for the city galleys to manoeuvre, manned by crossbowmen who could direct a lethal fire on anyone who had managed to get past the gateway. Even so, Saladin had no reason to expect more resistance than at Sidon a few kilometres up the coast which had fallen easily. When he lay siege to Tyre the commander, Reynaud of Sidon, a charming, elegant gentleman who spoke Arabic and was rumoured in Damascus to have the Koran read to him during meals, seemed quite ready to hand the city over. He had fought at Hattin and survived, making his escape with Raymond of Tripoli. He received Saladin's yellow banners with a view to flying them from the battlements at the appropriate moment. However, these civilized arrangements were upset by the unexpected arrival of a fugitive from Byzantine justice.

He was Conrad of Montferrat, whose dead brother had been Queen Sibylla's first husband. A soldier of fortune under the Emperor, he left Constantinople in a hurry because otherwise he would have been arrested for complicity in a murder. With a number of followers he set out in a pilgrim ship for Acre and arrived only ten days after the city had fallen to Saladin, although he was quite unaware of this fact. His suspicions were aroused by not hearing the harbour bells normally rung when a ship came into port. A pinnace shot out from the harbour with a Moslem officer in charge who wanted to know who the faces peering at him over the side were and where they came from. A bluffing reply was given. From the guarded exchanges that now took place the pilgrims understood the enormity of what had happened and the ship set off for Tyre just up the coast where, they learned, the remnants of the Frankish fighting force had taken refuge. Once in Tyre, such was Conrad's personality that he took charge. There would be no question of surrender. 'God's curse upon him,' wrote Ibn al-Athir, 'for he was a devil of a man . . . and of immense bravery withal.'

Conrad of Montferrat's arrival was a Frankish fluke. Without him Tyre would have fallen to Saladin and the city would never have served as the base from which the Franks were able to recover something from the disasters of 1187. Conrad saw the opportunity to snatch a dominion for himself and being confirmed in it by the new crusade that, he saw, must inevitably follow the fall of Jerusalem. Nothing would be capable of deflecting him in this ambition. His father, the elderly Marquis of Montferrat, had been taken prisoner at Hattin and Saladin now had him brought before Tyre, saying he would be killed if the city was not surrendered. Conrad said that the old man had lived long enough. His life would not purchase a single stone of Tyre, so Saladin, his bluff called, sent the Marquis back to his prison in Damascus. Saladin's reputation for clemency did him no service in this kind of confrontation.

Tyre did not fall, not only because of Conrad's resolution but because of Saladin's disinclination to tie his forces down in a protracted siege when he could be moving on to deal with less stubborn resistance. His failure to press the siege of Tyre was the most costly mistake he ever made. 'It was a habit of his,' said al-Athir, 'to tire of a siege when a town put up a firm resistance . . . thus when he and his advisers saw Tyre was a problem . . . they grew bored and decided to leave.' But this is to underestimate the real difficulty Saladin would have experienced with his own forces if he had insisted on pressing the siege. Winter was coming on and they just wanted to go home.

Saladin might have been able to keep his army together with substantial cash inducements but he had few reserves to draw on. He had no interest in accumulating any personal wealth and he also spent the contents of the war coffers in a way his advisers thought nothing short of improvident. They even took to concealing certain reserves from him for fear, said Beha al-Din, 'that some financial emergency would arise. For they knew that the moment he heard of their existence he would spend them.' But at the end of this glorious year of 1187 when he had destroyed the Latin Kingdom there were no reserves to conceal. Of the 220,000 dinars raised by the ransoms at Jerusalem, for example, Saladin kept nothing but spent it on the re-establishment of the Moslem Holy Places; the rest he distributed to the emirs, soldiers and such camp followers as the jurists, the preachers and the dervishes. Here, before Tyre, winter was coming on and rain was falling, turning the camp to a quagmire; there was no money over and above what was needed to purchase the immediate supplies of the army. The emirs were well aware of this and even anxious lest Saladin might ask them for loans. In spite of his urgings, in spite of his insistence that now if ever was the time for perseverance they were off, his nephew Taqi al-Din with his men in the lead, the armies of Mesopotamia and of Mosul marching away up the Litani valley and across the foothills of Mount Hermon. 'Let us go away and rest while the cold weather lasts and take up the fight again in the spring.' Imad al-Din wrote that they little realized 'how their short repose would be followed by bitter toil'.

Saladin wintered at Acre with his guard, the *mamluk* Halka, living in the citadel. Its harbour could not take such large ships as Tyre (which had a splendid westward-facing harbour protected by a mole and a great chain across its mouth) but Acre's advantage was that its harbour faced south and could be entered when most of the prevailing winds were blowing. It was a tight, snug fortress of a city. On the landward side were massive walls with towers overlooking, said Ibn Jubayr, 'a torrent course, along the banks of which, extending to the sea is a sandy plain. . . . As a course for horses there is none to compare with it.' In fact, there was a wide, sandy beach stretching for about 15 kilometres to the south along Haifa Bay. Like Tyre, the harbour had a mole and chain but it was also guarded by an island fort known as the Tower of the Flies because at one time it had been a place of execution.

Under Frankish rule merchants converged here from Mesopotamia, Syria and Arabia; and traders from Europe and the Maghreb came in their *nefs* with pilgrims, wool and weapons. All were given peaceable transit, subject to tolls, irrespective of whether the travellers were Moslem or Christian. Whole streets were owned by the cities of Genoa, Pisa and Venice and merchants traded according to their own law and custom. 'Its roads', said Ibn Jubayr, 'are choked by the press of men so that it is hard to put a foot to the ground.' He complained of the stink in the streets, 'being full of refuse and excrement'. But he paid tribute to the officers of the Latin Kingdom who treated him 'with civility and respect, and without harshness or unfairness'—in contrast to the behaviour of the customs officials of Alexandria when he had first landed in the East.

But now the Italian merchants had gone. Where once the Christian clerks of the customs house had sat on carpets spread over the stone benches, dipping their reed pens into ebony ink-stands ornamented with gold, speaking and writing Arabic under the direction of their master (known as the Sahib) there was now a guard of bearded warriors from Aleppo. The streets were crowded not with merchants but with armed men and labourers whose job was to strengthen the walls and defences of the city, as directed by the eunuch Karakush, builder of the Cairo Citadel. Theologians and lawyers, always numerous in their attendance upon Saladin and his armies, were housed in the Hospital of St John after it had been ceremoniously cleansed by prayer and rose-water of Christian contamination. The Bishop's Palace was turned into a hospital.

When spring came and Saladin's vassals reappeared it now seemed less important to press the siege on Tyre than to go campaigning in northern Syria. Apart from his dislike of protracted sieges, Saladin had another reason for the move. If there was to be a strong European response to the fall of Jerusalem it would surely be with an army marching, as the First Crusaders had marched, through Asia Minor and Lesser Armenia into the Principality of Antioch. The Second Crusade came this way too. It was important, therefore, to anticipate the invasion by picking up as many Crusader strongholds as possible in the County of Tripoli and the Principality of Antioch. So Tortosa was taken (the town, but not the keep itself with its superb Gothic cathedral) and Lattakia which Imad al-Din thought the most beautiful city he had ever seen; he deplored the way its marble buildings were wantonly destroyed by Moslem troops who saw in them only the evidence of infidel luxury. Six other strongholds were captured on successive Fridays, but the greatest castle in Syria the Hospitallers' Krak les Chevaliers with its garrison of up to 2,000 men and stores to last for years was too strong for Saladin and he marched past and to the north. Markab too defied him. Tripoli held out, having been reinforced by Conrad of Montferrat and William II of Sicily who had sent his fleet under Admiral Margaritus to the eastern Mediterranean, the first European ruler to come to the rescue of the beleaguered Franks. But for the most part Saladin's summer campaign of 1188 was almost monotonously successful and his troops were glutted with booty.

Margaritus was a sailor with so many successes behind him that he was popularly known as the King of the Sea. One of his captains rather boldly asked for a safe conduct to come and see Saladin with what seems to have been the crazy idea of doing a deal. 'You have achieved wonders,' he said in effect. 'You have done great damage to the Franks but now let them be. If handled aright they will be your slaves and soldiers; with them as allies you will conquer more provinces and kingdoms. And you will restore their country to them.' The implication was that he considered Saladin to be just a rapacious war-lord, an assumption that could easily be made by a Sicilian who would cheerfully have fought against Greek Christians just as he would against Turkish Moslems if there was profit in it. 'If you don't do this hand Palestine back to the Franks—a force will come against you that you will be unable to resist. Your situation will be painful and perilous.' To all this Saladin replied that he had no fear of those who came from beyond the sea. He would give them what he had given their brothers, death or imprisonment. The Sicilian made the sign of the Cross and took his leave.

Another Frankish visitor, this time at Saladin's invitation, was a Spanish knight who had taken part in sundry skirmishes with such spirit that Saladin's admiration had been aroused. He was known as the Green Knight because he bore a green shield and helmet. Saladin received him in his tent, gave him presents and tried to persuade him to change sides. The Green Knight, however, said he had come to the Holy Land only to fight the Moslems and he would not be deflected. They parted with mutual respect but the fact that Saladin should even have thought to suborn a Crusader knight is interesting. There was cultural arrogance on both sides of the great divide. When the Franks saw virtues in a Moslem, as they did in Saladin, they thought he had European blood in his veins, and was a Christian knight at heart. When, on the other hand, a Moslem prince was taken by the bravura of a Christian knight he wanted to buy him as he might want to buy a spirited horse.

The great objective of this northern campaign of 1188 was the Principality of Antioch, but by the end of August the Moslems were so exhausted by the campaign and rich from their successes that when Bohemond of that city made soundings for a truce Saladin was ready to agree; it would last until at least May of the following year when his idea seems to have been to have another go at taking the city. The impetus of his counter-Crusade seemed to be somewhat spent. This may have been because of Saladin's poor health. After the serious illness in Harran there had been recurrent bouts of fever and colic with the result that it became harder for him to assert his personal authority and dominate the councils where major policy decisions were taken. But he, rather than his vassals, remained the hawk. If there was any tendency to think of a more protracted truce it was to be found among his supporters.

But he went on releasing prominent Franks. Humphrey IV of Toron was returned to his mother even before his castle of Kerak in Moab had surrendered. The old Marquis of Montferrat was returned to his son Conrad in Tyre and most important of all King Guy was released to Tripoli, so honouring the agreement under which Ascalon had surrendered to Saladin. Guy went after taking a solemn oath never to bear arms against the Moslems again and to leave for Europe immediately. On arriving in Tripoli Guy was absolved from his oath by the Church, on the grounds that it had been made under duress and to a Moslem. He was soon recruiting an army from the local notables, from the Sicilians and, rather unexpectedly, the Pisans who turned up in some military force in a fleet of galleys. He quickly built up a surprisingly large army.

The number of Moslems making the pilgrimage to Mecca that year was big, many of the devout going to Jerusalem and Hebron as well, anxious to worship on holy ground now purged of the hated polytheism. The great Hajj from Damascus was led by none other than Ibn al-Muqaddam, the governor who had played an important part in handing the city over to Saladin on his arrival from Egypt after the death of Nur al-Din. He had proved a faithful supporter ever since, though there had been a dangerous moment when Saladin had displaced him from his governorship of Baalbek in favour of his brother Turanshah. The fact that in course of time he became Governor of Damascus again under Saladin shows there were no hard feelings on his side and respect for his ability on Saladin's. Ideally the first pilgrimage after the recovery of Jerusalem should have been led by Saladin himself—it would have been for the first time if he had gone and so fulfilled this basic religious obligation—but he was tied down by the war. The pilgrimage was a triumphant thanksgiving to God for the liberation of the Holy Places and al-Muqaddam was not only honoured to be in charge but zealous for the honour of Saladin. Other caravans set out from Cairo and Baghdad.

The Baghdad Hajj was made up of pilgrims from Iraq and Persia; it made its way directly across the desert following the line of wells dug at the expense of Zubeida, Haroun al-Rashid's wife, and was led by a certain Tushtigin, one of the Caliph al-Nasir's most senior officers. What followed was an indication of the poor relations existing between Baghdad and Damascus. The two caravans met outside Mecca, at Arafa, on 9 February 1188 and the leaders, Tushtigin and al-Muqaddam quarrelled about their rights. As Tushtigin saw it, he was representing the supreme authority in Islam, the Prophet's successor, the Commander of the Faithful, Caliph of Baghdad and as such could not possibly give way. In an ordinary year al-Muqaddam might have agreed but this was a special thanksgiving pilgrimage and Saladin had claims to the gratitude of Islam that could be recognized by allowing the Damascus pilgrims to beat drums and clash cymbals during the ceremony that took place at Arafa. He made his preparations accordingly and when the order to desist was ignored Tushtigin felt it necessary to get his soldiers into the saddle. The Syrians had no right to beat drums and cymbals. What had been an argument now became a quarrel and it got out of control. Men slashed at each other with their swords.

In trying to stop the fighting al-Muqaddam was wounded and Tushtigin, angry but conscious of the scandal that might result from the affray, had him taken to his tent so that he might be looked after, but to no avail. Beha al-Din was on the spot when al-Muqaddam was mortally wounded and saw him carried to Mina where he died on Thursday, the day of the great feast, when rams, he-goats or she-camels are sacrificed in commemoration of Abraham's sacrifice of the ram instead of his own son, Isaac—or, as Moslems believe,

[131]

Ishmael their ancestor. Death in such a place and at such a time was significant. Ishmael was spared but God, in his wisdom, took al-Muqaddam into Paradise as a reward for his honourable life. His funeral oration was given the same evening and he was buried in al-Maala, the chief cemetery of Mecca where the graves of many of the Companions of Mohammed were to be found. 'He could have had no happier fate,' said Beha al-Din. 'This occurrence touched the Sultan deeply.' But when the Caliph al-Nasir heard what had happened he complained to Saladin about al-Muqaddam's behaviour.

The Caliph would naturally be sensitive to any disturbances in the homeland of the Faith. Mecca and Medina had been within the Abbasid Caliph's sphere of influence before the Fatimids took them over but ever since Saladin had despatched his brother Turanshah to march through the Hedjaz in 1174 on his way to the conquest of Yemen the Holy Cities had come to accept Saladin's special status there. The Spanish pilgrim Ibn Jubayr referred to him as Lord of the Hedjaz. He paid Mukthir, the independent prince of Mecca, an annual sum of 2,000 dinars, handed over regular supplies of wheat and set aside estates both in Yemen and Upper Egypt to provide annual consignments of food. These payments did not always arrive punctually (there were times when Saladin found it difficult to raise the money). The Prince would then demonstrate his independence by taxing the pilgrims on his own behalf and, if they failed to pay up, even threatening them with prison. But usually the subsidies were paid and the pilgrims were accordingly grateful. At the mention of Saladin's name during Friday prayers in the Great Mosque there were murmurs of appreciation; when the pilgrims returned to their native countries they testified to Saladin's virtues as the champion of Islam. At the time of Reynald of Chatillon's raid he had demonstrated that his forces alone stood between the Holy Cities and desecration. From Baghdad it looked like a take-over and so, in a sense, it was. But not for territory. It was for the minds of men. The more powerfully Saladin was presented as the pillar of orthodoxy and the leader of Holy War the better would be his chance of maintaining his authority over his allies and vassals. Al-Muqaddam was a victim of the uncertainties and suspicions that Saladin's policies had aroused.

This same year Ibn al-Athir, travelling from Mosul to follow

Saladin's armies, passed near the battlefield of Hattin and saw bleached bones shining in the sun, lying where the hyenas had left them. A critical, even hostile, witness, he was nevertheless impressed by the way Saladin took his place among the guards who stormed the castle of Barzuya and spurred them on. His determination to share the rigours and dangers of the campaign with the ordinary soldier gives the impression at times that Saladin was deliberately shaming a reluctant fighting force into more determined action; as at the siege of Safed, for example, when on a night of torrential rain he stayed up all night to supervise the setting up of five mangonels. Belvoir was another castle taken in heavy rain and high wind, after a breach had been made in the wall. Kerak in Moab, Reynald of Chatillon's stronghold, was starved out by Saladin's brother after the garrison had eaten their horses and entrusted the women and children to the local Beduin. But there was one castle where the siege was conducted quite differently from the others.

This was Beaufort, so placed high on Mount Lebanon and on the edge of the Litani gorge that a stone or a condemned man could be tossed from the battlements straight into the turbulent waters 350 metres below. The castle was held by the same Reynaud of Sidon who had been on the point of surrendering Tyre when Conrad of Montferrat had arrived so unexpectedly, and he now took it into his head not to pull up the drawbridge and post men on the battlements, but to ride down the steep hill to Saladin's camp and explain that in his view this fighting between Moslems and Christians was a sad waste of time for civilized men. Making use of his good Arabic, he said he was quite prepared to hand over the castle to Saladin and go and live the rest of his days peaceably in Damascus, perhaps as a Moslem, perhaps as a Christian, provided he was given time, say three months, to bring his wife and family from Tyre where Conrad would certainly give them a bad time if he realized what was afoot. In Damascus, Reynaud hoped, he would be granted an appropriate income and establishment. He dined with the Sultan and, says Beha al-Din, 'argued with us on the subject of our religion . . . He talked very well and expressed himself with great moderation and courtesy. . . . His manners were truly charming.'

In the high summer of 1189 Saladin waited three months before Beaufort, entertaining Reynaud from time to time, talking religion and poetry, while all the time Reynaud's men were strengthening

[133]

the fortifications and stocking up with foodstuff bought in the local markets. Saladin probably enjoyed the respite in the mountain air. His health benefited. They were so high that at nights clouds packed into the Litani gorge below them; in the moonlight they looked like sheep flocking west from serene, high Hermon to the dark night air over the Mediterranean. Cicadas shrilled incessantly as Reynaud tried to explain that the doctrine of the Trinity was consistent with belief in one God. Saladin quoted from the Koran and Traditions to prove that although the Christians had been given a genuine communication from God they had trivialized and corrupted it. How could a mere man be God? Reynaud would have let him win a few arguments knowing that Saladin's vanity was touched by the possibility of making a convert. In fact, we do not know what precisely they talked about.

Not so very far away, on the road between Aleppo and Damascus, was the small town of Ma'arra where the blind poet Abu 'l-Ala had lived and written some hundred years before. He had unconventional religious views in spite of the Sunni beliefs he formally professed. Abu 'l-Ala said that whether a man was a Moslem, a Christian, a Magian or a Sabian depended entirely on circumstances. If you were born into a Christian household you were a Christian. A man would be a Moslem if, as a child, he had received Moslem instruction from his elders. His contemporary al-Ghazali had said much the same thing but Abu 'l-Ala went on to say that one creed was no better than another.

> We mortals are composed of two great schools,
> Enlightened knaves or else religious fools.

He also parodied the Koran to disprove the claim that its literary excellence was a proof of its divine origin; he thought his own work was just as good. Although a misanthrope he became rich from teaching and lived to be 84. For Reynaud of Sidon, a man poised between two cultures, Abu 'l-Ala's scepticism would have been congenial and if he had wished to be provocative he could have regretted to Saladin the passing of a time in which the poet had freedom to prosper. Saladin would have said: 'Had he lived in my time he would not have prospered,' and this was no more than the truth.

Aleppo, in contrast to orthodox Damascus, was still an intellectually tolerant community with a strong Persian influence and it is not surprising that Abu 'l-Ala should have come from this territory. Even as Saladin and Reynaud of Sidon sat and talked there were circles in Aleppo where advanced and unorthodox ideas about religion were discussed, most openly by a certain al-Suhrawardi who was an outstanding scholar and mystic. He has been variously described as an advanced Sufi, a theosophist, a man whom even al-Ghazali, with his own sympathetic understanding of mysticism, would have regarded as being so extravagant in his beliefs as no longer to be a Moslem. But Saladin's treatment of this man is the most cruel example of his belief that the stability of the state and the success of the Holy War depended on a strict observance of the ideological line. On Saladin's orders al-Suhrawardi, at the age of 38, was strangled in the castle at Aleppo and his body hung on a cross for some days.

After three months' delaying tactics Reynaud asked for another nine months' respite 'to make a complete year' but Saladin, realizing at last how he had been played with, gave Reynaud an ultimatum— surrender, or else! Speaking in Arabic Reynaud called on the garrison to surrender and then privately charged a priest with a message in French ordering them to do nothing of the sort. The garrison was largely made up of Templars who, in any case, would have surrendered only on the instructions of the Master of their Order. No surrender was forthcoming and Reynaud went to prison in Damascus in silver chains and with the satisfaction of knowing he had tied Saladin down long enough for Tyre to be strongly reinforced by sea. King Guy in Tripoli had been given time to muster an army. Taking Saladin by surprise, he marched south, first of all on Tyre where Conrad would have nothing to do with him because he wanted the Kingdom for himself, and so kept the gate at the end of the causeway shut. Guy then, very audaciously, marched on Acre.

It was a tremendous gamble and the real beginning of the Third Crusade.

9

Before Acre

The story of the next two years is very largely one of Moslem Acre under siege by a Christian army which, in turn, is under attack from Saladin. Quite new armies were brought into the field, notably those of King Philip of France and King Richard I of England, both financed out of a special tithe levied on the revenue and movable possessions of all laymen throughout their territories, the so-called Saladin Tithe. Unlike earlier Crusaders they came by sea. Most dangerous of all potentially was the army, estimated at some 200,000 men, which the German Emperor, Frederick Barbarossa, was already leading towards the Holy Land across the Balkans, having challenged Saladin to battle 'on the field of Zoan', which sounds as though his geographical knowledge was poor. Zoan is in Egypt. Frederick, then getting on for 70, was no stranger to this part of the world (he had taken part in the siege of Damascus in 1148) but this vast contingent of Germans was unprecedented. The Germans had not so far played a great part in the Crusades or the defence of the Latin Kingdom and Frederick, as full of ardour as if he had been forty years younger, thought to crown his life by the liberation of Jerusalem.

Saladin's information about this threat came largely from his ally, the Emperor Isaac Angelus, who was unable to stop the German Crusade from entering his territory as he would have liked. He sent an ambassador with a letter bearing a gold seal with an impressed portrait of himself. It was written in Greek and Arabic, an imposing document which was examined with some curiosity in Saladin's secretariat. The gold seal itself was weighed and valued. Note was taken of the protestations of friendship, but also of the document's undoubted testiness. The Emperor denied rumours that he had given succour to the Germans. In fact, it was only with great difficulty that they escaped his brave imperial troops. 'It is not surprising that my enemies should propagate lies to serve their own ends.' He doubted whether they would even reach Saladin's dominions. That being so, he was astonished that Saladin had not communicated his defence plans to Constantinople. 'It seems to me that the only result of my friendship with you has been to draw down upon myself the hatred of the Franks and of all their kind.' News of Frederick Barbarossa also came from spies at the court of the Seljuk Sultan of Iconium, Kilij Arslan. Such was Kilij Arslan's rivalry with Saladin that, fellow-Moslem though he was, he had agreed not to hinder the German Emperor and even to help with supplies; this, in the fullness of time, did not stop Frederick from plundering his capital. Saladin could not accept the Emperor's assurances that the Germans were no real danger to him. But King Guy with his army outside Acre was a more immediate problem.

By now Saladin was 50 years of age, his short, dark beard rapidly turning grey, unnaturally spare from the severity of his constant campaigning. There was Koranic dispensation from fasting during illness or at time of war provided the arrears were made up at the first opportunity which Saladin tried to do. Fasting did not suit him. Al-Fadel or, in his absence, Beha al-Din, were under instruction to keep a tally of the Ramadan fast days he had missed but just as all the money at his disposal was not revealed to him for fear he might spend it, so, one suspects, the proper quota of fast days he ought to make good were played down by the learned Cadis out of regard for his health. He was unusually devoted to his family and, in particular, missed the company of his children in whom he delighted. But these hardships and deprivations would, from now on, only intensify. The most testing time of his life was just beginning.

He had been taken aback by Guy's audacity in marching on Acre. The fact that Guy was in breach of his solemn oath did not really surprise him (the word of a Christian, he now recognized, meant nothing even when sworn on the Gospel) but he was surprised by the large force Guy had put together—about 9,000 men, not counting the Pisans. He wanted to intercept Guy as he came along the coast road but his war council disagreed. 'Let them take up their position before Acre and we shall cut them to pieces in one day,' said an emir, and Saladin, who had summoned the forces of Hamah, Aleppo, Mosul and Mesopotamia to join him, marched on Acre via Tiberias. Events were to prove Saladin right and his emirs wrong, but his failure to have his own way in the council, perhaps because illness had sapped his vitality, was a pointer to the future. He managed to reinforce the Acre garrison and on Friday, 14 September 1189, launched an attack on Guy's army at the hour of prayer, as was his custom.

He had the advantage in numbers. There was so much confidence among the Moslems that al-Fadel wrote from Cairo that the victory proclamation had already been drawn up. Attacking on the extreme right wing, Taqi al-Din managed to lead his troops into Acre itself and the Sultan was able to walk on the wall and inspect the enemy's camp, pitched at the foot of the ramparts and defended by hastily thrown up earthworks. The Franks were more formidable than he had expected because Conrad of Montferrat had been persuaded to join in and there were about 30,000 men down there, French, Italian, Pisans, Germans, Templars with their distinctive banners and decorated tents. There were lines of tethered horses. Saladin wanted to press the advantage gained by the link-up with the garrison but his emirs disliked the idea of attacking an enemy so well dug in. It was Saladin's practice to set up camp in the formation actually to be used in battle, himself in the centre based this time on a hill some 8 kilometres east of Acre with his two sons, al-Afdal and al-Safir. On the extreme right were Syrians under Taqi al-Din, on the extreme left were the *mamluk* veterans of Shirkuh's Egyptian campaigns; in between were the contingents from Mosul and Mesopotamia, men from Diyar-Bekr, and Kurdish tribesmen from the upper Tigris, some of them inexperienced in set battles.

A few days later the Franks attacked in four divisions, Guy himself commanding on the right with the Gospel (the next best thing to the Relic of the True Cross lost at Hattin) carried under a satin canopy. Taqi al-Din, under strong pressure from the Templars on the extreme right wing, adopted the traditional Turkish tactics of a feigned retreat. Thinking he was in trouble Saladin sent reinforcements from the centre and was immediately attacked by Conrad of Montferrat. The contingent from Diyar-Bekr took the full force of the charge, were completely demoralized and bolted. Some of them did not stop until they reached Tiberias. The Count de Bar even led a charge through Saladin's headquarters camp and rummaged triumphantly in the Sultan's own tent.

Saladin's coolness saved the day. He saw that the Frankish charge was not supported. The left wing of the Moslem army was still intact and much of the centre. Characteristically, he was able to rally his bewildered battalions and launch such a fierce counter-attack that the Franks were routed. Conrad of Montferrat was saved only by King Guy's intervention and this the King lived to regret; Gerard of Rideford, Master of the Temple and chief advocate of the disastrous march on Hattin, was the most notable Christian killed. Heavy casualties were inflicted. After the battle Beha al-Din sat on his mule and watched the Frankish dead being thrown into the river by Moslems to pollute the water. The remnant of the Franks had shut themselves up in their camp, behind the earthworks. As for the Faithful who had died, Beha al-Din described the battle as a market in which they had sold their lives to gain a great profit, Paradise. The old mercantile attitudes were as strong as ever.

Now was the time to press the Moslem advantage. Saladin addressed his assembled emirs. 'Only a small number remain. If we leave them in peace they will, in time, receive large reinforcements by sea, whereas we have no great reinforcements to draw on. Let us attack them forthwith. But let each of you say what he thinks.'

These words are as reported by Beha al-Din long after the event and they are informed by a knowledge of what subsequently happened, but there is no reason to doubt that Saladin was all for finishing the Franks off whereas the emirs, incredible as it may seem, decided this was the moment to go home. They were tired out. For fifty days they had been under arms and were entitled to a rest. 'Much better to wait for reinforcements from Egypt, muster the troops again who had run away, and see to the restoration of our own property.' So much for cutting the Franks to pieces in one day.

It was perfectly true that in the early stages of this first Battle of Acre the Moslem camp followers had plundered the emirs' tents. Saladin gave orders that all was to be restored. He had all the stolen goods placed in front of his own tent and said that those who recognized their property could take a solemn oath and carry the stuff away. But on the really important issue he had no support at all. The Franks might have lost a lot of men but they were not going to be dislodged without the kind of hard slog in a confined space the Moslem light cavalry had no stomach for. Saladin, who had been too preoccupied with the fighting to eat properly for many days and was so weakened by a further attack of colic that the weight of his body armour seemed too great for him to support, reluctantly allowed himself to be talked into breaking off the campaign. The units from Mesopotamia made their way home and Saladin was left to see the winter through supported by his own guard and his brother al-Adil who arrived with some regiments from Egypt. Admiral Lulu, the same who had chased Reynald of Chatillon out of the Red Sea, brought an Egyptian fleet into Acre harbour with provisions and 10,000 troops, so if it had not been for the news about the approaching German Crusade the Moslems would have felt in a strong position to take up the fight once more in the spring when the allies returned. But that was the time when Frederick Barbarossa was expected to arrive.

Saladin did not think he could throw him back with the forces at his disposal and sent Beha al-Din off to Baghdad to ask for the Caliph's support. The Caliph al-Nasir was more interested in the attempt he himself was making to capture towns in Upper Iraq (including Saladin's birthplace, Tikrit) and actually called on Saladin for support in this domestic quarrel. He also wanted the surrender of one of Saladin's cities, Shahrizur, a demand that aroused great indignation among Saladin's emirs when they heard of it; but he had learned politics from his father and, whatever his private thoughts, said: 'The Caliph is the Lord of Mankind and the repository of the True Faith. If he were to join us here I would give him all these lands—so what of Shahrizur?' He really did hand Shahrizur over and was rewarded by the Caliph with a token offering of *naft* (a form of naphtha used for incendiary warfare), arrows, spear-shafts and the underwriting of a loan of 20,000 dinars he was authorized to raise in the Caliph's territories. Saladin certainly needed the cash but he was so displeased with the niggardly offer that he turned it down and appealed elsewhere for help.

A measure of the Caliph's generosity was provided by one of Saladin's emirs, the Kurd Abu al-Heija ('the Fat'), so called because he was so huge (when mounted his belly touched the horse's neck) and he had to sit in the Sultan's presence as his legs could not easily support him. Nevertheless he went into battle. He was such a popular figure that the potters made a kind of jug in his likeness, rather as Toby jugs were later made in England. More to the point, in the year the Caliph made his financial offer Abu al-Heija spent no less than 50,000 dinars of his own on the wars, two and a half times greater than the offer of the Commander of the Faithful himself. Men were having to dig deeply into their own pockets. The fighting had disrupted the trade with Europe that had brought in so much revenue, particularly to Egypt, and cash for the army dried up. In addition to the military threat there was an economic crisis. In parts of Syria the peasants and small traders were being squeezed so badly by the local *iqta* holders (who were being pressed by Saladin's commissariat) that they were in a state of near revolt.

The Moslem potentate who would have been capable of providing effective military support was the quite independent Almohad Sultan of the Maghreb. He had a powerful fleet of war galleys at his disposal and could have done something to cut the Crusaders' sea links with Europe. But the Sultan was nursing a grievance. He still resented the incursions made by Taqi al-Din into his territory and did not even reply to Saladin's letter; later it was learned that he had allowed Genoese craft, in transit to King Guy's camp outside Acre, to victual at his North African ports. The fact was that in all the territories of Islam except those under Saladin's own control, there was only indifference to the new threat from Europe and envy of him personally.

He often contrasted the piety and sacrifices made by the Christians with the shortcomings of many Moslems. One wretched prisoner on being questioned said that his mother, a poor widow back in France, had sold all she had, her house, so that he could be fitted out and transported to the Holy Land where his fate was now to be a slave in a Moslem household. Saladin himself questioned a Christian prisoner who was so old that he was toothless and could scarcely put one foot before the other. Through an interpreter he said that he had no thought but to make a pilgrimage to the Church of the Resurrection in Jerusalem. Saladin was so touched by his condition and this answer that he provided a horse for the old man to be taken back to his own camp. If only there were more self-sacrificing devotion among the Moslems! But this is to choose the exceptional example from one's enemies to reprove the general behaviour of one's friends. In his army Saladin had volunteers and dervishes who had walked out of Persia to join him. It was the princes, like the Seljuk Sultan, Tughril, away in Isfahan, who showed lack of interest and even understanding; he had a revolt on his hands and wanted Saladin's help in putting it down!

Before Acre

As Frederick Barbarossa came nearer Saladin made his preparations, with a touch of desperation. He was so sure the Germans would burst into Palestine that he had the defences of key cities dismantled—Tiberias, Jaffa and Caesarea among them. Al-Fadel reproached him for defeatism but Saladin thought he was only being realistic. Al-Fadel and Imad al-Din continued indefatigably to write around, trying to drum up support for the Holy War at this time of grave emergency, but to remarkably little effect. In Saladin's own camp the approach of Frederick necessitated a reduction in its own strength. No sooner had the forces of Sinjar, Mosul and other cities in the Jezireh arrived before Acre than Syrian contingents, mainly from the right wing of the army, went north to protect their home territories of Aleppo, Hamah and Baalbek against German attack. Emirs from more remote areas where the Germans were not expected to advance nevertheless sent home to provide for an emergency. At harvest time one of them wrote to instruct his bailiff to sell none of the crops. Not long after, he changed his mind and countermanded the order. Asked for an explanation, he said: 'When we got news of the German king's advance we were convinced he would drive us out of Syria and I took precautions to ensure a good reserve of provisions. But when God destroyed the Germans there was no need.'

For that is what it looked like, divine intervention. The news came from the Armenian Catholicos who wrote from his stronghold on the upper Euphrates in a letter which, although it came from the head of a Christian Church, might have been written by a Moslem. He described himself as the Sultan's *mamluk* and asked God to prolong the prosperity of 'our lord and master' who had reunited the faithful. Something must be allowed for the Armenian sense of what it is tactful and flattering to say, but the letter is a reminder of the eagerness with which oriental Christians identified with the Moslem East rather than the Christian West. The news he gave was that the Emperor Frederick Barbarossa was dead.

While fording the shallow river Calycadnus in Cilicia on 10 June 1190, Frederick's horse stumbled and threw him into the water. The Armenian Catholicos's version was that he went for a bathe in the cool water. Some say he drowned. There is some uncertainty about what actually happened but agreement that the chill of the water, in contrast to the intense heat of the day, brought on a fatal seizure and

[142]

Before Acre

command of the army had to be taken over by the Emperor's son, Frederick of Swabia. It disintegrated. Christian soldiers too saw the hand of God at work and they were having a very bad time anyway. Depleted by disease, starvation, the rigours of the journey, attacks by Moslem cavalry on any weak point and, above all, by the demoralization that followed the death of their almost super-human leader, a mere 5,000 ill-disciplined men entered Antioch instead of the huge army that had originally set out.

Isaac Angelus had been right after all. They were no longer a serious danger to Saladin whose real problem now was the steady arrival of reinforcements to the Frankish army before Acre by sea. They did not need a harbour. The galleys or *nefs* sailed in as close to the shore as they could, and men waded to land. Horses were driven into the water and made to swim for it. On one occasion a horse escaped and swam into the harbour of Acre where it was caught by the Moslems. For some of the new arrivals there were small boats and rafts. Princes were carried shoulder high. It was a precarious beachhead and under constant Moslem threat, the fighting these men were coming to would be the bloodiest most of them had known, but they splashed ashore laughing and shouting. The Egyptian navy could do little to stop them. The most important arrival was Henry of Champagne with 10,000 men, Count Heri as the Moslems called him.

But before that there had been ferocious battles at intervals. When things were quiet, though, there was a surprising amount of fraternization between Christian and Moslem soldiers. They sang and danced together to the lute and the drum. Mimic fights were arranged between Moslem and Christian youths, wrestling in a ring of cheering supporters. Less endearingly, Moslem soldiers would raid the Christian camp at night on kidnapping expeditions. A three-month old baby was seized in this way (it was normal for women and children to be in the Christian front line; with the Moslems, never) and sold in the market. The distraught mother walked into the Moslem camp and appealed to Saladin in person. He bought the child himself, returned it to the mother and had them both put on a mare to be taken home. Moslem writers repeatedly commented with amazement on the sexual licentiousness of the Franks. Imad al-Din went into a great deal of lascivious detail, presumably some of it imaginary, about the brothels in the Frankish

[143]

camp. He heard that '300 lovely young Frankish women had arrived by ship, offering themselves for sin . . . They maintained this was an act of piety without equal, especially to those who were far from home and wives. . . . The men of our army heard tell of them and were at a loss to know how such women could perform acts of piety by abandoning all decency and shame.' Imad al-Din went on to record regretfully that 'a few foolish *mamluks* and ignorant wretches slipped away [through the Frankish lines] under the fierce goad of lust.'

The Frankish camp was always disease-ridden and frequently starving; the garrison within the walls of Acre were in constant danger of famine even though Saladin had built it up as his main forward depot. Frankish superiority at sea made all the difference. There was no repetition on any scale of Admiral Lulu's success in ferrying Egyptian troops and supplies into the city though in June 1190, a sea battle was fought off Acre that resulted in some supplies getting through. In this particular battle a Frankish galley was seized by grappling irons and boarded. A dromon from Constantinople with a passenger list of Germans wanting to reach Acre as soon as possible was rowed incautiously into the fight, was also captured and towed into Acre harbour. But once in the harbour the Egyptian fleet found it hard to get out again because of the vigilance of the Frankish galleys. Conrad sailed up to Tyre with a small flotilla and brought back wood for the construction of siege engines. In September three Egyptian ships appeared with provisions at a time when the garrison and population of Acre had supplies for only one day more. They were set upon by the Frankish blockaders and Saladin himself came down to the beach to watch and pray 'like a parent robbed of a child'. A breeze sprang up and with the help of their auxiliary sails the Egyptians managed to round the Tower of Flies and a great welcoming shout went up for them.

By this time such was the stranglehold exerted by the Franks that Saladin could maintain communication with the garrison only by carrier pigeon, fast skiffs at night, or swimmers with letters and money wrapped in oiled silk. One was a man called Aisa who failed to arrive and some days later his body was found within the city limits still with the letters and money intact. 'Never before,' said Beha al-Din, 'have we heard of a dead man delivering a message entrusted to his care.'

[144]

Before Acre

Every device of early medieval siegecraft was used by the Franks at Acre. The attacks, the sorties, the mining by sappers to collapse a part of the walls, the bombardments and the use of incendiaries provide, when documented and studied, a comprehensive textbook of one of the last great sieges before the coming of gunpowder. With the wood brought back from Tyre by Conrad siege towers 30 metres tall and on wheels were constructed. They had five platforms capable of accommodating 500 men. On the roof was a rock-hurling mangon and crossbowmen to keep the defenders on the city walls and towers at bay while the fosse was filled in so that the tower could be wheeled right up to the battlements and out-top them. The idea was that the 500 men would rush up ladders and across a wooden bridge made ready for the occasion and so into the city. As in the navy, hide screens soaked in urine or vinegar were used as a protection against the incendiary bombs. But on this occasion in vain.

After the usual naphtha bombs had failed to set the towers on fire a young metal-worker from Damascus said he knew how to do it. His interest in experimental science had been ridiculed by his friends but Karakush regarded the towers as such a menace that he was ready to try anything and decided to give the young technician his head. He asked for 'certain materials' which he mixed with naphtha and placed in metal pots. Each pot was then projected by a ballista (a kind of enormous crossbow normally used for shooting heavy bolts of sometimes red-hot metal) until the towers were plastered. Then he began firing the pots before they were shot—'each of them was thus full of fire'—and the towers when hit became pillars of flame, inflicting savage casualties on the wretched besiegers. Just what the mixture was we do not know.

For 1,000 years highly combustible materials had been used in war, mainly pitch, naphtha, sulphur and charcoal. A native of the town where Saladin was brought up, Baalbek, had been responsible, some 500 years before, for a refinement. He was an architect called Callinicus who took flight from the invading Arab armies and went to Constantinople where he presented the Emperor with his recipe for 'wet fire' which could be ejected from siphons. The formula of this 'Greek fire' was jealously guarded, though as water seemed to play an important part in the combustion the likelihood is that quicklime was the new secret ingredient. The Byzantines were currently developing means of discharging this Greek fire from earthenware cylinders, perhaps by an hydraulic pump.

The young man from Damascus plainly depended on ingredients that were fairly easily available so quicklime (produced by roasting chalk or limestone) would not have been one of them. Saltpetre, or nitre, used in the preservation of meat and in common supply may well have played a part. Whatever the nature of this new secret weapon it was devastatingly successful and undoubtedly postponed what was now becoming to look inevitable, the fall of Acre. Saladin offered to reward the young chemist but he refused, saying he required no payment for serving God. It was a reply after Saladin's own heart but there is no record of his then doing the obvious thing and asking for the formula so that it could be made greater use of. If the experimenter from Damascus survived the siege he probably went home again to carry on with his cauldron-making.

When Frederick of Swabia arrived at the head of a small force of Germans, Saladin's spies reported that he meant trouble; he was all for asserting himself by an immediate show of arms. The rest of the Franks took this as was intended, a rebuke for what the Count regarded as their inactivity and no doubt they took a certain melancholy satisfaction in the ease with which Saladin's personal guard of *mamluks* drove Frederick back with many losses. Frederick now master-minded an attack on the walls of Acre with a huge battering ram. This was a tree trunk with an iron head suspended by chains from perpendicular beams and swung by sixty men who were protected by a penthouse roofed with iron plates. One way of dealing with a battering ram was to drop a heavy forked beam over the head just as it struck the wall, preventing it from swinging back. Another device had a head like the share of a plough. It was called a 'Cat' because of the way it clawed its way into the walls. On this occasion there was a desperate sortie by the Moslems, the Cat was set on fire and the Ram itself dragged back into the city from where the head, looking like the axle of a mill-stone, was somehow taken out to the Moslem camp and laid before the Sultan himself.

During these early months of summer Saladin had been welcoming the arrival of Zengid princes from the Jezireh and others with the kind of elegance judged necessary for their *amour propre*. He was never allowed to forget the underlying resentment over his ascendancy, particularly at a time when fortune seemed to be turning against him, money was short and, for the first time, he seemed to be asking his vassals and allies to remain in the field indefinitely. The reception of Imad al-Din Zengi of Sinjar was typical. Saladin put his troops on battle alert so that he could be free to go out and meet Imad al-Din himself. After leading him to a point where he could view the Frankish camp Saladin then welcomed him to his own tent where a banquet was prepared with the finest delicacies known to Damascene cuisine. Gifts were presented and the guest was placed on a cushion next to the Sultan's own. A satin cloth was spread for him to walk on and eventually a special tent was pitched for Imad al-Din on the left wing of the army close to the river, this being the sector where he and his troops would see action. In the same way were received the other Zengid princes of the Jezireh and of Mosul.

This did not stop them deserting when the bad weather started. One of them, Moezz al-Din, was so worn out by his experiences before Acre that he went off with his little army and Saladin sent a message after him saying: 'At one time you asked my protection out of fear of members of your own family. Now look out for another protector.' Moezz read this angry declaration near Tiberias, ignored it and then had the misfortune to run into Taqi al-Din who quickly sized up the situation. He was, says Beha al-Din who tells the story, 'a very resolute character who was ready for any emergency and afraid of no man'. He said to Moezz al-Din: 'Go back or I shall make you.' Moezz did as he was told, made his peace with Saladin but was nevertheless so fearful of the consequences of what he had done that he asked permission to pitch his tent close to Taqi al-Din's for protection, plainly thinking he needed it. Imad al-Din Zenghi of Sinjar, who had been received by Saladin with such honour and was Moezz al-Din's uncle, was the next to insist on going. Saladin wrote to him with his own hand: 'I should like to know what advantage it would be to you to lose the support of a man like me.' Imad al-Din stayed where he was. At the same time as he was trying to keep his army together Saladin was having to fight a new kind of slow-motion war, with frequent forays and less frequent set battles, which could go on without a break for years. There came a time when even Taqi al-Din grew impatient and certain political changes in Mesopotamia provided him with the occasion to show it.

The rich city of Irbil was one of the remotest of Saladin's

dependencies, away to the east of Mosul, and when its ruler, Zain al-Din, unexpectedly died the question of his successor was important; Irbil was on a frontier that could be threatened by not only the Seljuk Sultan of Persia but by the Caliph himself. Eventually it was decided that Zain al-Din should be followed by his brother, Geukburi, who had welcomed Saladin into the Jezireh back in 1182, had commanded the left wing at Hattin, and was now his brother-in-law. Geukburi's move meant the surrender by him of his fiefs of Harran, Edessa and Sameisat which Saladin now thought proper to confer on Taqi al-Din to hold in addition to his existing important fiefs, including Hamah, in Syria. Saladin was clearly going out of his way to placate his ambitious nephew, even to the extent of giving him permission to leave the camp at Acre with his own *mamluk* regiment of 700 guards, on condition that his mission was solely to organize his new fiefs and raise more troops for the war. He was particularly warned against any fighting with Saladin's other vassals in the area.

It was a surprising decision because Saladin's forces, particularly the garrison of Acre, were considerably weaker than before and he could ill afford to lose the services of his most successful commander, as Taqi al-Din undoubtedly was. One reason for weakness was a botched relief of the garrison; misunderstandings, a wooden-headed insistence on bureaucratic procedures by Coptic clerks who seemed obsessed with inventories and accountancy correctness at this most inappropriate of times, even deliberate sabotage—all this, coupled with the reluctance of men to volunteer as replacements for that part of the garrison being evacuated, led to a most undesirably sharp reduction in the number of men available to man the parapets under their Kurdish commander, al-Meshtub. Nevertheless Saladin let Taqi al-Din go. Possibly it was the lesser of two evils. If he stayed his impatience might have led to some rash demonstration.

Taqi al-Din was relieved to get away from the boring stalemate at Acre and into open cavalry country where the kind of mobile warfare he enjoyed was possible once more. As he had been unable to establish himself as an independent ruler in Egypt or Tripolitania perhaps he could carve out a kingdom for himself and his sons in the Jezireh and Armenia. Saladin might be cut down by a stray arrow at any time. His attacks of colic and fever were becoming more frequent and his life could be expected to last only a few more years anyway. What would Taqi al-Din's fate be when his uncle's personal empire disintegrated and his cousins ruled separately in Aleppo, Damascus and Cairo? As he took the road for Tiberias Taqi al-Din may already have decided never to return to Acre and, as he passed the spot where he had turned back the young Moezz al-Din only a short while before, thought how no one could turn him back. Only Saladin himself was strong enough and he had Saladin's own authority to depart. It was an irony that God, in his wisdom, no doubt intended.

He ignored Saladin's warning. He took possession of Harran, Edessa and Sameisat and then, having raised more troops, set about fighting Saladin's various vassals in the Jezireh, annexing towns and territories in his own name and even assuming the title of Sultan. To ease his conscience about deserting from the Holy War he persecuted the Christians of Armenia, which he now invaded, with such vigour that Ibn al-Athir compared him to Julian the Apostate. His aggression damaged Saladin in a number of ways. Over a wide area his vassals preferred to stay at home and defend their own interests against Taqi al-Din rather than send contingents to support the Sultan at Acre. (Saladin felt so strongly about this he subsequently blamed Taqi al-Din for the loss of Acre.) The ruler of much of the territory near Lake Van, Bektimur (to whose assistance Saladin had once marched) was defeated in battle by Taqi al-Din and complained to the Caliph al-Nasir in Baghdad, who immediately wrote to Saladin for an explanation. Is this the way you fight the Holy War, by attacking fellow-Moslems? As well as a reply to the reprimand, the Caliph asked for Saladin's adviser al-Fadel to be sent to Baghdad, ostensibly to provide information about Saladin's circumstances.

It was a time when Saladin came near to despair. His letters to Cairo had been so gloomy that al-Fadel had himself come to Acre to provide what encouragement he could. In council, he and al-Adil advised Saladin that he had no alternative but to disavow Taqi al-Din's behaviour, saying that he had been authorized merely to collect troops and would soon return with them to take part in the Holy War. Al-Fadel wrote to Baghdad himself, in Saladin's name, saying this and as for the Cadi al-Fadel, 'he suffers from numerous physical indispositions and his lack of strength precludes a strenuous journey to Iraq.'

[149]

Before Acre

Taqi al-Din died in Armenia on 10 October 1191, after an illness. He had deserted and injured his uncle yet when the news of his death reached Saladin by letter he wept, and those standing by wept too, without knowing what had caused the Sultan so much distress; he had broken the seal of the letter and read it silently. When he told them that Taqi al-Din was dead there were renewed lamentations until Beha al-Din said: 'Ask God's forgiveness for allowing yourselves to give way in this manner. Remember Almighty God and submit to what has been determined and pre-ordained.' He was reminding them of the Prophet's warning against crying over the dead.

Saladin replied, 'I ask pardon of God.' When some years earlier he had learned, also from a letter, that his son Ismail had died he had not given way so openly. He was now that much older and more exhausted. Besides, Ismail had been a child and Taqi al-Din, in spite of his conduct, was a great general and his death was of public consequence. Saladin believed that if he had lived he would have returned to the Holy War with new recruits. But God had decided otherwise. Perhaps He had willed the death of Taqi al-Din as a way of rebuking True Believers for their shortcomings. Perhaps this great new wave of Crusaders from Europe was a solemn warning too. The only possible course for the Faithful was prayer, the waging of Holy War and total submission to the will of God. Saladin bathed his eyes in rose-water and ordered a meal to be served which all present would share.

This was not the end of the trouble sparked off by Taqi al-Din's defection. His son al-Mansur asked for his father's fiefs and, when Saladin imposed conditions because of his inexperience, went into open rebellion, even threatening the possibility of an alliance with his father's old adversary Bektimur of Khilat. But all this was in the future. For the moment Saladin had to reckon realistically with the fact that at the very time his own strength was weakened by this domestic and dynastic in-fighting the Crusaders were powerfully reinforced. After the arrival of Henry of Champagne in 1190 with a sizeable French army there now followed the King of France himself, Philip Augustus, with a well-stocked war chest, and a well-equipped army and new siege engines. On 8 June, seven weeks later, an even more formidable foe arrived, Richard Coeur-de-Lion of England who had, almost casually, conquered Cyprus en route and was now anxious to chase Saladin back to the desert in the shortest possible time.

From their vantage point on the hills 5 or 6 kilometres east of Acre Saladin and his headquarters staff could watch the incoming galleys. The English could see them too, 'an unnumerable army of Turks swarming on the mountains and valleys, the hills and the plains, and having their tents, bright with coloured devices of all kinds, pitched everywhere'. The English were in good heart because they had intercepted and sunk a Moslem ship from Beyrout with stores, provisions, military equipment and 650 soldiers bound for Acre. The Moslem version was that its captain had scuppered the ship to prevent its cargo from falling into Richard's hands, but whatever the truth of the matter the ship was lost. It was a heavy blow. That night bonfires were lit in the Christian camp to celebrate the King of England's arrival. From this moment on the siege was intensified.

In spite of falling sick Richard supervised the construction of stone-slings, mangonels and a wooden tower designed for setting up in front of the main gate. King Philip set about mining a section of the wall and with some success. His men burrowed under the foundations and started a fire there, causing a part of the wall to give way. But it did not collapse, it remained standing at an angle, and when the French troops tried to scramble over it the garrison were able to drive them back.

Saladin was well informed about the new arrivals. Beha al-Din said: 'The King of England was very powerful, very brave and full of resolution. . . . As regards his kingdom and rank he was inferior to the King of France but he outstripped him in wealth, in valour and in fame as a soldier.' This is accurate so far as it went. Richard was in his 34th year, an enormously headstrong and arrogant man, with a rough sense of humour, who had once paid public homage to Philip Augustus for his continental possessions in order to secure an advantageous but temporary alliance. The two men had conflicting ambitions in Europe. They were a great contrast to one another—Philip Augustus, a patient, even cold character who took pleasure in the long drawn-out details of a siege, Richard eager to be off down the coast and up into the Judaean hills for the assault on Jerusalem which he regarded as the main object of his Crusade. It was entirely characteristic of Richard that one of his first acts on arrival was to seek a meeting with Saladin himself, no doubt to see whether he could talk the Sultan into giving up Jerusalem without a fight. Saladin replied: 'It is not customary for kings to meet unless they have previously laid the foundations of a treaty; for after they have spoken together . . . it is not seemly for them to make war upon one another.' Richard, who had not scrupled to make war on his own father and brothers, could not have understood such delicacy. But what applied to kings did not, in Saladin's eyes it seems, apply to their lieutenants, and his brother al-Adil struck up quite a friendship with Richard which led later to his son being knighted or, at least, being given the belt and spurs of knighthood by Richard himself. At Acre, even though peace negotiations were not immediately possible and the fighting continued, there was nevertheless a ceremonial exchange of gifts.

Moslem and Christian princes, even when at each other's throats, went in for this kind of gesture because it accorded with their sense of what their own dignity required. The making of a conspicuous gift to an enemy was almost a sign of contempt. Such is my wealth and the strength of my position that I can afford to confer blessings on you, being less fortunate. Awareness that this was the possible reason for the gift had made it necessary for any gift to be returned by another of precisely the same value; otherwise anyone who made a 'profit' out of the exchange would be seen as losing face. So when Richard wanted to give Saladin a present of hunting falcons al-Adil agreed with this important proviso, that an exchange present of equal value be received by Richard. But there was another reason for the gifts, other than the one of mildly humiliating the recipient; they were an important part of intelligence gathering.

In this way Richard sent a Moslem prisoner—a Maghrebi, possibly a sailor—as a present to Saladin with a promise of the hunting falcons to follow. The envoy made the best of his opportunity to examine Saladin's camp and even to visit the market where the comparative luxury of the Moslems was evident. There were 7,000 shops and 1,000 baths where, for a dirham, a warrior could plunge into a clay-lined hole filled with hot water. Saladin presented the envoy with a robe of honour in spite of the knowledge he was just gathering information. Richard, who liked to tease, asked his envoy to say that as for the falcons they were not in good condition and needed feeding up before they could be handed over. Perhaps a few fowl could be sent for this purpose. Al-Adil was quick to respond. 'I suppose the king needs the fowl for his own use and this is the way he tries to obtain them.' This bantering tone was often used in exchanges between the two men.

Saladin never met Richard nor, in spite of the romances, did they ever confront each other directly on the battlefield. Their style of command was entirely different. Richard was enormously strong and led his knights in person, laying about him with a great sword or battle axe when the fighting was at close quarters. Saladin was more the general who took up a point of vantage the better to direct his troops. Later, when peace was eventually made, Saladin received the Bishop of Salisbury in Jerusalem and they spoke of Richard. 'Not to speak too severely of him,' said Saladin, 'he often runs unnecessary dangers and is too prodigal of his life. . . . I would rather be gifted with wealth, so long as it is accompanied by wisdom and moderation, than with boldness and immoderation.'

From the beginning it was evident to Saladin that he now had to contend with an enemy more formidable than King Guy, Reynald of Chatillon or even Conrad of Montferrat. For all King Philip of France's status and resources he too was less to be feared than Richard whose reputation for furious fighting had preceded him to Acre. More than that, he was known to be a shrewd and hard negotiator. He was always ready for a deal and even stuck to an agreement until it suited his interest to break it. He also made it clear that his stay in Palestine would last no longer than was necessary to re-establish the Latin Kingdom under King Guy who was his vassal in Europe. This he expected to do quite quickly. As a general he saw no rival—certainly not King Philip whom he despised—and since he boasted of descent from the Devil himself he felt free from the constraints of ordinary men. He was the Moslem idea of what a dashing and dangerous Frankish knight could be; as was appropriate for a king, his presence seemed larger than human.

✤ 10 ✤

Driven Back by the
Third Crusade

Saladin gained some reinforcements—they came from Egypt and
Sinjar and Mosul—but in nothing like the numbers that would have
ridden out of Mesopotamia if only Taqi al-Din had behaved himself.
Even Geukburi, one of the heroes of Hattin and Saladin's brother-
in-law, stayed behind in his newly acquired city of Irbil, where he set
about establishing himself in a manner that was talked about many
years after the splendour had faded, giving alms to all and sundry,
building hospitals, listening to all-night concerts of Sufi music and
every year celebrating the birthday of the Prophet (rather daring
this, not approved of by the conservative orthodox) with a great fair
where wooden pavilions were built; there were choirs and bands of
musicians, exhibitions of Chinese shadow puppets. Immense
numbers of camels, oxen and sheep were sacrificed and roasted. It
went on for four days. Geukburi's passion for the Holy War was
now being diverted into other channels and at the time when
Saladin, who felt increasingly helpless to relieve Acre, had most
need of him.

Saladin was unable to entice the Crusaders to come out and
attack him in force, even though he placed himself and his headquarters staff in an exposed position to act as bait. Whenever an
attack was made by the Christians on the city wall the fact was
signalled to Saladin by the beating of drums, who then gave orders
for his own drums to sound and for an attack to be launched,
designed to draw off enemy strength, but in vain. The Christians
seemed impregnable behind their trenches and earthworks and they
went on filling in the ditch before the city walls so that their wheeled siege engines could be moved into place. Rubbish of all kinds,
dead horses and even human corpses, were thrown in. The greatest threat to them was from disease. Among those who had died
was Guy's wife, Queen Sibylla, a death that was of considerable

political importance because he had been king largely by virtue of being her husband.

The remaining royal heiress was Sibylla's half-sister, Isabella, who had married the young Humphrey of Toron in the castle of Kerak when Saladin was attacking it. Humphrey had no royal pretensions and in any case was not the kind of virile leader the Franks were now looking for. Conrad of Montferrat was and Humphrey, regretful but nevertheless compliant, found Isabella taken away from him, a divorce pronounced, and Conrad usurping his place as Isabella's husband to challenge Guy for the kingdom. Not only that, he took his bride off to Tyre and abandoned the Christian camp to the bickering that went on between the King of France and the King of England, to its near-starvation and to its killer diseases. The Moslems marvelled at the extraordinary role women played in Frankish society. But it was not lost on Saladin that Guy's claim to the throne was championed by no less a person than Richard himself and there was still the possibility of playing upon the dissensions that would undoubtedly arise between the factions of Guy and of Conrad.

Much to Saladin's anger and in defiance of his orders the garrison commanders in Acre now opened negotiations with the Crusaders for the surrender of the city. Al-Meshtub went personally to King Philip who demanded an unconditional surrender which al-Meshtub said was impossible. He pointed out that his master, the Sultan, had taken many cities. 'Even when we carried them by storm we have been accustomed to grant terms to the vanquished and we have had them taken to the places in which they wished to take refuge, treating them with all kindness.' To this Philip replied coldly: 'Those you took were our servants and slaves. I shall see what I shall do.' Quite apart from being untrue—many Frankish men and women from Balian of Ibelin downwards, and not servants or slaves, had been treated by Saladin exactly as al-Meshtub claimed— Philip's words were a rejection of the Moslem code of warfare. He may have thought he was merely behaving as Saladin had at Jerusalem when initially he too declined to grant surrender terms. But that was because he had made a vow to take Jerusalem by storm. A vow was a serious matter and he had sought advice from the theologians on how to get round it; they had proposed a fiction, that Saladin could accept the surrender and then treat the inhabitants as though he had taken their city by the sword, as prisoners of war who could ransom themselves. But King Philip had taken no solemn vow to storm into Acre. Al-Meshtub's reply to him was very like Balian of Ibelin's to Saladin at Jerusalem before the theologians produced their peace formula. 'We will rather kill ourselves than surrender the city, and not one of us shall die until fifty of your greatest have fallen.' King Philip was, in fact, prepared to grant terms, very harsh ones, but the garrison took his reply to al-Meshtub at its face value and were in despair.

There were desertions. A group of officers and men escaped from Acre in a boat under cover of darkness. Saladin managed to secure one of the leaders and had him imprisoned. When he now tried to lead an assault on the enemy lines there was mutiny. Troops not only failed to support him, they actually demonstrated, shouting: 'You will destroy all Islam.' This city 'for which the whole world contended', to quote a later chronicler, was not to be saved, even by an army of phantom warriors who made their appearance when the earth trembled and a thunderous noise was heard (probably an earthquake) rousing both the Moslem and Christian armies. The phantoms were dressed in green to show that they were the dead martyrs of Islam. Ghostly warriors or not, it was evident, after the failure of Saladin's assault, that the city could not hold out and he gave orders for the garrison to break out during the night. This was a fiasco.

Al-Meshtub and Karakush were no longer able to defend Acre, so Saladin learned from a letter brought by a swimmer. They were too weak to defend the breach made by King Philip's sappers and knew they would all be massacred if the city were taken by storm. They proposed, therefore, to surrender the city and all it contained, to commit Saladin to the payment of an indemnity of 200,000 gold dinars (plus 4,000 gold dinars for Conrad of Montferrat because he had returned from Tyre to play a decisive part in the negotiations), to hand over 500 ordinary Christian prisoners and 100 more prisoners of distinction whom the Franks would name. In addition they would undertake to return the Relic of the True Cross. In exchange for all this the Moslems, with their families and personal possessions, would be allowed to leave. Saladin, with an undefeated army in the field, felt under no obligation to accept these conditions which he regarded as disgraceful.

Even as he sat debating the terms of his refusal with his council Christian banners were seen floating from the walls of the city with crosses and pennons bearing the devices of the French, English and German leaders. Celebratory bonfires were lit on the ramparts. Ominously it was a Friday (12 July) and at a time towards the middle of the day, the hour of prayer when in the past he had launched so many successful attacks. Now he saw no honourable alternative to accepting the terms of the agreement that had been made in his name. The loss of Acre was the greatest reverse he had ever experienced. He took it badly, 'like a mother who has lost her child', but this did not prevent him from sending perfumes and wearing apparel to King Philip who, being ill, soon left for the greater comforts of Tyre; nor from displaying the True Cross to two of King Richard's officers who prostrated themselves on the ground before it so that their faces were smudged with dust.

Now that King Philip had gone, leaving the French forces under the Duke of Burgundy, Richard was commander-in-chief and there was trouble—or so Richard said—over the timetable arranged for implementing the terms of the treaty. At regular intervals during a three-month period instalments of gold dinars would have to be paid, prisoners handed over and eventually the Relic of the Holy Cross returned. Saladin seems to have been in some difficulty in keeping to the timetable, particularly in the matter of the named prisoners (some could not be found) and proposed two possibilities; he asked for the release of the Moslem prisoners taken at Acre and offered hostages for the named Christian prisoners he had so far been unable to produce. Either that, or he must have hostages for the Moslem prisoners until he could meet the full instalment of money and prisoners then due. Richard's envoys accepted neither alternative and were unwilling to release any of the Moslem prisoners until the instalments were paid in full. When that was done 'accept our solemn oath that your comrades will be sent back'. Saladin did not believe them. He had no faith in a Christian oath and feared that once he had honoured his side of the bargain Richard would renege on his. Neither side trusted the other. Richard thought that Saladin was deliberately delaying the settlement and he would have had good reason to do so. Beha al-Din had already reminded him that now the fate of Acre had been decided the other cities of the coast and Jerusalem itself must be defended and one way of doing that would be to tie Richard and his army down until the bad weather began. But four months of fighting weather still remained and Saladin could not have hoped to drag the negotiations on that long. There is no evidence he even had this possibility in mind. Whatever the reason for the hold-up, Richard's patience snapped.

He realized that although the loss of Acre was a terrible setback for the Moslems, the Franks too had lost a great deal; they had been pinned down at Acre for nearly two years and lost 100,000 men, rather more of them from disease than in battle. Saladin's own army had suffered much less from disease and was largely intact. Time was on his side. He would stay in this land until he died, but Richard needed to get home with reasonable speed to frustrate the possibility that the King of France—now on his way to Europe from Tyre —would partition his realm with Prince John, Richard's brother. Richard was an impulsive man and he was in a hurry. The Moslem defenders of Acre were reluctantly admired by the Franks for their fighting qualities and they now presented a problem. If the situation had been reversed, and they were the Christian prisoners of the Moslems, they could have been marched off to the slave markets. Richard did not have this option. He was not prepared to release them until Saladin had honoured his agreement in full and yet he could not set out for Jerusalem and leave them behind under guard. So he ordered these men, mainly *mamluks* from Egypt, to be slaughtered.

Three thousand Moslem prisoners, tied together with ropes, were butchered by sword and lance before the hill of al-Ayadiya under his personal supervision. Their wives and children died with them. Only prisoners of note and rank like al-Meshtub and Karakush were spared. Saladin's troops, seeing what was happening, tried to interfere but in vain. They were driven off with casualties but not without killing a number of Franks. Although Saladin was grieved and angered by the atrocity he would not have been shocked or surprised. It was typical Frankish behaviour. In the Moslem camp it was surmised that Richard had intended the killings all along, once Saladin had fulfilled his treaty obligations, out of revenge for the Christians killed by the Franks, though no one seemed to think the murders after the Battle of Hattin were particularly in Richard's mind. One consequence of Richard's ruthlessness was a Moslem reluctance to be inside a city when Richard was laying siege to it, so that for Saladin the defence of Jaffa or Ascalon or Jerusalem was to become all that more difficult. Another consequence was a change in Saladin's treatment of prisoners. Taken during the fighting at Acre they had been honourably treated. In winter the knights among them had been given furs before being sent on to prison in Damascus. Ordinary soldiers were fed and sent to the slave market. From now on Saladin regularly ordered the killing of prisoners. The difference between Hattin and Acre was that Richard had murdered men whose lives he had guaranteed if the terms of the treaty were properly observed and Saladin had no intention other than observing them. Hence his anger.

Richard's barbarity and Saladin's killing of Frankish prisoners did not prevent courtesies between them, the exchange of gifts, the giving of banquets, the provision of fruit and snow when Richard was suffering from a fever, even the well-attested offer of a remount when Richard was unseated in battle. Honour and the codes of chivalry applied, it seemed, to the officers who took pleasure in a sometimes ostentatious display of magnanimity if it contributed to their self-esteem, but the men did not rate this treatment. It was unusual for a prisoner of rank on either side to have his head cut off (Reynald of Chatillon was a special case) because a knight or an emir was worth money and could be ransomed, but Other Ranks were either slaves to the Moslems or forced labour to the Christians; and they were dead men if not physically up to it. Status and cash decided one's fate. So courtly elegance between princes and emirs was seen to flourish as ordinary, helpless soldiers were done to death. King Philip of France had spoken of such men as slaves and servants. In Islam there was equality before the religious law, in theory if not always in practice, which mitigated rule through strength; all men were surrendered to the will of God, and in those perspectives Sultan, merchant and slave prayed side by side in the mosque on Fridays. But worldliness crept in. Top people lived by different rules. Saladin would not have regarded Richard as a war criminal. His victims had been ordinary men. He was a king, as such deserving of honour, and Beha al-Din continued to refer to him with respect and even admiration.

From the fall of Acre on 12 July 1191, until Richard embarked for Europe on 9 October in the following year, it was the English king who dictated the course of events. He had a large army and, leaving

Acre garrisoned, he was able to march three divisions south along the coast towards Ascalon with the intention of establishing a firm base there, or at Jaffa, before striking up into the hills to Jerusalem. The army came from all parts of France and from England: Templars in the van, followed by Bretons, by men from Anjou and, under King Guy's command, men from Poitou for which his family acknowledged Richard Coeur-de-Lion as their feudal lord. Then came Normans and English with the two-lioned standard of Richard in a cart, stepped tall as a minaret. Hospitallers brought up the rear. When they marched along the shore of Haifa Bay Saladin sent a force under his son al-Afdal to cut off the last of them, but was beaten off by infantry armed with crossbows.

The march of the Crusader army south was remarkable for the firm discipline Richard maintained. His steel-helmeted knights in chain-mail body armour were well-nigh arrow-proof and so were the infantry in the heavily padded tunics, called gambisons, which the Moslem arrows could not penetrate from any distance. Horses, as had been shown at Hattin, were the vulnerable part of the army. Here the Crusaders were protected by the sea on the right and Richard saw to it that the infantry, to protect them, were always between his cavalry and the Moslems who menaced his left flank from the east. When the Moslem horse-archers shot at the Frankish infantry the arrows simply stuck in the gambisons. Yet if they came within range of the Frankish crossbows they were in danger. Their horses, too, were vulnerable and although they had gambisons like the Franks, often over chain-mail, the greater penetrating power of the crossbow, or arbalest, put them at a disadvantage. Although it had less range and a slower rate of shooting than the Moslem bow it could put an arrow through chain-mail and padding as well. The usual missile was a square-headed bolt, called a quarrel, which could knock a man off a horse, shatter an arm and certainly break a horse's leg.

To begin with Saladin thought Richard might strike inland towards Jerusalem and so took up position on the hill of Shafram which commanded the route into the plain of Esdraelon. But when he saw Richard make for the Carmel headland to follow the line of the old Roman road along the coast Saladin himself rode over the Carmel ridge to inspect in advance the route they would have to follow. There was plenty of time for him to choose a site where a major attack could be launched; the Franks rested every other day because of the intense heat. There was a shortage of beasts of burden and foot-soldiers carried the baggage and tents. As everyone was in battle order human endurance was tested severely though—as the Moslems noted—the infantry was divided into two, taking it in turns to protect the cavalry and to march along the beach with the baggage as a respite. Another reason for the slow pace was Richard's need to keep in touch with the fleet of galleys that accompanied his march; the prevailing westerlies did not make for a quick passage round Carmel.

South of the Carmel headland and west of the ridge were scrub, thickets, marsh and woodland, even an extensive oak forest towards Arsuf and, using the cover provided, the Moslems were able to launch attacks from the hills. They attacked fiercely near Caesarea but the Frankish infantry maintained their steady march, looking like hedgehogs with arrows sticking in their gambisons. Their patience and discipline were all the more remarkable from the Moslem point of view because they were blindly obeying orders without, as Beha al-Din said, who watched them from a distance on his mule, 'any participation in the management of affairs or deriving any personal advantage'. This was in contrast with Saladin's troops who, thinking that the tide of affairs was turning against them, were ready to question, to challenge and even to mutiny.

Richard put out a peace feeler and Saladin authorized his brother al-Adil to protract the negotiations until the Turkoman reinforcements he was expecting came up. Saladin had renewed his urgent appeals for help to his Ortoqid vassals in upper Mesopotamia and to Geukburi at Irbil. The Almohad Sultan in Tunis had been told that his naval help would be more welcome than ever. For the first time rulers who owed no allegiance to Saladin responded to his appeal, the Prince of far away Erzerum for one and, a little surprisingly, also Bektimur of Khilat whom Taqi al-Din had fought. But they could not move quickly enough for Saladin's needs. Better a troop of undisciplined and mercenary Turkoman tribesmen who were at hand than Bektimur's battalions who were still on the other side of the Tigris. Saladin waited in his camp in the hills above the forest of Arsuf hoping the Turkomans would arrive before the negotiations between Richard and al-Adil were broken off, as he foresaw they inevitably would be. Apparently the two delegations were dressed with as much magnificence as the battle conditions permitted. The proceedings were conducted in Arabic, the young Humphrey of Toron translating and making a favourable impression on the Moslems not only with his linguistic ability but with his handsome appearance, even though he followed the ugly Frankish custom of shaving his beard. But, in spite of all this, negotiations broke down when Richard demanded the surrender of Jerusalem and all other territories taken by Saladin since Hattin.

Whenever a Moslem army set up camp for any length of time, as before Acre, a market soon sprang up where the troops could buy food and clothes. The market at Acre was abandoned so quickly that the merchants were unable to get all their goods away and had to abandon supplies the Moslem army would now have welcomed. It was calculated that each soldier could carry enough supplies to last a month but that time was up and they were buying food from the local peasants, barley at 4 silver dirhams a quart and bread at a dirham a kilogram, much above the normal price. And these were real silver coins, not the debased kind circulating in Egypt. If it was profiteering Saladin was too preoccupied with other matters to do anything about it. The Moslems and the Crusaders were watering their horses in the same stream, just 20 kilometres apart.

The battle of Arsuf when it came on 7 September was a highly intensified version of the running fight that had been going on for some time and it was on ground of Saladin's choosing. The oak forest of Arsuf extended for about 25 kilometres parallel with the sea and at points only 4 kilometres from it, so there was room enough for him to deploy his cavalry and yet have the forest and the hills to fall back on if he had to. During the march from Acre individual knights and emirs had left the ranks and fought as champions in the space between the two armies, but now hordes of Moslem skirmishers emerged from the wood to attack the Christian infantry; they were Nubians from Egypt or other blacks from even further south, followed by half-naked Beduin from the desert armed with spears, bows and bucklers. The woods and hills echoed to the sound of drums and trumpets, timbrels, rattles, gongs and war cries. The Crusaders continued their steady progress towards the thickets and gardens of Arsuf, the defensive line of infantry fighting off the attacks as they marched. At the rear they even marched backwards, so as not be taken by surprise, with their crossbows at the ready.

Driven Back by the Third Crusade

Saladin tried to isolate the rear division which was made up, apart from the infantry, of Hospitaller knights. They had to withstand an attack by Moslem cavalry who had 'laid their bows aside and were thundering upon the rearguard with their scimitars and maces like smiths upon anvils'. So wrote the author of Richard's *Itinerarium*. Richard's orders had been that even an attack like this should be endured until the whole Moslem army, and not just a division, had committed itself to close combat when he would order the sounding of six trumpets. This would be the signal for a general charge of the knights along the whole line. But the pressure Saladin was exerting on the Hospitallers was more than they could bear; their Master rode to seek Richard's permission to launch a counter-attack but still Richard refused. At this the Hospitallers took matters into their own hands, the infantry parted to let them through and squadron after squadron wheeled round to the attack. Without general support there was a danger the Moslems might cut them off so Richard ordered the sounding of the trumpets. In a matter of minutes there was a general charge of the knights and, for all the terror of the moment, Beha al-Din could not withhold his fearful admiration. At Acre there had been no assault on this scale. The charge of the knights was famous and he was witnessing a major demonstration of its power.

Beha al-Din took refuge with the centre of the army but it broke up in disorder. He kicked up his mule to hasten to the left wing but that had taken to its heels. Eventually he found Saladin himself with only seventeen men but with his standards still flying and the war drums beating to rally the fugitives. Al-Afdal charged so violently that a blood vessel burst in his face which was masked in blood. The Mosul squadron in particular distinguished itself in the counter-attack but the Crusaders' charge could not be turned and they did not, as Saladin hoped, gallop wildly into the oak woods where they might be separated and cut down. There were 7,000 Moslem dead. Saladin counted the day as a defeat and he seemed overwhelmed by it, would not listen to the consoling remarks that were addressed to him and only reluctantly took a little food. His own tent had been lost and an awning was rigged up to protect him from the sun.

Arsuf has been described as the most complete and typical of all the victories of the Franks and it is certainly true that the Moslems were so mauled that Saladin was never ready again to meet the full strength of the Crusaders head on. But it would be an exaggeration to claim that his victory made Richard master of the situation. Saladin managed to stem the wild flight of his troops and gathered his army together again, pretty well intact as a fighting force. Richard was fully aware of the tenacity of his opponent and proceeded cautiously. By firm march discipline and by his own heroic efforts, he had succeeded in bringing his army down the coast to within striking distance of Jerusalem. But he could not immediately follow up his victory, which is what Saladin would have liked him to attempt, and took part in a service of thanksgiving in the church of Arsuf before moving on to Jaffa which he took without a serious fight. The defences of the city, like those of Arsuf, had been destroyed by Saladin during the Frederick Barbarossa scare and the Crusaders now set about restoring them.

Saladin withdrew his army to Ramleh, some 25 kilometres to the south-east and continued to take the odd prisoner or two who always seemed singularly ready to give information about their countrymen's movements and preparedness for battle, hoping to save their lives. Usually they had their heads cut off, in spite of their willingness to collaborate. What Saladin now wanted to know was which city Richard intended to move on, Jerusalem or Ascalon. He lacked the strength to defend both. Jerusalem was poorly garrisoned at the moment. Ascalon, the key to Egypt, was of great strategic importance; its loss would expose Egypt to invasion by the Crusaders with everything that meant in the loss of money, supplies and soldiers. But it was known that Richard's time in Palestine was limited and Jerusalem, because of its overriding religious signi-ficance, would probably be his first objective. So Saladin's Council advised defending Jerusalem and abandoning and even destroying Ascalon, to prevent the Crusaders gaining anything there. Also present in their minds was what had happened at Acre. Moslem troops did not want to be caught again, as they might be in Ascalon, between a Frankish fleet of galleys and a besieging army of Crusaders with the likelihood that they would be massacred by Richard if he took the city by storm or massacred by Richard even if they surrendered.

Saladin was in anguish. 'I take God to witness I would rather lose all my children than cast a single stone from the walls, but God wills it; it is necessary for the Moslem cause, therefore I am obliged to carry it through.' This was no conventional expression of distress. He did not use the name of God lightly and in calling on Him to witness that he valued Ascalon more than his children the possibility would have been present in his mind that divine providence would save the city. But at what cost? He had spoken before of his hope of dying a martyr while fighting the infidels. He would joyfully die if, at the same time, he brought about the destruction of the enemy and, before Acre, had quoted the proverb: 'Kill me and Malik; kill Malik with me,' which referred to a famous fight in which the hero struggled on the ground with his enemy and asked his men to put a lance through his assailant even at the cost of his own life. Saladin had seen himself as a possible sacrifice for the Faith but never before had thought of his children as offerings to God. He was devoted to them, as Abraham had been devoted to his son, but was nevertheless prepared to sacrifice him if it had been God's will.

Troops and labourers hired from the local population spent more than a month destroying this once attractive city, the home of al-Fadel. The inhabitants in distress had to abandon their houses and what possessions they could not take with them on the journey either to Egypt or to Syria, which was done mostly on foot because they had no money to hire camels, mules or donkeys. Their houses and other buildings were set on fire. Demolishing the walls and towers that defended the town was a prodigious task. Under Saladin's personal supervision the towers were filled with wood and fired, cracking the stone and making it that much easier to prise the great blocks apart. The citadel overlooking the sea was so solidly built that the workmen's picks could make no impression on it and, here again, wood was stacked up and fired to make the stone more friable. Richard's army was camped not much more than 48 kilometres away and Saladin was concerned that his scouts might see the rising columns of smoke from afar and bring down an attack he was not well placed to resist. But Richard did not learn what was afoot until it was too late. Such were Saladin's exertions that he again fell ill and kept to his tent for two days, taking no food. The task now was to stand between Richard and Jerusalem.

The rest of the Moslem world showed an unawareness of the significance of what was happening that would have been comical if, from Saladin's point of view, it had not been so dispiriting. A minor ruler from Anatolia turned up to ask for the Sultan's support against

[165]

his father, Kilij Arslan, and brothers who were trying to take his possessions from him. The raising of this domestic dispute was extraordinarily inopportune but, choosing to regard it as a tribute, Saladin sent al-Adil to give the traditional welcome. More inopportune still was the behaviour of Taqi al-Din's young son, al-Mansur Mohammed, who now asked that his dead father's fiefs in Syria and elsewhere should be conferred upon him. Saladin hesitated because al-Mansur was still in his teens and lacked the experience to rule in areas where, even now, the old Zengid hostility could bubble up; eventually he agreed but with the imposition of certain strict conditions. During the winter, at a time on the Jerusalem road when the morale of the Moslems was at its lowest, al-Mansur went into open rebellion, possibly with the connivance of Bektimur of Khilat from the other side of the Tigris; Bektimur had recently promised to send assistance for the Holy War, but was now considering whether it would be cleverer to exploit Saladin's difficulties. The Sultan had seriously to consider the possibility of war on two fronts.

Al-Adil was acutely aware of the danger presented by family quarrels and tried to act as a peace-maker, but Saladin was so angered by the demands made in a letter from his great-nephew that he tore it up. The instinctive reaction of most of the emirs now gathered in Jerusalem was to urge the Sultan not to deal harshly with al-Mansur. But disloyalty of this kind and at such a time could not be tolerated and al-Afdal was despatched to Aleppo where he was instructed to seek the assistance of his brother, al-Zaher, in taking over all Taqi al-Din's old fiefs which were now conferred on him. Al-Mansur had lost his inheritance. There was consternation in Jerusalem and al-Adil set about the difficult task of asking his brother to reconsider his action. He sounded opinion among the emirs. Abu al-Heija, 'the Fat', was their spokesman and he emphasized the danger of al-Mansur making an alliance with Bektimur and the consequent threat to carrying on the Holy War. 'We cannot carry on two wars at the same time. If the Sultan wishes us to fight the Moslems he must make peace with the infidels; then we will cross the Euphrates and fight but it must be under his leadership. If he wishes to keep on the Holy War, let him pardon the Moslems and grant them peace.' In other words, climb down. Al-Adil supported this view. Saladin marvelled that a boy in Mesopotamia could be the cause of so much trouble. It was a harsh reminder of the strategic importance of the land beyond the Euphrates and how right he had been to assert his authority over the city states there, Harran, Sinjar, Edessa, Sameisat, right up to Mosul itself, to guard against just such a stab in the back as this. It would have been easier to bear if the hand that held the dagger was Zengid rather than that of a member of his own family.

His calculations were complicated by an unexpected move from Conrad of Montferrat, who sent a delegation to Jerusalem led by none other than Reynaud of Sidon, the man who had hoodwinked Saladin before his castle of Beaufort. Presumably he was one of the 'named' prisoners released after the fall of Acre. Saladin seemed to bear him no ill-will and treated him with some ceremony. The message he brought was that Conrad, then in Tyre with his royal wife Isabella, was prepared to made a break with Richard and even work for the return of Acre to Saladin, in return for recognition of his right to the territories he already held and for Sidon and Beyrout in addition. He drew the line only at actually fighting Richard. Reynaud put this extraordinary proposal with his usual charm and in spite of the experience at Beaufort Saladin found himself, once more, falling under his spell. Reynaud's Arabic must have been if not good at least appealing.

The same day another Arabist appeared, the young Humphrey of Toron, who had been sent by Richard also to discuss a peace. Ever since the Battle of Arsuf Richard had been making peace proposals with the usual unacceptable minimum demands. 'As to Jerusalem, we are fully resolved never to give it up, even though we have but one man left; touching the land, you must restore it to as far as the other side of Jordan; and lastly, as regards the Cross—to you it is nothing but a piece of wood but it is very precious in our eyes and if the Sultan will graciously give it into our hands we will make peace and breathe again after continual weariness.' These demands were rejected. 'As concerns the Cross,' Saladin had replied, 'its possession is a great advantage to us and we cannot give it up except if we should thereby gain some advantage to Islam.' So there was deadlock.

Richard had then proposed that al-Adil, whom he described as his friend and brother, should marry his sister Joan who, having been widowed in Sicily, had accompanied him to Palestine. If not Joan (because the Pope's approval to her marriage would have to be sought and that might not be given) then Richard's niece Eleanor of Brittany, who was his ward and would have to do what he told her no matter what the Pope said. After the marriage the pair would rule jointly over Palestine, peace would return and Moslems and Christians would be brothers. It would help if al-Adil became a Christian. Saladin had taken this proposition in the way it was intended. He consented because he knew very well that Richard had no intention of securing a peace on any such basis; it was all trickery and mockery. So he said 'yes' three times, believing that nothing would come of the idea. Rumour among the Moslems had it that the lady Joan was furious when she heard of the plan (al-Adil already had several wives) and the fighting went on.

But now Humphrey of Toron was bringing more realistic proposals based on the idea of a division of territories, even the partitioning of Jerusalem between al-Adil and Richard or, more accurately, a future Frankish king yet to be decided. It was this uncertainty about the identity of the future king that lay behind the rival negotiations but the problem, as Saladin and his Council saw it, was to know whom it was better to treat with, the Marquis or the King of England.

In their deliberations they did not wonder whether the future king would be Conrad or Guy. Conrad was supported by the majority of the barons but his claim was undermined by the scandal of his marriage to Humphrey of Toron's wife when Humphrey was still alive and, indeed, negotiating on behalf of Richard. Guy, on the other hand, had been crowned king, however questionably, and been recognized as such by all. Moreover he was Richard's candidate. Richard could not understand the antipathy to Guy and went up to Acre to sort matters out. Conrad's expectation was that Richard would not only be against his candidature but would attempt to dispossess him of Tyre. To resist such a move Conrad thought he would need Saladin's help; this calculation lay behind his approach to the Sultan. In fact Richard reluctantly came round to the view that Guy lacked the support a king of Outremer needed and agreed that Conrad should be proclaimed King. But to the Moslem Council all this was unknown or imperfectly understood and they judged between the rival proposals of the Marquis and the King of England from the point of view of immediate advantage.

Al-Adil played an important part in the to-ings and fro-ings. He and King Richard dined together, first on French dishes, then on oriental, but he also struck up a cordial friendship with the Marquis's emissary, Reynaud of Sidon, and went on hunting trips with him, much to the annoyance of Humphrey of Toron who happened to see the pair ride out together. In contrast to the bestialities that took place on the battlefield and particularly those committed by the Crusaders in the towns they took and sacked, the exchange of courtesies, compliments and gifts that went on at the highest negotiating level was remarkable. On Palm Sunday of that year Richard personally girded al-Adil's son, a future ruler of Egypt but then a boy of 12, with the belt of Knighthood. Balian of Ibelin who had surrendered Jerusalem arrived in Saladin's camp and was given a splendid reception that included a special tent with a canvas enclosure inside fitted out with cushions and carpets. Saladin's courtly behaviour made a great impression on the Franks. Only a confident and therefore very powerful prince could afford such magnanimity. That was how it struck them and no doubt that was how it was intended to strike them. The reality was different. Saladin just felt the strength oozing out of him.

But which was it to be, the King or Conrad—King Conrad as he now was? The Council of State and the emirs, including al-Adil, had become so defeatist they wanted a truce with Richard that would allow them to go home. On the whole Saladin was more disposed to treat with Conrad. He did not trust Richard to honour any agreement whereas Conrad was likely to observe a treaty that was so much in his own interest. Saladin's principal objective remained to drive Richard and all his forces into the sea. His emirs were not totally behind him but if this opportunity were missed it would never come again. The state of his health was such that his life might not have long to run. 'If we make peace with these people,' he said, 'there is nothing to protect us against their treachery. If I were to die it might be difficult to get an army together such as this, and meanwhile the enemy would have waxed strong. The best thing to do is to persevere in the Holy War until we have either driven them all from the coast, or we ourselves die in the attempt.' He was against peace.

Saladin's belief that Richard was not a man to be trusted was confirmed when the consequences of al-Mansur's rebellion became even more threatening in Mesopotamia and Richard broke off peace negotiations in the hope of profiting if the Moslems started fighting each other. Following the handover of al-Mansur's claimed provinces to al-Afdal the rebel had made an appeal to al-Adil for intercession on his behalf. This al-Adil did. He had not approved the giving of all these fiefs to al-Afdal for two reasons, one being the provocation it would give to that difficult young man, al-Mansur, who regarded them as his own; and the second lay in his estimate of al-Afdal's character. In spite of his bravery in battle he was giving promise of developing into a self-indulgent sensualist, a wine-drinking sybaritic, who was in no way qualified to govern in that highly sensitive frontier area, the Jezireh. Al-Adil expostulated with Saladin and the row that followed can only be imagined because there is no record of it. The outcome was, however, that Saladin (never a man to stand on his dignity and always open to reason) agreed that perhaps he had made a mistake in giving so much responsibility to his eldest son and this must be put right. He sent al-Adil off after his nephew to take over his newly acquired possessions himself. Al-Afdal was so angry when his uncle caught up with him and told him of the Sultan's decision that he too became mutinous and, for some time, refused to rejoin his father's forces. Al-Mansur was compensated for his disappointment with the news that he could have his father's Syrian fiefs after the lapse of a year. But al-Afdal sulked for a long time and only rejoined the Moslem armies at Jerusalem when directly ordered to by his father who rode out to meet him. Because of this family row both Saladin's brother and his eldest son were absent from the defence of Jerusalem at a time when Richard had returned to the attack, but even so Saladin thought fit to dismount at Bethany, the place where he met al-Afdal, as a mark of honour to soothe his feelings.

On 28 April 1192, while walking back to his palace for dinner through the narrow streets of Tyre, King Conrad was stabbed by two Assassins disguised as Christian monks and died within a matter of minutes. This was taken as bad news by the Moslems who regarded the Marquis as a potential ally against Richard and some thought that Richard had paid the Grand Master of the Assassins, Sinan of Masyaf, to have the work done. This was believed by the French and Germans. Another rumour was that Saladin had paid Sinan to remove not only Conrad but Richard as well. This was the view of the Zengid historian Ibn al-Athir, who does not explain what advantage the death of the Marquis was to Saladin. The true promoter of this murder has never been established but it was not usual for the Old Man of the Mountain to act as a hired murderer unless, as in the attempts on Saladin himself some years before, there was ideological purpose in it, and that seems lacking on this occasion. As it happens Sinan had reasons of his own for the murder of Conrad.

The Assassins had profited from the fighting between the Moslems and Christians to strike advantageous bargains with both sides, strengthen their castles and generally increase their wealth by commercial speculation. Sinan was running a state like any other state and, becoming part of the Syrian political scene, it later paid tribute to the Templars and Hospitallers. Assassinating one of them was pointless because he was replaced, the Orders carried on as before, so the Assassins had to come to terms with them. Sinan's state traded internationally. One of its more considerable ventures, a merchant ship with a valuable cargo, was piratically seized by Conrad and this seems a possible explanation of the murder for which, incidentally, Sinan's successor apologized to the Franks some years later. It is an agreed fact, however, that the murderers of Conrad made a confession in which Richard was implicated. They may have been lying but the removal of the Marquis was certainly welcome to Richard. As ex-King Guy was too unpopular to be a candidate for the succession one was found in Henry of Champagne. He was the nephew both of Richard and the King of France, was liked by them both and so unlikely to cause any further dispute between them. Henry was married so quickly to Conrad's widow to make him King (it was her third marriage and there was to be a fourth, such was the destiny of queens born royal) that it was wrongly believed by the Moslems that the nuptials were consummated although Isabella was already pregnant. It was the sort of gross sexual behaviour, specifically forbidden in the Koran, that Moslems had little difficulty in attributing to the Franks.

Neither Saladin nor Richard was in a position to achieve their respective war aims. For Richard this would have been the taking of Jerusalem and the crowning of Henry and Isabella as leaders of a secure state by the Latin Patriarch in the Church of the Holy Sepulchre. The relative strength of the two armies, in spite of Saladin's difficulties, were too finely balanced to make an attempt by

[171]

Richard on the Holy City anything but a gamble. During the winter the rain turned the rough roadways to mud and even the 240-kilometre journey from Jerusalem to Damascus could take nineteen days. Richard's first direct approach to Jerusalem came to a halt almost within sight of the city when torrential rain and high winds made it impossible even to camp, the sodden tents were blown across the rocks, animals died, and the biscuit and bacon rations rotted. In spite of the foul weather there were bands of Moslem horsemen in the hills quick to pounce on stragglers. As Saladin and his remaining troops (many contingents had been sent home) were cooped up in Jerusalem the winter gales fought for him more effectively than any raiding regiments he could send out. In summer the natural defences were of a different kind. Jerusalem is a hill city with little natural water for miles around and if Saladin took it into his head to pollute the few wells that did exist—as he eventually did—an advancing army might have to endure the killing thirst of Hattin all over again. Richard set about rebuilding Ascalon in what looked like preparation for an invasion of Egypt and Saladin, lacking the strength for another pitched battle, attacked the Crusaders' lines of communication, staged ambushes, and waited for the return of the Mosul, Sinjar and other eastern contingents while the peace negotiations went on and on.

In these the Relic of the True Cross continued to feature prominently though it is not certain whether the one in Saladin's possession was the one taken at Hattin. That was sent to the Caliph who had it buried under a Baghdad city gateway where Moslem feet could tread on it. If so, what was the Relic shown to the Crusaders at Acre? No one suggested that imitations had been made. Richard never doubted that Saladin possessed the authentic Relic, nor did the Emperor Isaac Angelus who chose this moment to write and ask for it; also the handing over of all the Jerusalem churches to the Greek rite, all this in return for an offensive and defensive alliance. Saladin's answer was no. In spite of his lack of money he also refused a huge bid for the Relic, 200,000 gold dinars, from Georgia which was then at the zenith of its power and wealth under Queen Tamara. Saladin either recovered the Relic from Baghdad or acquired another and equally authentic or fraudulent fragment, like the one shown to Richard by the abbot of a monastery near the Crusaders' camp in the Judaean hills before the storms drove him back to the coast.

⚜ 11 ⚜

The Defence of Jerusalem

Egypt's contribution to Saladin's war effort was prodigious. Three-quarters of all national expenditure went on the army and navy. Military strength was concentrated in the large cities for the defence of the country but tens of thousands of troops regularly marched across Sinai or were ferried up by the navy to fight in Palestine. The financial strain on the Treasury was so great that Saladin's administration there under his son al-Aziz reduced the gold and silver content of coins as an alternative to cutting soldiers' pay. Gold was scarce anyway because the traditional supply from West Africa was now interrupted by the Almohad Sultan in Tunis. Silver coins were so debased that they contained only 50 per cent silver, in contrast to Syria where the coins remained of good standard. Egyptian devaluation was to the advantage of Syrian merchants who found their purchasing power in the markets of Fustat greatly increased, a state of affairs much resented by Egyptians who felt their national interests were being sacrificed for the benefit of the Turks, as they called them. If the Turkish war in Palestine could be stopped Egypt's profitable European trade would pick up once more and Egyptian wealth would cease being drained by the Damascus caravan. Al-Fadel, who was now the head of al-Aziz's administration in Cairo, did his best to represent these views to the Sultan.

The importance of Egyptian supplies was dramatically illustrated by what happened to one great convoy on its way from the Delta. It was so large it had been divided into three, one part to travel the old route south-east of the Dead Sea and up past Kerak as though making for Damascus, another to travel through the desert somewhat further west, and a third, much the largest apparently, rather rashly taking the short route through Hebron. Richard, having taken Darun, the last Moslem stronghold on the coast before the River of Egypt, was in the area and learned from the Beduin that a particularly rich caravan from Egypt was within striking distance. He could hardly believe his luck. To make sure he was not being bluffed he sent out another Beduin whom he trusted and two soldiers disguised as Beduin to inspect the caravan as it camped for the night. There was a full moon and the night was brilliant. The scouts confirmed that the caravan was indeed there. By dawn Richard was on ʾhe scene with a sizeable force and took the caravan after a brisk fight, lifting 3,000 horses, 3,000 camels, an unspecified number of mules, foodstuffs in vast quantities, weapons including much-needed arrows, lances and body armour. The Egyptian reinforcements for the army at Jerusalem were scattered. Only one baggage train escaped the general disaster and that was because of the heroism of the officer in charge. It happened to belong to Saladin himself.

The loss was disastrous because it occurred when Moslem morale was already very low. Beha described it as a disgraceful event. The caravan commander should have known the risk he was running by deciding to camp when he ought to have been hurrying the convoy on under cover of darkness, a common practice anyway at the height of summer as this was. Even so the other two parts of the caravan apparently got through. If they were comparable in size to the part that was lost the very number of animals involved must be an indication of the extent to which Saladin was stretching Egypt's resources. 'Never was the Sultan more grieved or rendered more anxious,' Beha wrote. He knew how badly the loss would be taken by his personal troops, the Kurds and the *mamluks*, who had been campaigning without a break in a way almost unprecedented for a Moslem army of the time and were now looking for the arrival of fresh mounts, replacements for weapons lost and, above all, reinforcements. Saladin called a meeting of his Council. He had information that Richard was marching once more on Jerusalem and could not be sure the Moslems were sufficiently determined to defend the city.

The proceedings were opened by Beha al-Din as Cadi of the Army. He spoke of the sacred duty of fighting a Holy War and suggested they adjourned to the Sacred Rock, there to take an oath to fight on under the Sultan until death. Abu al-Heija sat in his chair hardly able to move. Al-Meshtub was there, having been ransomed from Acre where he had been held prisoner. Both these men were

Kurds. Other leading officers present were Turks who had served under Saladin's uncle Shirkuh, men who had seen perhaps a quarter of a century in the service of the Ayyub family. There was no move to go to the Sacred Rock after Beha al-Din had finished speaking. Instead there was silence and men were so still that, as the saying went, it was 'as if a bird perched on each of their heads'.

Saladin watched them and when he eventually spoke it was to say that the responsibility of all within that tent was a heavy one. 'If you give way—which may God forbid!—the Franks will roll up this land [and he quoted the Koran] like the rolling up of a scroll. You will be answerable. You undertook to defend this land. You have received money from the public treasury and on you alone depends the safety of Moslems throughout the land.'

The plain fact was that the *mamluks*, whether they were veterans who had served under Shirkuh or not, did not want to defend Jerusalem from within its walls. The memory of Acre was too vivid for them. But the Kurds present had, over and above their military pride, a pride of race too. They were Kurds in the presence of their Kurdish leader and it was one of them, al-Meshtub, who spoke.

'My lord, we are your servants and slaves. You have been gracious to us and made us great and mighty and rich; we have nothing but our necks and they are in your hands. By God! not one of us will turn back from helping you until we die.' His words had special weight because they came from a survivor of Acre but it was noticeable that he argued for carrying on the fight out of personal loyalty, which some of the Turks present may not have shared; Saladin had hoped for a more religious commitment. There was no further discussion. The meeting broke up, a meal was served, but there was no move to the Sacred Rock for the taking of the oath as Beha al-Din had asked. Instead, some time later when all had dispersed Abu al-Heija, the great go-between, came back, walking with ponderous slowness, and reported to Saladin that there had been further unofficial talk between members of the Council. The *mamluks*, in spite of their silence in the tent, were still of the opinion that they should not shut themselves up behind the walls of Jerusalem but take their chance in the open. Even if the army was defeated, enough soldiers would survive to fight another day. If Saladin insisted on defending Jerusalem from within the walls either he or one of his family must stay with the garrison because Kurds would not take orders from Turks, nor Turks from Kurds. It would be wiser if Saladin's person were not risked. Eventually, a great-nephew, Bahram-Shah of Baalbek, was nominated. Saladin remained deeply anxious, even distressed.

The Crusading army had marched up once more to the place in the Judaean hills, Beyt Nuba, from where they had been driven by the weather the previous winter. But now it was July. The King of England stayed in this position for a surprisingly long time, surprising, that is, until it was realized that he was waiting for the new King Henry to arrive with his reinforcements. There was no doubt in Saladin's mind that his army was about to be put to the final test; and when the *mamluks* made it plain they would not defend the Holy City in the way he wanted he could not sleep. Beha al-Din found him still watching at dawn and begged him to take an hour's rest.

After the ritual washing, the necessary preliminary to the morning prayer which the two men now said together, Saladin was reminded by the Cadi that it was Friday, the most blessed day of the week when prayer was most heard. 'Your Highness is weighed down with anxiety, your soul is overburdened with care, you can hardly bear up. Earthly means are useless. You can only turn to God Almighty.'

The account is Beha al-Din's own and occcasionally, as here, his tone is a little self-regarding. His remarks would certainly have been what Saladin most wished to hear. He had done his best. For some inscrutable reason the Mosul, Sinjar and Diyar Bekr contingents, which had been on their way for some time, were dallying near Damascus. Perhaps they too did not want to be shut up in Jerusalem. All was as God willed and Saladin determined to surrender himself to that will by devoting this Friday to nothing but religious observance.

This involved the giving of alms. In Islam there was no provision for the relief of poverty out of public funds. Instead the giving of alms was regarded not just as praiseworthy but a religious duty which, if neglected, led to damnation and the fires of hell. Extra merit was acquired if the alms could be distributed so that no one knew the giver. This was the method chosen by Saladin on that Friday, 2 July 1192, and we would have known nothing of it if Beha al-Din, his intimate adviser, had not told us. But the source of the silver coins that now appeared in the begging bowls of Jerusalem would have been no great mystery to the beneficiaries, nor would the reason for the giving. The Sultan was observing one of the five pillars of Islam as a way of asking God to protect the Holy City.

He uttered the Creed, the first of the five pillars: 'There is no God but God and Mohammed is his prophet.' This *shahada* is the only dogmatic profession required of a Moslem. Its utterance formed a part of another indispensable duty, another pillar, the five daily performances of liturgical worship. Saladin, as was his habit, scrupulously observed the necessary ablutions and the required movements of the body, the bowings and the prostrations. As an act of supererogation he performed two *rak'a*, the reciting of verses from the Koran and making two inclinations of his head for each. The Al-Aqsa Mosque was crowded for the noon prayer. The ranks of armed men prostrated themselves and prayed with the precision of the parade ground. Saladin himself led the prayers, prostrating himself so that his nose and forehead touched his prayer carpet. Beha al-Din, who prayed with him, observed the tears that fell on the carpet and, when he stood up, glistened on his beard.

Fasting was not a religious obligation at this time in the Moslem year, the month was not Ramadan, but Saladin had many fast days to catch up on because of campaigning. It would have been in character for him to fast that Friday as one of them. A religious duty he had so far failed to perform was the Hajj, the pilgrimage to Mecca, and the omission—which he intended to put right as soon as he was able—might weigh against him on this fateful day. Was his conscience clear that he had postponed the obligatory pilgrimage for good and sufficient reason?

The only acceptable excuse for not making the Hajj was ill health or poverty. When he was a young man he could easily have gone. Nur al-Din went when Saladin was one of his entourage at Aleppo. I Iis father Ayyub went, so did his uncle Shirkuh, they all made the pilgrimage, but Saladin did not accompany them. He had thought there was plenty of time before he need fulfil the obligation. This was evidence, like the wine he drank, of no great early piety. Later, in Cairo or Damascus, there were political responsibilities he could not turn his back on, even for the two months or so the Hajj would have taken up. Another excuse was the cost. The Hajj, for a ruler of his prominence, involved considerable expense. This could not be met out of the public purse because canonical taxes were intended mainly for war, not the religious duties of the ruler. He had little money of his own. But in his heart he knew that this, and nervousness about being away from his centres of power, would not justify him in the eyes of God who might already have decided there was no other way to salvation for him but a martyr's death.

From the towers and walls of Jerusalem there were moments in the early morning when the scouts of the enemy could be detected in the hills to the west as the sun caught their lances and helmets. The King of England might have been among them, seeing the city from afar—or not seeing, as the case may be, because it was later said he put up his shield in front of his face to avoid the tantalizing sight. That Saturday news came, from spies or Franks taken prisoner, that the Christian High Command was undecided what to do. The following day, Sunday, the Crusading army poised to launch its attack on Jerusalem broke camp instead and began the march back to the coast. For Saladin, who rode out to watch them go, it was a clear result of Divine intervention. Information reached him later about what had happened. As Acre was a warning to the Moslems, so Hattin was to the Christians and Richard came to the conclusion that an attack on the city would be a risky business. In the height of summer they would be without drinking water; an army with tens of thousands of horses and beasts of burden needed enormous quantities of it. There was, too, the nagging thought that even if the city were taken it could not be held. The Crusading troops looked for no home in Palestine. They were pilgrims and once they had performed their vows they would have no thought but to return to Europe. The decision was finally taken by a council which Richard presided over; it was for retreat in favour of an attack on Egypt. The French complained loudly but there was nothing they could do about it and peace negotiations began all over again.

The attack on Egypt did not take place but the importance attached to the fate of Ascalon in the negotiations shows how live the Egyptian issue was. The Crusaders had started to rebuild Ascalon after its destruction by Saladin but it was a shadow of what it once had been. Its significance lay in the site, threatening communication between Egypt and Syria. Once the walls had been rebuilt it was a forward base for the major attack on Egypt which Western opinion increasingly considered would not only be profitable in itself but the centre from which to destroy Moslem strength in the East, to dominate the invaluable Red Sea trade routes and to recover the Holy Land. Saladin would never agree to handing Ascalon over to the Franks but, such was the war-weariness of his troops, he was prepared to see it and Darun declared a neutral zone, to be left waste and not occupied by either Moslems or Franks. Richard was even prepared to abandon his claim to Jerusalem except for the Church of the Holy Sepulchre there (this Saladin was prepared to grant) and free access by pilgrims, but he really must insist, Richard said, on retaining Darun and Ascalon. With his usual robust candour he said he had spent a lot of money on rebuilding Ascalon and did not want to be out of pocket! He was anxious to clear these details up because he had to return to England where there were problems calling for his attention. To show good will he sent Saladin a brace of falcons.

On both sides there was a desire for peace. Richard's recognition that Jerusalem was beyond his grasp was not only bad for his prestige in general, it aroused the contemptuous anger of the French and the least he could realistically do for his reputation was to insist on keeping Ascalon. But Ascalon was the sticking point for Saladin, too. At the suggestion of al-Meshtub he was prepared to compensate Richard for his expenses by some other land deal, even the surrender of Lydda. Knowing that Richard intended to leave for Europe in the near future, and that the Third Crusade had spent itself, Saladin thought he had everything to gain by waiting. Richard, without finalizing the peace terms, marched off to Acre with the intention of moving on to Beyrout, still in Moslem hands, which he would take and plunder before leaving for England. Southern Palestine was, therefore, unprotected by the person of the King, and the temptation for Saladin was too great. He sent al-Afdal to pick up the Mosul, Sinjar and Diyar Bekr contingents still near Damascus and march to the support of Beyrout. He himself took his Kurdish, Turkoman and *mamluk* forces down to Jaffa and, after sharp fighting, broke into the city.

What followed was the last and in some ways most striking clash between Saladin and Richard. It was a long time since the Kurds and Turkomans had had an opportunity for plunder and they went on the rampage, killing a few citizens who resisted. But it was property they were after, not lives, and there was no general massacre. Saladin formally accepted the surrender of the city from its garrison commander on the same terms as he had taken Jerusalem: safe conduct for those who ransomed themselves. But he could not maintain discipline over his troops. He advised the new Patriarch of Jerusalem who happened to be in the city (Heraclius had died) to get as many of the defenders as possible into the citadel for their own safety; he then ordered his personal guard of *mamluks* to recover the loot. When the Kurds came out of the town gates with 'fine stuffs, abundance of corn, furniture, even the remains of the booty taken from the caravan from Egypt' the *mamluks* set about them, beat them up, and stacked the plunder for disposal in accordance with the terms of the surrender, much of it to be returned to the owners. A less scrupulous commander than Saladin would have turned a blind eye. To set one section of his army on to attack another in the interests of probity was the act of a man still passionate for his honour; and like many who put their own integrity before gratifying the wishes of others he aroused bitter resentment.

News came that Richard, hearing of the attack on Jaffa, was hurrying back from Acre by sea, his army marching in support. The possession of the citadel now became of prime importance. A number of knights, about fifty together with their wives and their horses, left the citadel under safe conduct and, once again, there were scenes astonishing even to the Christians. The Kurds and Turkomans in the streets had to be beaten back by the *mamluks* to ensure that Saladin's safe conduct was honoured. But when Richard's rescuing fleet of fifty vessels came into sight the rest of the Christian garrison decided to stay in the citadel and fight on. First to beach was Richard's galley, painted red, covered with a red awning and flying a red flag. Still in his boating shoes and without armour he waded ashore brandishing an axe. In less than an hour he had got his men disembarked, mainly troops from Pisa. Beha al-Din, now acting as Saladin's aide-de-camp and riding a horse not the customary mule, watched with incredulity how Richard and his men, though heavily outnumbered, attacked the Moslems with such ferocity they broke and ran away. Saladin, still in his tent, had the embarrassment of seeing his panic-stricken troops in full flight while he himself was still talking to two of the Patriarch's envoys who did not know that Richard had landed. The Moslems ran for five miles before reassembling.

What is striking about the taking and retaking of Jaffa, all within two days, is the disproportionate strength of the two sides. Saladin was reputed to have about 60,000 men at his disposal, Richard less than 3,000, including 54 knights (with only 15 horses between them), 400 crossbowmen and 2,000 Pisan infantrymen. Saladin, who had stayed where he was with a squadron of light cavalry when the rest of his army ran off, was determined to drive Richard into the sea and the fact that he was unable to do so is an indication of the poor heart his men were in, the resentment leading to near mutiny over the removal of their plunder, and the fear they had of European troops. Beha al-Din, during the siege, had spoken of the terrifying sight presented by the wall of Christian halberds and lances and by the stern discipline of the men who held them.

Richard made another bid for peace. 'Greet the Sultan from me, and tell him in God's name to grant me the peace I ask at his hands,' he said to Saladin's emissary. 'This state of things must be put a stop to. My own country beyond the seas is being ruined.' He even offered to accept Saladin as his liege-lord if he were given Jaffa and Ascalon. 'The troops I leave there will be always at your service and, if you have need of me, I will hasten to come to you.' Saladin did not believe him and would not give up Ascalon on any terms, not even as a fief to Richard.

'It is absolutely impossible for us to give up Ascalon,' he said. 'I am an old man now. I have no longer any desires for the pleasures of this world. I have had my fill of them and have renounced them for ever. . . . I believe I am furthering God's cause in acting as I do. I will not cease therefore until God grants victory to whom He will.'

Whereupon Saladin tried to attack before Richard's reinforcements could arrive—tried, because his men would not budge after their first attempts had been beaten off, except for the squadron under his son al-Zaher. This was the famous occasion when Richard's horse was killed and Saladin sent him two remounts so that, the story goes, he would be at no disadvantage. But the day was chiefly remarkable for the refusal of the Moslem troops to go on the offensive. 'I have been assured,' wrote Beha al-Din, 'by men who were there that the King of England, lance in hand, rode along the whole length of our army from right to left and not one of our soldiers left the ranks to attack him.' More serious, in spite of Saladin's exhortations, was the way the squadrons of Moslem cavalry held back. No less a person than the brother of al-Meshtub (the Kurd who had commanded at Acre and supported Saladin in his Jerusalem Council) now turned savagely on the Sultan, saying, 'Give your orders to those *mamluks* of yours who beat up the troops as Jaffa and took their booty away from them.'

Al-Zaher was a son of whom Saladin was particularly fond. Yet after the near-mutiny before Jaffa Saladin showed such anger that al-Zaher did not dare to come into his sight for fear of what might happen. Alone among the emirs he had charged the enemy with such vigour that Saladin had to order him to retire for his own safety. So what can this fear mean? That al-Zaher thought his father capable of ordering the arrest or punishment of his own son and quite unjustly? It appears so. He confessed to not having the courage to enter his father's tent until he was summoned. The other emirs felt certain the Sultan would show his displeasure by having a great number of them crucified as he had crucified Omara and the other conspirators in Cairo twenty years before. These men knew what Saladin was capable of. Cowardice in the face of the enemy can be a capital offence in modern armies. Deserters from the Moslem garrison at Acre had been killed. Now that his authority had been directly challenged he would have been thought well within the rules if he had decided to make an example of one or two trouble-makers, al-Meshtub's brother to start with.

Saladin rode away from the battlefield, seeing that his troops would do no good that day. When al-Zaher entered his tent he saw that a quantity of fruit had arrived from Damascus.

'Send for the emirs,' said Saladin, 'let them come and taste.'

The crisis was past. They entered apprehensively but were so well received that when they left they were ready to march as though nothing had happened. But not quite. They had shown how little stomach they had for fighting and Saladin, for all his conviction that the war had to be fought to the bitter end could not order them against Richard's wall of spearmen and the crossbowmen who stood behind. And there was a wider disillusion with the Holy War. For more than two years the supply of volunteers from Egypt, Syria and Iraq, who had played an important part at Hattin, had dried up. Saladin was no longer leading a popular movement and that it was a movement at all depended entirely on his own personal dedication. 'Unlike other princes,' he said, 'I do not prefer a life of ease to the Holy War.'

The Defence of Jerusalem

Al-Fadel now wrote to him: 'None among all the Moslems will help in the Holy War except by empty words. No one will follow you except for money. You summon them in the name of God and it is as though you were summoning them for yourself. You ask for personal commitment and it is as though you were asking for the supererogatory.'

Much use was made of the word 'peace', but there was never any question in anyone's mind of concluding a real peace treaty with provisions intended to stand for ever. In the eyes of Moslems there could not be permanent peace with the polytheists; for the Christians, too, there would be no peace without Jerusalem. What was in prospect was a truce—just like the other truces Saladin had made in the past with Antioch, Tripoli and the Kingdom of Jerusalem—designed to last for a limited period, after which fighting would start again. The truce of 2 September 1192 was made possible because Richard, who had fallen seriously ill and was provided by Saladin with fruit and snow, decided he had to go back to England So he conceded Ascalon. It was to be demolished once more. The Franks retained the cities they had taken, from Acre to Jaffa, and there were provisions for the free access of Christian pilgrims to Jerusalem, and for Moslems to travel, as they had before the Crusade, throughout the Sahil. The truce was to last for three years and eight months, which seems an odd period to choose until it is remembered that an exact three years would have expired just before the bad weather came. Fighting, it was envisaged, would start again in the late spring or early summer of 1196. Richard hoped to be back in person but if not, King Henry, the Masters of the Temple and the Hospitallers, all of whom took the oath to observe the truce, would make another bid for Jerusalem. It was an appointment.

By that time Saladin would have been in his late fifties. His health was bad. Even if he lived that long the rigours of another campaign fought with the intensity of the one just ended might be beyond him. For this reason he was deeply reluctant to agree to the truce. He had just received reinforcements from Egypt and the Jezireh. The opportunity was surely too good to miss. Richard would be away to England, truce or no. Why then should the Moslems not deal with the rest of the Frankish army? But the emirs had had enough and wanted to go home. So he gave in, warning them about the future. He did not say that when he was dead such unity as existed among

[183]

the Moslems would disintegrate. But he did say: 'The enemy will increase their forces and come out of the lands we are leaving in their possession and recapture those we have taken from them. Each of them will make a fortress on some hill top. But I cannot draw back from the truce now.' He would, in his heart, have preferred Richard not to give way over Ascalon.

The Third Crusade was over and Saladin sat in Jerusalem observing the throng of pilgrims who came up from Richard's army, among them Hubert Walter, the Bishop of Salisbury. Saladin had a long conversation with him through an interpreter, showed him the Holy Cross and then invited the Bishop to ask for a gift. Whatever he asked would be granted. Saladin may have thought the Bishop would ask for the Holy Cross itself, but instead he asked that Latin priests should be allowed to celebrate Mass in the Holy Sepulchre, in addition to the Syrian Jacobite priests already there. Saladin was so pleased with this request that he granted the petition and for the Latin rite to be celebrated at Bethlehem and Nazareth too. So much for Isaac Angelus's request that the Holy Places should be handed over to the Orthodox Church. News of the peace had come as a disappointment to Constantinople. The Emperor had hoped that Saladin would do better, even to the extent of enabling him to recover Cyprus, but that had never been a possibility. Richard soon sold the island to the Templars who in turn sold it to Guy of Lusignan whose dynasty reigned there for nearly 300 years. The dynasty of his conqueror at Hattin was to be nowhere near as long-lived.

The war had ended better for Saladin than at one time he had feared. All the territory he had gained since the Battle of Hattin had been retained except for the coastal strip and the admittedly key cities of Jaffa and Acre. His failures to take Tyre and to stop Guy marching on Acre have been judged harshly by historians who, like al-Athir, think the Third Crusade would not have been possible had he acted more decisively. But the Crusade was pinned down, its attacking force blunted, for two years. If Saladin had taken Tyre and stopped Guy in his tracks the Kings of France and England could still have landed further north at Tripoli and, using the impregnable castle of Krak les Chevaliers as their base, marched on Homs and the vital route between Aleppo and Damascus; if Frederick Barbarossa had not died in Cilicia the combined European armies would have rolled down into Palestine. Saladin, who had shown his awareness of this possibility by ordering the destruction of so many city defences in Palestine, knew, once the threat from the north had disappeared, that Acre would delay the Crusaders longer than they could afford and might even bleed their army to death. The strategy had been forced upon him but by his personal tenacity he made it work. When Richard finally boarded his ship for Europe Saladin had been campaigning almost without a break for over five years, never quite knowing whether the men who went home at the beginning of each winter would return to join him in the spring. That most of them did was a tribute to his personality; he persuaded men by his conduct that they could be as dedicated as he was himself.

During these final stages of the Third Crusade there had been no improvement in the relations with the Abbasid Caliph; paradoxically Saladin and Richard I had a greater regard for each other than existed between Saladin and the Caliph al-Nasir. Ever since he had succeeded to Nur al-Din's territories and started the struggle for power with the Zengids there had been suspicions of Saladin's real motives. For these suspicions there was, it must be admitted, a lot of justification. As time went by, and the Caliph still failed to show full acceptance of Saladin's claim to be the disinterested champion of Islam and provide real support, Saladin became disillusioned and angry.

The Caliph could not plead poverty. Although concerned by the threat to his own security presented by the Seljuks of western Persia and the Khwarizm Shah he had not, like Saladin, had to meet the costs of a major war and there was an economic boom. The Caliph's new theocratic state was afloat on a flood of silver coming from new mines in Iran. The population of Baghdad grew rapidly and new suburbs were built. Elsewhere in Iraq new villages were founded, irrigation canals dug and the peasants, freed from non-canonical exploitative taxation, were nudged in the direction of greater productivity. The merchants of Baghdad, Tikrit and Basra accumulated vast fortunes and the Caliph's own trading activities flourished too. In spite of his professed aim to order the state on truly religious lines he lived ostentatiously, in contrast to Saladin. When the news came from Jerusalem that a peace had been made the Caliph's councillors, members of the Divan, took the view that Saladin must be placated in case he took it into his head to make good

[185]

the economic hardships of his own territories at the expense of the Caliph's. The view was acted upon but not to the extent of the Caliph or his Vizier approaching Saladin himself. A rebuff at this level would be a serious matter. Accordingly the Assistant Vizier in Baghdad, Ibn al-Nafedh, sent an ambassador to al-Adil asking him to be an intermediary. Would he please do what he could to persuade his brother to show more respect to the Caliph? Relations between Baghdad and Jerusalem would be much improved if the Cadi al-Fadel were sent to the Caliph's court as ambassador. Anything along these lines that al-Adil was able to arrange would be so much appreciated by the Divan that great benefits would come his way, his influence would be of the greatest, and so on. The ambassador was not precise about al-Adil's reward.

Saladin's response, when he heard of this approach, showed how wise the Divan had been not to approach him direct. He was so angry over the Caliph's indifference to the needs of the Holy War and so resentful of the petty rebukes and reprimands that had come his way from Baghdad that he was all for al-Adil sending the ambassador back with some disobliging message. The Cadi al-Fadel had been asked for before. The answer had been no then and it was no now. Saladin was not prepared to let anyone think that the Caliph had any influence with him at all—a great change from his earlier deference. But the Caliph had never joined Saladin in Palestine, the war was over, his help was no longer needed. That was the difference. No, he had no respect for the Caliph, whose leanings towards the Shiah had become a scandal to the orthodox. Saladin no longer needed the Caliph's diplomas for territory he controlled and he could no longer regard himself as the Caliph's commander in the field as once, before the taking of Jerusalem, he had.

Many leading members of Saladin's Council had left for their homes in Mesopotamia by this time. Some of them would have rejoiced at Saladin's refusal of the olive branch, seeing the possibility of pickings at Tikrit or elsewhere down the Tigris or Euphrates if relations became really bad. But the discussions, which were lengthy, took place between the two brothers alone. Al-Adil was all for conciliation. Time was needed to restore the economy, particularly of Egypt where extra taxes had been imposed and, uncharacteristically, at Saladin's insistence. Al-Adil would have reminded his brother that he had proposed a special income tax of

1 per cent, only to be told it was not enough for the needs of the war and must be increased. At Alexandria and Damietta foreign traders were having to pay taxes amounting to 25 per cent of the value of the cargoes they shipped into and out of the country. Some crops had failed. That very year the price of beans had doubled in the markets of Fustat. There had even been pro-Fatimid demonstrations in Cairo.

As for Syria, it was well known that there were administrative abuses so outrageous, farmers being exploited by their *iqta* owners, that there had been disturbances, fighting and deaths in the Damascus area. Much needed to be done. There was evidence that taxes were disappearing on their way to the Treasury. The State was without money. As al-Fadel, writing from Egypt, had said: 'Even if many of our misfortunes have ended, an empty treasury may prove the greatest catastrophe of all.' This was no time for any break with Baghdad. The Caliph was the source of all power. To defy him was to defy orthodoxy and that was not politically possible. There were still Zengid sympathizers. A story was going round that when, only the previous year, Moizz al-Din (a Zengid prince) had held Saladin's stirrup for him to mount, an acknowledgement of subordination, a bystander had been heard to say: 'Son of Ayyub, you will rest easy no matter how you may die. The son of a Seljuk prince held your stirrup.' The old Turkish ascendancy was not to be trusted. The Franks were not to be trusted either. If they saw an advantage they would not hesitate to break the truce. There were many dangers. Nothing was to be gained from delivering a rebuff to Baghdad.

Saladin remained insistent that he would not allow al-Fadel to go to the Caliph's Divan. He was much too distinguished a figure to take orders in Baghdad. But it was reluctantly agreed that a less prominent person, a one-time Cadi of Damascus, should go and in this way diplomatic negotiations were resumed after the break. This Cadi, al-Dia esh-Sheherzuri, was charged with the responsibility of making it clear to the Divan that when Saladin made the pilgrimage to Mecca as he planned it would have no political significance. He had no wish to stir up any religious fervour in a way the Caliph might regard as threatening his own status or interests.

Before having these discussions Saladin's main thoughts had been on the preparations for this pilgrimage. Those who intended to accompany him were invited to put their names down. A quarter-master's department was set up to organize supplies for the winter journey, letters were sent to Egypt and the Yemen (where Saladin's brother Tughtigin still ruled) saying that part of the journey might be by sea and asking for ships to be made available. Camels and horses were assigned. But al-Adil, backed up by al-Fadel and the emirs, urged Saladin to reconsider. A pilgrimage would be more acceptable in God's sight once he had done something to repair the damage to civilian life the war had brought about. Much better to postpone the pilgrimage and undertake a tour of inspection. Above all, go to Egypt! Al-Fadel was particularly worried about Egypt but even here in Palestine there were administrative scandals that must be put to rights.

As a young man Saladin had been an honest city administrator and he assumed, all too easily, that the men he appointed were equally incorruptible. Al-Meshtub was an example. Saladin felt under some obligation to him because of his bearing at the Jerusalem Council and would have liked to see him Governor of Jerusalem. But there was opposition not only from Saladin's sons and brother but also from leading religious figures such as Beha al-Din. General consultation led to the appointment of the long-serving emir Jurdik, one of Shirkuh's men in the invasion of Egypt, and a leader of the *mamluks* in Jaffa who had so angered al-Meshtub's brother. What ruled al-Meshtub out was his bad showing as governor of the smaller city of Nablus where, even in the brief period he held the appointment, he had provoked the people into complaining direct to Saladin of the oppressive way he had treated them. Nizam al-Mulk, who had described the ideal administrative system when the Seljuk Sultanate was at its greatest and whose advice was still taken to heart, specifically warned that local governors and tax-collectors needed constant surveillance even if it meant using spies. Saladin preferred the tradition that a Moslem ruler should be available at fixed times to listen to complaints and petitions, and this he did at Nablus. The experience was disturbing. If a man like al-Meshtub could be found wanting just how many of his other local governors were above reproach? Saladin never succeeded in getting the administration of his empire on the same efficient basis as his armed forces.

The postponement of the pilgrimage, now decided upon, was largely due to the insistence of his advisers that it was urgently necessary to take decisions about the administration of Egypt and, now that the Franks had an agreed presence on the coast, to ensure that the various Moslem strongholds along the border were strengthened and properly manned. Before returning to Damascus Saladin undertook a tour to set this defence work in motion. The Frankish territory of Antioch had taken no direct part in the Third Crusade and Saladin had always made it an object of his policy to keep it as isolated as possible from the other Frankish states, even if it meant giving Count Bohemond (nicknamed the Stutterer) who ruled there specially favourable treatment. Count Bohemond had no voice in the peace negotiations between Saladin and Richard for this reason. He now approached Saladin for recognition of his authority in Antioch and the two men, in as much splendour as the hard times permitted, met in Beyrout.

Bohemond was quite ready to put his pride in his pocket and do homage for any township or strip of land Saladin thought fit to make him a present of. Saladin decided that his friendship had considerable value if the Franks to the south broke the truce and he returned to Bohemond the Plain of Antioch, taken from him in 1188. This was rich agricultural land worth 15,000 gold dinars a year and it made a considerable difference to Bohemond's standard of living. He resisted the idea, however, that he should become a Moslem even though the case was persuasively put by Saladin himself who, as with Reynaud of Sidon, enjoyed playing the proselytizer. They parted on good terms and Saladin, with his retinue, set off on the last stage of the journey to Damascus.

It was November and the rains had set in early. On the pass over Mount Lebanon black ice formed during the night and the horses slithered. The Beka'a plain was invisible because of cloud. When the cavalcade descended into it there was mud to flounder about in. The track into the foothills of the Anti-Lebanon leads to the upper reaches of the Barada, little more than a stream here, slipping through the rocks to the ravines and valleys that lead down to Damascus. The track twists and turns between the hills as though it could not possibly lead to anywhere of importance. Suddenly small, cultivated fields could be glimpsed through the rain. Peasants came out of their shanties to wave and the children ran to keep up with the horses. Poplar trees appeared and, beyond them, a falling away of the hills on either side. The way could be seen leading down to the walls of Damascus. Beyond was the blue dome of the Great Mosque. It was the first time that Saladin had been back to the city he regarded as his home since he set out on the journey, more than four years before, that led to the Battle of Hattin and he was never, except for the briefest journey, to leave it again.

✤ 12 ✤

Return to Damascus

Saladin's homecoming and the reunion with his family cannot be written about because here there is a blank. We know little about his several wives except the names of two of them, Ismat, previously married to Nur al-Din, and Shamsa, the mother of al-Aziz and three other sons. Of Ismat he must have been particularly fond because during his Mesopotamian campaign of 1186 he wrote a long letter to her every day. Because of his serious illness at that time the news of her death in Damascus was kept from him for two months in case it should affect his recovery. But when his biographers mentioned the joy he took in his family they mean, exclusively, his children, particularly the boys—how he took pleasure in teaching them with the help of a Moslem creed which had been specially prepared for him by the learned Kutb al-Din al-Naisapuri. He held the book while the children repeated the contents from memory. Or again, here in Damascus in the wet, cold winter of 1193, we have a glimpse of him with his younger children when quite unexpectedly some Frankish envoys are announced who so alarm the children with their strange cropped heads and shaven chins that one of them begins to cry and Saladin sends the Franks away. But there are no women in sight. The seclusion of the harem is complete. The subjection of women and the practice of polygamy had a lot to do with the failure of medieval Moslem societies to establish stable dynasties.

It would be a mistake to think that women had no political influence but, as Nizam al-Mulk said in his *Book of Government*, it was for the bad and was to be discouraged. Family unity in princely establishments was constantly threatened by the harem system. Brothers were often only half-brothers and each mother intrigued for her own son's advancement. Family quarrels were equally violent in the monogamous West, but as the elective theory of monarchy there had given way to one of inheritance by the eldest

[191]

son there was agreement about what constituted political legitimacy. For one thing there were not so many sons with a claim and, if
born of the same mother, there was the principle of primogeniture to
sort them out. The demise of the crown was not the constitutional
crisis it was in the East where a number of sons of roughly the same
age but with different mothers saw themselves as candidates. Later,
under the more barbarous Ottomans, the successful candidate,
usually the eldest living male in the family, eliminated his brothers
and half-brothers but in Saladin's time manners were milder. The
dying king tried to get his lords to swear allegiance to his eldest son,
but not necessarily for all his territories. There seemed to be an
unspoken agreement that Saladin was such an exceptional man, who
had taken power by force, that he could not be succeeded by any one
son. His empire would be divided up among a number of them. Yet
if he had thoughts about the succession he took no action, perhaps
because he was uneasy about the way his eldest son, al-Afdal, was
turning out. He had a higher regard for al-Zaher who ruled in
Aleppo.

The last time he had seen al-Afdal was in Jerusalem when, for
some reason, he had reprimanded the young man. But now they
were reunited in Damascus, al-Afdal not the slightest bit put out by
being in disgrace. Al-Zaher came down from Aleppo to take part in
the feasting and to listen to the poets who were so full of themselves
that they tried to burst into the Sultan's private apartments to
declaim their eulogistic verses. When the time came for al-Zaher to
leave Saladin gave him advice. 'Beware of bloodshed. Trust not in
that. Spilt blood never sleeps.' He was not thinking of warfare but of
state security. 'Win the hearts of your people . . . and of your emirs
and ministers. Such position as I have was won by gentleness and
conciliation.'

Al-Adil arrived from the Jezireh. The two brothers rode out into
the desert to hunt gazelle in the crisp winter sunshine that had
temporarily taken over from the rain, this being in al-Adil's view the
kind of relaxation that Saladin was greatly in need of. The beaters
made it an easy hunt. They galloped and screamed, driving the
gazelle towards the hillock where Saladin had taken up position and
the Ayyub brothers galloped in parallel with their flight, shooting
from the saddle. At night, under the flaring stars, they talked mainly
of Egypt, the country which was near to al-Adil's heart and from

which he had been separated by political necessity. If there was to be another invasion from the West, another Crusade, it would have as its immediate objective not Palestine but Egypt, and the country urgently needed to be put once more in a state of preparedness. But no firm decisions were taken. Al-Adil was concerned. The Sultan seemed not to be concentrating properly.

About al-Adil himself it is often said that towards the end of his elder brother's life he had ambitions of his own and Saladin became suspicious of him, presumably because they could only be at the expense of his own sons. There is an implication that ambition in al-Adil, if it existed, would be unworthy and disloyal. Al-Adil had not previously shown himself as self-seeking; on the contrary he had been conspicuously loyal to Saladin and aware of the need for good relations with his young nephews (witness the conversation with al-Zaher and al-Aziz before they went off to their fiefs of Aleppo and Egypt) though in supplanting al-Afdal, his eldest nephew, in his Mesopotamian fiefs he had certainly built up trouble for the future from this resentful and arrogant young man. It was not disloyal, now that he saw the poor state of his brother's health, for al-Adil to consider his own future. None of Saladin's sons inherited their father's statesmanlike qualities. They were jealously watchful of each other, they were unpredictable and, in the case of al-Afdal, a bit foolish. They had no grasp of the political need their father had felt for being more orthodox than the Caliph to ensure the unity of Islam in face of the European invaders. Al-Adil foresaw quarrels between them. He had no real secure base of his own like the other surviving brother, Tughtigin, away in Yemen, and if things turned out badly he could easily find himself reduced to living on some modest fief in the Jezireh, but still regarded as a threat to whatever the new power structure might be and in danger of elimination. In the absence of an overlord with the personality of Saladin the only law, apart from Sharia, that effectively operated was the law of the jungle. Al-Adil was not ambitious as Turkish *atabegs* like Zengi had been ambitious, he just wanted to keep his end up and to make sure his brother's empire held together, because the alternative was anarchy.

After a second hunting trip in the desert that lasted two whole weeks, when the two brothers were out of immediate touch with Damascus, al-Adil returned to his fiefs on the other side of the

Euphrates, understanding that as soon as the weather improved Saladin would leave for Egypt. They did not meet again. Al-Afdal, popular because of his easy-going ways, was the centre of court activities back in Damascus and when Beha al-Din arrived from Jerusalem in February he found the young man surrounded by the throng in the audience chamber. He had expected to see Saladin there but the Sultan was still in his private quarters preparing for the audience. The exceptionally bad weather had made the roads almost impassable and Beha al-Din's arrival had been much delayed. Hearing of it Saladin asked for the Cadi to be admitted before all the others. Much moved by the sight of the man who embodied so many of the qualities he believed in, devotion to the Faith, to Holy War and to learning, of undoubted courage and loyalty, Saladin stood up to receive him. It was four months since they had last met and Saladin, his eyes filled with tears, embraced the younger man.

Three days later he rode out on a raw day to meet the caravan of pilgrims returning from Mecca. It was a festive occasion and crowds came out of the city. Beha al-Din arrived just as Saladin met the Hajj but could not approach him because al-Afdal rode up and took the Cadi on one side to speak to him. At this moment Beha noticed that the Sultan was without the quilted jacket he invariably wore when riding and was so concerned that he broke away from al-Afdal to urge the Sultan (he invariably referred to him by this title), who seemed like a man waking out of a dream, to ask for the garment. But the master of the wardrobe could not be found. Beha thought this ominous. The following day Saladin was running a high temperature and al-Afdal sat in his place at table. The sight so upset Beha al-Din that he withdrew without sitting down.

For the ordinary citizen the rule of a good prince meant more than anything else the maintenance of law and order; his death created uncertainty and this usually meant trouble. If leading members of the court were at each other's throats ordinary people took the law into their own hands. The mob would be out, houses pillaged and under cover of the general confusion old scores settled. When it was learned that Saladin's life might be ebbing away there was intense public anxiety and al-Afdal asked the emirs publicly to swear allegiance to him. Saladin, possibly because he refused to admit the gravity of his illness, had not done this himself yet it was necessary to affirm a proper transfer of power so that public order could be maintained. The city was already in such commotion that merchants had started carrying their goods out of the bazaars for safe-keeping. The form of the oath was drawn up by the Cadis, the intention being to get the emirs to promise support for Saladin as long as he lived and for al-Afdal when he died. The terms were very tough. They included the acceptance of penalties if the oath were broken; the emirs would have to divorce their wives, set their slaves free and go barefoot on the pilgrimage to Mecca. Divorce, incidentally, was an easy matter, depending entirely on the declaration of the husband. A man could divorce his wife twice and each time take her back, but the third time was irrevocable until the woman had been married and divorced by another husband. Al-Afdal asked for the penalty of this triple divorce by the declaration: 'I divorce thee three times,' and some of the emirs refused, saying they had never taken an oath that contained such a condition.

Others wanted guarantees and concessions. Never again would there be such an opportunity to strike a bargain. Civil war after the death of Saladin seemed a real possibility to some and they wanted assurances that they would never be asked to fight against any of al-Afdal's brothers. Others required confirmation they would continue in the possession of their existing fiefs. Those without a fief wanted one. Somehow al-Afdal managed to satisfy most of them and, while his father lay dying, invited everyone to a banquet. No attempt had been made to require oaths of allegiance from the emirs of Egypt, Aleppo and from the Jezireh because their masters were al-Aziz, al-Zaher and al-Adil respectively, who saw themselves as independent magnates. Al-Afdal recognized that his territory was Damascus and its dependencies alone. They stretched all the way from Sinai in the south to Lattakia in the north.

The account of Saladin's last illness has been vividly recorded by Beha al-Din who, together with al-Fadel, was in constant attendance. Saladin's humility repeatedly surprised Beha, particularly when it took the form of tolerating clumsy servants. It was well known that once, when recovering from an illness, he stepped into a bath where the water was too hot. He asked for cold, the bath boy tripped with the pitcher and Saladin had a chilly douche. All he said was: 'If your aim is to kill me just let me know.' Now, in his last illness, he called for water to drink. First it was too hot, then it was too cold. Beha said he did not get vexed or angry, but only said:

[195]

'Perhaps there is no one who can make the water of the right temperature'. These servants were slaves who under a different master could well lose their lives for a misdemeanor. Usamah recalled how as a boy he stabbed to death one of his father's slaves who had been impertinent to him. Zengi's slaves were so afraid when he caught them drinking his wine that they did not hesitate to murder him; they knew he would have not the slightest mercy. Saladin, however, was incapable of domestic brutality. He saw all Moslems as equal in the eyes of God, not only because this was a fundamental teaching of Islam but because it came naturally to him.

Beha al-Din said that Saladin's mind wandered during his last illness and was clear only at intervals. During one of these the Sheikh Abu J'afer was reciting from the Koran, saying: 'He is the God than whom there is no other God; who knows the unseen and the visible,' when he heard Saladin say: 'It is true.' He died smiling, in expectation of Paradise. This was on 4 March 1193, when he was in his fifty-fifth year. He left no money to pay for his funeral, not even enough to buy straw for the sun-baked bricks with which his tomb was lined, and the cost had to be borrowed, though al-Fadel paid for the grave clothes, the simple bier and the piece of striped cloth that covered it. Saladin left nothing. No goods, no house or any other property. In the West the story soon circulated that on Saladin's instructions his standard-bearer went through the streets of Damascus after his death with part of his shroud on the end of a lance, crying that even so great a ruler took no more than this to his grave. The story is evidence of European belief that Saladin was austerely religious, but he would not have gone in for such ostentatious humility and in any case he had no shroud. What is true is that his youngest sons went into the streets to receive the condolences of the ordinary citizen and these were given with tears. One observer said it was the only time a ruler's death had been truly mourned by the people.

Al-Afdal was critical of his father's policy. He thought the old man had become a grim fanatic, obsessed with the idea of Holy War when it was clear to everyone that fighting for religion was somewhat out of date. Times had changed. War was all very well, no doubt, but now that the Franks had been pinned back to their little strip of coast the realistic course was to strike bargains over trade and fight only when immediate practical advantages were to be obtained. Less ideology and more pragmatism was the new line. He dismissed his father's closest advisers, to show his independence, and appointed in their place the brother of the historian al-Athir, a certain al-Ziya who, by implication, was a Zengid sympathizer at a time when there were plans in Mosul to revive Zengid autonomy in the area. Saladin would have been angered. Al-Ziya certainly helped to undermine al-Afdal's authority. He was believed to have dealings with subversive factions and did nothing to distract al-Afdal from the gay and irresponsible life he chose to lead. Many of Saladin's ex-ministers left the country for Egypt where they were made welcome by al-Aziz.

Prominent among his father's ministers and advisers dismissed by al-Afdal were Imad al-Din, his Secretary of State, al-Fadel of Egypt and Beha al-Din, the Cadi of the Army. For them the great days were over and they lived with their memories, in particular Imad al-Din, now 68 years old; he decided there was no future for him elsewhere and stayed in Damascus to write and live out his time in disappointed seclusion and in poverty. His autobiography was called *al-Barq as-Shami* (the Syrian Lightning), to indicate how rapidly the early happy years had passed. In spite of his unusually florid style he was an accurate recorder of the facts as he saw them even when they tell against Saladin—he was not uncritical—but if the unmarked grave beside Saladin's is indeed Imad's, as tradition says, those who placed him there knew of the deep admiration he had for his master and of the close relations between them. He died in 1201 having, it is said, not left his house for several years.

Al-Fadel was happy to leave Damascus and return to Egypt where he became al-Aziz's senior administrator. He was much more of a statesman that Imad al-Din had ever aspired to be and he did not hesitate to express unwelcome truths. He was a humane, passionate man who cared a great deal about the well-being of Egypt. He had been the real brains of Saladin's empire and its chief propagandist. There was no coherent alternative to Ayyubid power and he remained faithful to it for the rest of his life, 'a frail old man, all head and heart,' as one of his visitors wrote, 'who dictated with all kinds of movements of the face and lips, so eager was he to get the words out.'

Beha al-Din went to Aleppo where at first he was much occupied with trying to patch up the quarrels between Saladin's sons.

[197]

Al-Zaher made him Cadi of Aleppo and, being not yet 50, he became active in his original profession of teaching. Of all Saladin's chief counsellors and advisers Beha did best. As the years went by he became modestly well-to-do, was able to found a college and mosque, later a school for teaching the Traditions, and he even became the chief administrator of Aleppo when al-Zaher died and his young son was in the care of an *atabeg*. In his old age he had a salon. People went to see him after Friday prayers to enjoy his conversation which was usually about literature. In winter he constantly wore a fur coat and sat beside the charcoal brazier. Before he died, in 1234 at the age of 90, he was described as being weak like a bird just hatched and his legs had so little flesh on them that they were like thin sticks. He bequeathed his house to a fraternity of Sufis.

By this time there had indeed been war between the brothers and between the brothers and their uncle al-Adil. At one point al-Adil was shut up in Damascus for six months besieged by al-Zaher and al-Afdal but he was too clever for them, winning over many of his nephews' vassals with the result that the siege was lifted. Al-Aziz of Egypt died prematurely in a hunting accident near the Pyramids, al-Afdal was pensioned off as an incompetent to cities in the north of the Jezireh and al-Zaher was forced to acknowledge his uncle's suzerainty. By 1201 al-Adil was in control of all Saladin's territories. The historian al-Athir had noticed that when a new dynasty was established it was rarely by direct succession from father to son. There was always some powerful brother or cousin ready to take over from the much younger sons and this was certainly the case with the Ayyubids.

Beha al-Din lived long enough to see Jerusalem in the hands of the Franks once more, as Saladin had feared, when the Emperor Frederick II negotiated its surrender in 1229 with al-Kamil, that son of al-Adil, who had been 'knighted' by Richard Coeur-de-Lion and was now the ruler of Egypt and Syria in his father's place. The Mongols, who were to destroy the Abbasid Caliphate, had already taken control of large parts of Persia. As the reports of the massacres came in, Beha al-Din could not have foreseen the scale of the disaster that was about to befall Islam. Knowing Saladin's preoccupations he would have been more concerned with Frankish attacks on Egypt but there was nothing he could do. He had a bad cough and kept indoors. Like Saladin in his illness he forced himself to his feet for the recital of the Friday prayers. The example, even after the passing of so many years, was unforgettable.

Not much more than 100 years later Dante located Saladin in the First Circle of Hell, the Limbo where virtuous Pagans dwell: 'I saw great Saladin, aloof, alone.' Strictly speaking, the First Circle was for highly regarded Pagans like Homer who lived before Christ and therefore could not be Christians. Saladin is here because of his moral stature, a man who chose to remain outside Christianity yet whose life exemplified the Christian virtues. For the West he became a figure of myth and legend, appearing in minstrels' tales, metrical romances, novels and plays, from the thirteenth century onwards, but no tribute is more impressive than Dante's. The Crusades were living history to thirteenth-century Italians. Dante's own ancestor Cacciaguida died on the Second Crusade in 1147; the Italian trading cities, particularly Pisa, had close and continuing links with Palestine so, in addition to William of Tyre's outstanding *History* and other chronicles, there was a wealth of information circulating, and out of all this emerged Saladin, the honorary Christian.

There was no comparable myth-making process at work in Islam; Saladin is not even mentioned in the *One Thousand Nights and a Night*. In popular esteem he fell short of the *mamluk* Sultan Baybars, who came to replace him two generations later and whose legendary exploits were told in a great romance that was built up over the years and recited by professional story-tellers right into modern times. Just why this is so, and why Moslem historians see Saladin's achievement as less significant than Baybars' can only be understood if the role of the Caliphate and later history are borne in mind. The suspicion with which he was viewed by the Caliphate had something to do with his glory being dimmer among the Moslems than in the West. The Caliph had reservations and in conservative, orthodox minds this caused worry. For all his fame in recovering Jerusalem there was still room for argument about Saladin's status. And after the loss of Acre his military achievement was not thought impressive either.

In Egypt he was regarded by some as the strong man who came down from Syria, destroyed the ruling Fatimids, put the country on a war footing and then drained it of money and men, first of all to fight fellow-Moslems far off in the north and then the Franks in Palestine, but without exacting as much booty for general distribution as he might. He had drawn attention to the wealth of Egypt, so the Fifth Crusade and the later Crusade under St Louis made straight for the Delta which the Europeans now saw as the key to Jerusalem. Egypt was parcelled out in *iqtas* between *mamluks*, the system Saladin had introduced to control the country through a body of men with loyalties personal to himself; it became increasingly oppressive when Saladin and al-Adil were not there to check abuses. So, for all the respect and devotion Saladin inspired, in spite of his reputation for fairness and justice, he was seen by many Egyptians as an alien war-lord in whose time and under whose successors Egypt was exploited.

When the Ayyubid dynasty petered out, power was seized by the strongest and most determined of the *mamluks*. This was how Egypt and much of the Near East was governed for the next two and three-quarter centuries, until well after the fall of Constantinople to the Ottoman Turks. The greatest of these *mamluks* was Baybars, the inspirer of the popular romance. He was bought as a youth in the Damascus slave market, showed unusual ability as a soldier and murdered his predecessor to become Sultan of Egypt in 1260, a big, blue-eyed and brutal Kipchak Turkoman who, unlike Saladin, was not in the slightest degree embarrassed by the envy of the Abbasid Caliph, for by that time the politico-religious system based on the Successors to the Prophet, the Caliphate, had been wiped out. In 1258 the Mongols under Hulagu sacked Baghdad and massacred the population, including al-Mustansir, the 37th Abbasid Caliph and his entire court. There were no more real Caliphs, only pseudo-Caliphs who were kept like canaries in a cage by the *mamluks* in Cairo and may, or may not, have been descendants of an obscure survivor of the Abbasid house.

So Baybars really was the Champion of Islam. There was no one else. The Mongols had transformed the East and threatened to drive down into Egypt. If they did there would be no Moslem state left of any consequence east of Morocco, but in one of the really decisive battles in history Baybars led the vanguard of the Egyptian army at Ain Jalud, the Pools of Goliath, in Galilee, where the Mongol army was destroyed. His prestige could not have been higher. He went on to break the back of Frankish resistance in Palestine and Syria, sacked and massacred without mercy (rather as the Crusaders had before him): he finally disposed of the Assassins, he took the oldest of the

Return to Damascus

Crusader states, Antioch, and battered the city beyond recovery. General Moslem opinion understood this more easily than Saladin's generosity. Baybars had saved Egypt and the country never forgot it. More than that, he was responsible for starting a new phase of Egyptian well-being and of culture, founding mosques and schools. But the ruthlessness of the man throws into relief the personality of Saladin.

They are buried not far from one another in Damascus, Saladin under a simple ribbed cupola just outside the Ummayad Mosque and Baybars in the Zahiriye Madrassa, now the National Library, in a room brilliant with mosaics. The contrast between the two is appropriate. When all allowance is made for the hagiography in the testimony of his contemporaries, Saladin still stands out as an honourable, truthful and simple man at a time when these qualities were rare in princes. Even so hostile a witness as his contemporary al-Athir was finally moved to describe him as 'the marvel of his time, a man rich in fine qualities'. His name within the family was Yusif bin-Aiyub, which, if fully Englished, could be taken as Joseph Jobson. This, rather than the magnate buried under all those honorific titles, sounds like the man who allowed himself to be hoodwinked by clever opponents like Reynaud of Sidon, who gave money away so readily that his treasurer kept secret reserves, who was always true to his word and so easy in his manner that soldiers and learned doctors were familiar with him, sometimes to the point of rudeness; yet he was capable of exemplary sternness not only to others but, more particularly, in his austerities and tireless campaigning, to himself. If he had been a domineering, headstrong man like his uncle Shirkuh he would not have succeeded. He was a good learner. The bringing together of Egypt, Syria and the Jezireh was achieved by a mixture of force and persuasion of which his father, the exemplar, would have approved. In other respects Saladin modelled himself on that ideal Moslem prince, Nur al-Din, but his natural geniality broke through.

Nur al-Din's tomb, a few minutes' walk from Saladin's, is visited by the devout and the indifferent alike because in addition to being the resting place of an acknowledged martyr (one did not have to die on the battlefield to earn that title) it has a fountain, the characteristic amenity of the city, and anyone can drink water, still with some of its mountain chill, from the chained metal cups provided.

These three, Nur al-Din, Saladin and Baybars, were the dominant Moslem leaders in the Fertile Crescent of Mesopotamia, Syria, Palestine and Egypt in the twelfth and thirteenth centuries, that period after the great Seljuk Empire had broken up, when the Fatimid Caliphate came to an end, when the Abbasid Caliphate itself was destroyed by the Mongols and the Frankish states were first of all severely cut back and then eliminated. If Saladin had been the somewhat aloof figure Nur al-Din had been, or the cruel and uncompromising Baybars, he would never, for all his achievement, have entered the European imagination. The Crusaders were fascinated by a Moslem leader who possessed virtues they assumed were Christian. To them, to his Moslem contemporaries (even those who opposed him) and to us, it still remains remarkable that in times as harsh and bloody as these a man of great power should have been so little corrupted by it.

Bibliography

Works consulted
The main sources of information about Saladin are the writings of
his contemporaries, the Mosul historian Ibn al-Athir, the Head of
the Damascus Secretariat Imad al-Din, and the Cadi of the Army
Beha al-Din ibn Shaddad. They are extensively printed in the
original Arabic and in French translation in the *Recueil des Historiens
des Croisades (Orientaux)*, 5 vols. (Paris, 1872–1906).

Ibn al-Athir (1160–1233), the greatest Moslem historian of his
time, was a supporter of Saladin's rivals, the Zengids. His history of
the *Atabegs* of Mosul appears in vol. 2, part II of the *Recueil* and his
al-Kamil fi al-Tarikh (World History) in vol. 1 and vol. 2, part I. The
mannered but factually accurate diaries of Imad al-Din (1125–1201)
are mainly preserved in extensive quotation by a historian of the next
century, Abu Shama (1203–67) who wrote *The Two Gardens* (the
reigns of Nur al-Din and Saladin) now printed in vols. 4 and 5. Beha
al-Din (1154–1234) was with Saladin for the last five years of his life
and his eulogistic biography is mainly valuable for the detail in
which he records these years. It appears in the *Recueil*, vol. 3, pp.
1–393. An English version, *What Befell Sultan Yusuf*, was published
by the Palestine Pilgrims' Text Society (London, 1897).

Arab Historians of the Crusades, selected and translated by Francesco
Gabrielli into Italian and by E. J. Costello into English (London,
1969) consists of extracts, some from the *Recueil* but mainly from
original texts.

Other contemporary or near contemporary writers
The Memoirs of Usamah ibn-Munqidh (1095–1188), trans. Philip K.
    Hitti (New York, 1929)
Ibn al-Jubayr (1145–1217), *The Travels*, trans. R. J. C. Broadbent
    (London, 1952)

Bibliography

Benjamin of Tudela, *The Travels, 1160–73*, trans. and ed. M. Komroff (London, 1928)

Ibn Kallikhan (1211–82), *Biographical Dictionary*, trans. Baron MacGuckin de Slane, 4 vols. (Paris and London, 1843–71)

Ibn al-Qalanisi (1070–1160), *The Damascus Chronicle of the Crusades*, ed. H. A. R. Gibb (London, 1932)

Nizam al-Mulk (1018–92), *The Book of Government*, trans. H. Darke (London, 1960)

William of Tyre (*c.* 1137–85), *A History of Deeds Done beyond the Sea*, 2 vols., trans. E. A. Babcock and A. C. Krey (New York, 1953)

Itinerarium Peregrinorum et Gesta Regis Ricardi (1190–2), ed. W. Stubbs (London, 1864)

Ernoul (*fl.* 1187), *Chronique* (Paris, 1871)

Modern biographies

M. W. Baldwin. *Raymond III and the Fall of Jerusalem* (Princeton, 1936)

Andrew S. Ehrenkreutz, *Saladin* (Albany, 1972)

H. A. R. Gibb, 'Saladin, from the works of Imad al-Din and Beha al-Din', in *History of the Crusades*, ed K. Setton (Pennsylvania, 1969; Oxford, 1973)

H. A. R. Gibb, 'The Career of Nur al-Din', in *History of the Crusades*

Geoffrey Hindley, *Saladin* (London, 1976)

S. Lane-Poole, *Saladin and the Fall of the Kingdom of Jerusalem*, (London, 1898)

M. C. Lyons and D. E. P. Jackson, *Saladin, The Politics of the Holy War* (Cambridge, 1982)

Other works

T. W. Arnold, 'Arab Travellers', in *Travel and Travellers in the Middle Ages*, ed. A. P. Newton (London, 1926)

E. Ashtor, *Social and Economic History of the Near East in the Middle Ages* (London, 1976)

C. M. Brand, 'The Byzantines and Saladin', *Speculum* 37, 1962

Claude Cahen, *La Syrie du Nord à l'époque des Croisades* (Paris, 1940)

M. A. Cook (ed), *Studies in the Economic History of the Middle East* (London, 1970)

K. A. C. Cresswell, *Fortifications in Islam before AD 1250* (Oxford, 1954)

N. A. Faris (ed.), *The Arab Heritage* (Princeton, 1944)

C. E. Gibson, *The Story of the Ship* (London, 1958)

Bibliography

Philip K. Hitti, *History of the Arabs*, 10th edn (London, 1970)

H. W. L. Hime, *Gunpowder and Ammunition, their Origin and Progress* (London, 1904)

A. K. S. Lambton, 'Internal Structure of the Seljuk Empire' in *Cambridge History of Iran*, vol. 5 (Cambridge, 1968)

Bernard Lewis, *The Assassins; a Radical Sect in Islam* (New York, 1968)

D. B. Macdonald, *Development of Muslim Theology, Jurisprudence and Constitutional Theory* (London, 1903)

R. A. Nicholson, *Literary History of the Arabs* (London, 1930)

Charles Oman, *Art of War in the Middle Ages*, 2 vols. (London, 1924)

Steven Runciman, *A History of the Crusades*, 3 vols. (Cambridge, 1951–4)

E. Sivan, *L'Islam et la Croisade* (Paris, 1968).

R. C. Smail, *Crusading Warfare* (Cambridge, 1967)

Index

Index

Index

Index

Index